GERMAN
A SELF-TEACHING
GUIDE

LANGUAGE SELF-TEACHING GUIDES
FROM THE WILEY PRESS

French: A Self-Teaching Guide, Hershfield
German: A Self-Teaching Guide, Taylor & Haas
*Italian: A Self-Teaching Guide, Lebano
Practical Spanish Grammar: A Self-Teaching Guide, Prado
More Practical Spanish Grammar: A Self-Teaching Guide, Prado

*Forthcoming title

GERMAN
A SELF-TEACHING GUIDE
GUIDE

Heimy Taylor

Werner Haas

A Wiley Press Book

John Wiley & Sons, Inc.

New York · Chichester · Brisbane · Toronto · Singapore

Publisher: Stephen Kippur
Editor: Elizabeth G. Perry
Managing Editor: Katherine S. Bolster
Production Services: Publication Services; Champaign, IL

Library of Congress Cataloging-in-Publication Data

Taylor, Heimy F.
   German, a self-teaching guide.

   English and German.
   Includes vocabulary lists.
   Includes index.
   1. German language—Grammar—1950–   . I. German
language—Self-instruction.   3. German language—
Text-books for foreign speakers—English. I. Haas,
Werner, 1928–   . II. Title.
PF3112.5.T39   1986   438.2'421   86-1581
ISBN 0-471-82756-8
Printed in the United States of America

86 87 10 9 8 7 6 5 4 3 2 1

Some material in this text is taken from:
Deutsch Fur Alle: Beginning College German – A Comprehensive Approach, 2nd Edition by Werner Haas © 1983 John Wiley & Sons, Inc.
Sprechen Wir Daruber: German Conversation – A Functional Approach by Werner Haas © 1984 John Wiley & Sons, Inc.
Used with permission from John Wiley & Sons, Inc.

Contents

Preface

German: A Self-Teaching Guide is a simplified and practical beginner's course for anyone who would like to learn German. This book lends itself easily to self-learners, students in adult education courses, and those in short-term beginning German courses.

This book can serve as a survival course for those who wish to learn only the essentials of German grammar and want to acquire some basic vocabulary for everyday life and traveling in German-speaking countries. Be assured: whatever you learn in this text you can apply in speaking or in writing to communicate with German-speaking people. However, it lays no claims to completeness: on the contrary, rules have been shortened, structures simplified, and the vocabulary geared towards high frequency use. The objective of this book is to teach important communicative skills in German at the beginner's level.

Each chapter of this text contains most of the following features:

Culture Notes in English
Dialoge in German with English translations
Grammar Explanations
Exercises (Übungen) with answers in the back of the book
Review (Wiederholung)
Chapter Vocabulary (Wortschatz)

Before you begin with the first chapter, take a look at the introduction, *German Sounds and Spelling,* to orient yourself to spelling rules and pronunciation.
Here are a few hints for using this text:

Read the *Dialoge* aloud and study them carefully. Always check the English translation.
Then turn to the brief *Grammar Explanations* and try to do the *Übungen* (exercises).
Check the *Answers* in the back and see how well you did. Don't expect to bat 1000—hardly anyone does.
Analyze your mistakes and reread the grammar explanations.
Look up words in the vocabularies (chapter and end vocabulary).

A short tape which goes with *German: A Self-Teaching Guide* will assist you to improve your aural comprehension and speaking skills. Read aloud all sentences and exercises. Don't worry about your less than perfect pronunciation. It still beats "silent mumbling." This tape can be purchased by mailing in the Business Reply Card in the book.

The *Chapter Vocabulary* (Wortschatz) lists the new words appearing in that particular chapter. If you can't find a certain word there, look it up at the end of the book. There you will find most of the words used. Note that we have included *German = English* and *English = German* vocabulary lists.

German: A Self-Teaching Guide will not turn you into a polished speaker of German overnight. It will not enable you to deal immediately with every German text. But it will provide you with the basic tools to understand, to speak, to read, and to write simple German. It opens the gate to a very gratifying experience: to understand and appreciate the language and culture of the German-speaking people. "Viel Spaß mit Deutsch" (Have fun with German)!

H.T.

W.H.

Editor's Note: The margin notes throughout the book provide reminders of grammatical rules and irregular word forms. They are intended only to highlight material from the text, not to summarize it.

Introduction: German Sounds and Spelling

Basic Rules

As you read and write German you will notice that all nouns are capitalized; not only proper nouns like *England, Hamburg, Karin Braun,* but also common nouns like *Ball, Butter,* or *Mann.* Other words when used as nouns must be capitalized as well. Unlike English, German does not capitalize proper adjectives such as *englisch, amerikanisch, deutsch.*

The formal address *Sie* (you) and the corresponding *Ihr (your)* must always be capitalized. When writing letters, all pronouns of direct address are capitalized.

Note the letter ß which is pronounced like the s in bus; Fuß/foos/ (foot).

German has a graphic sign called *umlaut* (literally "sound transformer") which consists of two dots¨ placed over the vowels a = ä; o = ö; u = ü. They are pronounced differently than the regular a, o, and u. Watch out for these *umlauts* in speaking as well as in writing.

In German as well as in English certain syllables receive more stress than others. This stress is not indicated through a special mark, as in French. Generally speaking, most German words are stressed on the *first* syllable (wándern, trínken, Hámburg). In compound words usually the *first* word is stressed more than the second (Aútofahrer). Words of foreign origin are usually stressed on the last syllable of the stem (Studént, Universität). Separable prefixes like *ab, an, aus,* etc. are *always* stressed (ábfahren, ánkommen, áusgeben). Inseparable prefixes such as *be, ent, er,* or *ge* are *never* stressed (behándeln, entférnen, erkénnen).

Now let's look at the German vowel and consonant system in detail. Remember, the best way to learn to pronounce German is to imitate native speakers as accurately as possible. As you listen to the pronunciation tape, repeat all the sounds and words as carefully as you can.

Vowels

Vowels in German are either long or short. German spelling will help you in deciding whether they should be pronounced long or short. Note the following general pronunciation rules:

A vowel is pronounced long if...*

it is doubled	*Boot* (boat) /bōt/; say -o- as in English so
followed by an h	*nehmen* (to take) /naymən/;say -e- as in English nay, but don't glide the -e-
a syllable ends with a vowel	*haben* (to have) /hābən/; say -a- as in English father
an -i- is followed by an -e- which is silent	*lieben* (to love) /leebən/; say -ie- as in English see

Caution: though we have a tendency to glide our long vowels in English, you should avoid this glide in German.

A vowel is pronounced short if...

it is followed by a double consonant	*Mitte* (middle) /mitə/; say -i- as in English mittens
before consonant clusters	*Fenster* (window) /fenstər/; say -e- as in English met
if followed by ck, or tz	*Ecke* (corner) /ekə/; *jetzt* (now) /jetst/; say -e- in met and -j- as the -y- in you

German has three diphthongs which are easy to pronounce since they resemble our own. A diphthong is a combination of two vowels pronounced as one unit. German diphthongs are shorter than English diphthongs.

ei, ai	pronounced as the -i- in mine (mein, Hai)
au	pronounced as the ou in house (Haus)
eu, ä	pronounced as the oi in oil (Leute, Häuser)**

Here is the German vowel system in simplified spelling:

	Spelling	Phonetic Symbol
short	i ü u	/i/ /ü/ /u/
	e ö o	/e/ /ö/ /o/
	ä a	/e/ /a/
long	i ü u	/ee/ /ǖ/ /oo/
	e ö o	/ey/ /ȫ/ /ō/
	ä a	/ey/ /ā/
diphthong	au ei	/ou/ /i/
	äu (eu)	/oi/
unstressed	e	/ə/

*A line above the vowel indicates that it should be long.

**Note: -ie- is not a diphthong but the German long-i- which is always pronounced like English -ee-; *lieben* (to love) /leeben/.

Practice saying the following words:

German Spelling	Phonetic Symbol	Description	Examples
a (short)	u	Almost like the English -u- in hut or up	hat (has) - /hut/ packen (to pack) - /pukən/ Hammer (hammer) - /hummər/
ā (long) aa, ah	ā	like our -a- in spa; but open mouth wide and don't glide	ja (yes) - /yā/ Nase (nose) - /nāzə/ Bahn (track) - /bān/
e	ə	unstressed like in begin, locket	beginnen (to begin) - /bəginən/ leben (to live) - /leybən/
e (short)	e	like our -e- in met	Bett (bed) - /bet/ kennen (to know) - /kenən/ es (it) - /es/
e (long) ee, eh	ey	like our -ay- in say, but spread lips and don't glide	Beet (bed of flowers) - /beyt/ beten (to pray) - /beytən/ nehmen (to take) - /neymən/
i (short)	i	like our -i- in fit, mitten	mit (with) - /mit/ bitte (please) - /bitə/
i (long) ie, ih, ieh	ee	like our -ee- in see, me or bee; spread lips and don't glide	Miete (rent) - /meetə/ ihn (him) - /een/ tief (deep) - /teef/
o (short)	o	as in not, lot; don't open mouth too wide for -o-	Tonne (ton) -/tonnə/ hoffen (to hope) - /hofən/
o (long) oo, oh	ō	as in so, foe, open; round lips and don't glide	Lohn (wages) - /lōn/ Boot (boat) - /bōt/ Not (need) - /nōt/
u (short)	u	like our -u- in put or bush	muß (must) - /mus/ Kunde (customer) - /kundə/
u (long) uh	oo	like moon, shoe, or rule; but don't glide	Mut (courage) - /moot/ Huhn (chicken) - /hoon/ Schuh (shoe) - /shoo/
ä (short)	e	like the short German -e- or our -e- in met, let or wet	Bäcker (baker) - /bekər/ Blätter (leaves) - /bletər/
ä (long) äh	ey	similar to long German -e-; however, don't spread lips, rather open mouth wide	Käse (cheese) - /keyzə/ Fähre (ferry) - /feyrə/ Säle (large rooms) - /zeylə/
ö (short)	ö	tongue up front as for -e-, but lips rounded as for -o-; practice by going from short -e- to -ö-	Helle - Hölle (light, hell) /helə/ - /hölə/ Stecken - Stöcke (sticks) /shtekən/ - /shtökə/
ö (long) ö	ȫ	as long German -e- but with rounded lips	Sehne - Söhne (tendon, sons) /zeynə/ - /zȫnə/ Lehne - Löhne (arm-rest; wages) /leynə/ - lȫnə/

ü (short)	ü	tongue up front as for -i-, but lips rounded as for -u-; practice by going from short -i- to short -ü-	Kissen - küssen (pillow, to kiss) /kisən/ - /küsən/ Kiste - Küste (box, coast) /kistə/ - küstə/
ü (long) ṻ	ū̄	as long German -i- but with rounded lips	Biene - Bühne (bee, stage) /beenə/ - /būnə/ viele - fühle (many, feel) /feelə/ - /fūlə/
au	ou	as English -ou- in house	Haus (house) - /hous/ laufen (to run) - /loufən/
eu äu	oi	as English -oi- in oil	Leute (people) - /loitə/ Mäuse (mice) - /moizə/
ei ai ey ay	i	as English -i- in mine, or -y- in my	mein (mine) - /min/ Mai (May) - /my/ Meyer, Mayer (German names) /miər/ - /miər/

Practice

Say these pairs several times until you are comfortable with your pronunciation.*

kam	/kām/	Kamm	/kam/	Beet	/beyt/	Bett	/bet/·
Bahn	/bān/	Bann	/ban/	den	/deyn/	denn	/den/
Kahn	/kān/	kann	/kan/	stehen	/shteyən/	stellen	/shtelən/
Ofen	/ōfən/	offen	/ofən/	Mus	/moos/	muß	/mus/
Ton	/tōn/	Tonne	/tonə/	Ruhm	/room/	Rum	/rum/
wohne	/vōnə/	wonne	/vonə/	schuf	/shoof/	Schuft	/shuft/
Miete	/meetə/	Mitte	/mitə/	Öfen	/ȫfən/	öffnen	/öfnən/
biete	/beetə/	bitte	/bitə/	Höhle	/hȫlə/	Hölle	/hölə/
ihnen	/eenən/	innen	/inən/	Hüte	/hūtə/	Hütte	/hütə/
meine	/minə/	Miene	/meenə/	fühle	/fūlə/	Fülle	/fülə/
Leid	/litə/	Lied	/leet/	Maus	/mous/	Mäuse	/moizə/
reimen	/rimən/	Riemen	/reemən/	łauten	/loutən/	läuten	/loitən/
Wein	/vine/	Wien	/veen/	Laus	/lous/	Läuse	/loizə/

Consonants

Most German consonants are similar to their English equivalents. Double consonants are pronounced as the corresponding single consonants. They generally indicate that the preceding vowel is short.

The consonants b, d, g are pronounced almost as in English. However, their position in a word makes a difference in their pronunciation. Look at the chart.

The consonants p, t, k, f, m, n, h are always pronounced similar to their English counterparts p, t, k, f, m, n, h.

Examples: Papier (paper) = /paṕeer/   mit (with) = /mit/
Tisch (table) = /tish/   Hut (hat)   = /hoot/
Keller (cellar) = /kelər/   nein (no)   = /nine/
Fisch (fish)   = /fish/

*This is for pronunciation practice only. Don't worry about the meaning of the words. However, you can find the meaning in the glossary.

German Spelling	Phonetic Symbol	Description	Examples
b	b		Butter (butter) - /butər/ aber (but) - /ābər/ Biene (bee) - /beenə/ geben (to give) - /geybən/
d	d	at the beginning of a syllable, or between vowels pronounced like the English b, d, g	du (you) - /doo/ dann (then) - /dun/ reden (to talk) - /reydən/ denken (to think) - /denkən/ Geld (money) - /gelt/ gut (good) - /goot/
g	g		Magen (stomach) - /māgən/
b	p	at the end of a syllable, or before -s- and -t- pronounced like English p, t, k	ob (whether) - /op/ gibt (gives) - /gīpt/ und (and) - /unt/ lädst (load) - /leytst/ Tag (day) - /tāk/ fliegst (fly) - /fleekst/
d	t		
g	k		

Pay special attention to the following consonants:

German Spelling	Phonetic Symbols	Description	Examples
l	l	similar to English -l- but further to the front; tip of tongue should touch the gum ridge	leben (to live) - /leybən/ als (as) - /als/ Bild (picture) - /bilt/
v	f	generally as English -f-	Vater (father) - /fātər/
v	v	betwewen vowels like English -v-	Novelle (novelle) - /novelə/
j	j	as English -y- in you, yes, or year	ja (yes) - /yā/ Jahr (year) - /jār/
w	v	exactly as the English -v- in vine	Wasser (water) - /vasər/ Winter (winter) - /vintər/
s	z	at the beginning of a syllable and between vowels = -z- as in zoom	sagen (to say) - /zāgən/ Rose (rose) - /rōzə/ lesen (to read) - /leyzən/
s, ss,	s	single -s- at the end of a syllable, or double -s- and -ß- always -s- as in son	als (as) - /als/ lassen (to let) - /lasən/ Fluß (river) - /flus/
z	ts	always as English -ts- in sits, lets; note that English has this sound in final position, but never at the beginning of a syllable	Zoo (zoo) - /tsō/ Zeit (time) - /tsit/ zu (to) - /tsoo/ zwei (two) - /tsvi/

Pay particular attention to the *ch* combination in German. The pronunciation is very unfamiliar to speakers of English. *Ch* after *a, o, u, au* is pronounced in the back of the mouth (velum) where you also pronounce the *k*. However, it is much softer. If you can say the name for the Scottish lake *Loch* Lomond, with more breath or friction, you can say the German velar (back) *ch*. Listen carefully to the examples on the tape. Note that the phonetic symbol for velar ch is /x/. We will follow this pattern.

Nacht	(night)	/naxt/	lachen	(to laugh)	/laxən/
Buch	(book)	/boox/	Loch	(hole)	/lox/
Rauch	(smoke)	/roux/	Bauch	(stomach)	/boux/
hoch	(high)	/hõx/	nach	(after)	/nãx/

Ch after *e, i, ö, ä, ü, ei, eu and* after *n, r, l* is pronounced between the front of the tongue and the hard palate. It sounds very much like the English *h* in hue, huge, or human when pronounced with a lot of friction. Again, listen carefully to the tape. The phonetic symbol for palatal ch is /ç/. We will follow this pattern also.

ich (I)	/iç/	schlecht (bad)	/shleçt/
Licht (light)	/liçt/	leicht (easy)	/liçt/
echt (real)	/eçt/	München (Munich)	/münçən/
weich (soft)	/viç/	Küche (kitchen)	/küçe/

A Few Final Notes

1.   The German *r* never sounds anything like our American *r*. Using an American *r* in German sounds about as bad as using a German *r* in English. Most Germans say a uvular *r* for which the back of the tongue is raised toward the uvula. (The uvula is that little droplet of skin that you can see in the back of your mouth.) Probably the best way to learn the German *r* is by tipping your head back and trying a *dry* gargle. This might sound ridiculous, but it works. Don't let your tongue flip upwards. Listen to the tape and repeat as best as you can.

Rose (rose)	/rõzə/	Rand (edge)	/runt/
rund (round)	/runt/	Rhein (Rhine)	/rin/
Ring (ring)	/ring/	Rücken (back)	/rükən/
Rest (rest)	/rest/	reden (speak)	/reydən/
Ruder (rudder)	/roodər/	raten (guess)	/rãtən/

Note that when German *r* is *not* followed by a vowel, it tends to become vocalized, that is, it is pronounced almost as a vowel-like glide. Practice these examples:

Uhr (clock)	/oor/	mir (me)	/meer/
Tür (door)	/tür/	fährt (drives)	/feyrt/
Tier (animal)	/teer/	spart (saves)	/shpãrt/

2. *sp/st* at the beginning of a word is pronounced like *shp* or *sht*. Again, please practice.

Stuhl	(chair)	/shtool/
stehen	(to stand)	/shteyən/
spielen	(to play)	/shpeelən/
spannend	(exciting)	/spanənt/
sprechen	(to speak)	/shpreçən/

3. *sch* is pronounced like English *sh*.

Schiff	(ship)	/shif/
Schule	(school)	/shoolə/
Asche	(ash)	/ashə/
waschen	(to wash)	/vashən/

Kapitel 1

Greetings, Introductions, Useful Expressions

Culture Notes

The most common greeting in all German-speaking countries is "Guten Tag." It will suffice for most "hello/good day" situations during day time. "Grüß Gott" is also a popular equivalent to "Guten Tag," but only in southern Germany and Austria. "Grüizi" is used in Switzerland, but primarily among native Swiss.

"Guten Morgen" and "Guten Abend" are fitting greetings if used at the right time of the day. "Gute Nacht," however, is strictly used as a good-bye saying before turning in for the night.

And then there is the universal "Auf Wiedersehen" when one leaves. It is always appropriate.

There are a number of other informal greetings used by Germans, Austrians, and Swiss. "Grüß dich" (Germany and Austria), "Servus" (Austria), "Tschau" (Switzerland). Unless you are a close friend of the German-speaking people around you, you won't have much use for these greetings.

Shaking hands is a much practiced ritual among Germans, Austrians, and Swiss. They do it a lot more often than their Anglo-Saxon counterparts. They shake hands in everyday life, not just at receptions. A matter of courtesy: the gentleman is always supposed to wait for the outstretched hand when shaking hands with a lady.

If you introduce yourself: "Ich heiße...." or "Ich bin Walter/Erika" will be fine. Leave out "Herr, Frau, Fräulein" before your name.

However, if you introduce other people, the phrase: "Darf ich Ihnen Herrn/Frau/Fräulein...vorstellen" is the proper way of introduction.

If you can't remember that, just pointing at the person and saying: "Herr/Frau/Fräulein..." will do.

WICHTIGE AUSDRÜCKE	*IMPORTANT EXPRESSIONS*	
Ja.	*Yes.*	
Nein.	*No.*	These you need...
Bitte.	*Please.*	
Danke *oder* Danke schön.	*Thank you.*	

1

WICHTIGE AUSDRÜCKE	*IMPORTANT EXPRESSIONS (cont.)*
Vielen Dank.	*Many thanks.*
Nein, danke.	*No, thank you.*
Entschuldigen Sie *oder*	*Excuse me or*
Verzeihung.	*pardon me.*

BEGRÜßUNG UND ABSCHIED	*HELLOS AND GOOD-BYES*

Important... Guten Morgen / Guten Tag / Guten Abend / Grüß Gott / Auf Wiedersehen / Gute Nacht / Bis bald / Bis später / Tschüß

Guten Morgen is used to say hello in the morning.
Guten Tag is used to say hello at any time during the day.
Guten Abend is used to say both hello and good-bye during the evening.
Gute Nacht is a farewell late in the evening and at bedtime.
Auf Wiedersehen can be used at any time to say good-bye.
Tschüß is an informal farewell.
Bis später is equivalent to see you later.
Bis bald simply means see you soon.

IMPORTANT QUESTION WORDS

wann	*when*
warum	*why*
was	*what*
wer	*who*
wie	*how*
wie lang(e)	*how long*
wie oft	*how often*
wieviel(e)	*how much, many*
wo	*where*
woher	*where from*
wohin	*where to*

DIALOGE	*DIALOGS*

Herr B.:	Guten Morgen.	Good morning.
	Ich heiße Rolf Berger.	My name is Rolf Berger.
Herr C.:	Guten Morgen, ich heiße John Cook. Wie geht es Ihnen?	Good morning, I am John Cook. How are you?
Herr B.:	Danke, gut; und Ihnen?	Fine, thank you. And you?
Herr C.:	Danke, auch gut.	Fine.

Frau K.:	Entschuldigen Sie, wo ist die Luisenstraße?	Excuse me, where is Luisen Street?
Frau L.:	Die nächste Straße links.	The next street to your left.
Frau K.:	Danke schön.	Thank you.
Frau L.:	Bitte schön.	You are welcome.

Herr B.:	Darf ich bekanntmachen, mein Kollege, Erich Bürger. Herr Bürger, meine Frau, Jutta.	May I introduce my colleague, Erich Bürger. Mr. Bürger, my wife, Jutta.
Frau B.:	Sehr angenehm.	Pleased to meet you.

Frl. Lee:	Woher kommen Sie, Herr Klein?	Where are you from, Mr. Klein?
Herr K.:	Aus Frankfurt, und Sie?	From Frankfurt, and you?
Frl. Lee:	Aus Los Angeles.	From Los Angeles.
Herr K.:	Wie lange sind Sie schon in Deutschland?	How long have you been in Germany?
Frl. Lee:	Drei Wochen.	Three weeks.
Herr K.:	Und wohin fahren Sie jetzt?	And where are you going now?
Frl. Lee:	Nach Bonn.	To Bonn.

Herr J.:	Verzeihung. Wie komme ich zum Bahnhof?	Excuse me. How do I get to the train station?
Herr F.:	Fahren Sie mit dem Bus.	Go by bus.
Herr J.:	Wann fährt der Bus?	When is a bus going?
Herr F.:	Alle fünfzehn Minuten.	Every fifteen minutes.
Herr J.:	Vielen Dank.	Many thanks.
Herr F.:	Gern geschehen.	My pleasure.

HÄUFIGE FRAGEN

Wie heißen Sie?	*What's your name?*
Wie geht es Ihnen? *oder*	*How are you?*
Wie geht's?	*How are you?*
Wo wohnen Sie?	*Where do you live?*
Woher kommen Sie?	*Where are you from?*
Wohin fahren Sie?	*Where are you going?*
Was machen Sie heute abend?	*What are you doing tonight?*
Wie komme ich zum Flughafen?	*How do I get to the airport?*
Wie lange bleiben Sie?	*How long are you staying?*
Wieviel kostet das?	*How much does this cost?*
Wann fahren Sie nach Hause?	*When are you going home?*
Wieviele Kinder haben Sie?	*How many children do you have?*
Wie oft fahren Sie nach Hamburg?	*How often do you go to Hamburg?*
Warum bleiben Sie nicht hier?	*Why aren't you staying here?*

FREQUENTLY ASKED QUESTIONS

A. *Übung* (*Exercise*)

Stellen Sie Fragen! Write sentences with each one of the following question words.

> Beispiel: Wie = Wie heißen Sie?
> (Example)

1. Wo...
2. Wie...
3. Wer...
4. Was...
5. Wieviel...
6. Wie lang...
7. Wohin...
8. Woher...
9. Wann...

HÄUFIGE ANTWORTEN	FREQUENTLY GIVEN ANSWERS
Ich heiße Franz Kurz.	*My name is Franz Kurz.*
Ich komme aus München.	*I am from Munich.*
Ich fahre nach Hamburg.	*I am going to Hamburg.*
Wir gehen ins Kino.	*We are going to the movies.*
Wir bleiben vier Monate.	*We are staying four months.*
Wir haben drei Kinder.	*We have three children.*
Das kostet fünf Mark.	*That costs five marks.*
Ich wohne in Frankfurt.	*I live in Frankfurt.*

B.　Übung

Matching—find the appropriate answer to the questions below. Note that more than one answer may fit.*

Beispiel: Wie heißen Sie? = d. Karl Schmidt.
(Example)

1. Wo wohnen Sie?
2. Wie heißen Sie?
3. Wie geht's?
4. Woher kommen Sie?
5. Was machen Sie heute abend?
6. Wieviel kostet das?
7. Wann fahren Sie nach Hause?
8. Wie lange bleiben Sie?
9. Wohin fahren Sie?
10. Wie viele Kinder haben Sie?

Antworten (answers)

a. Fünfzig Mark.
b. Danke gut.
c. In Chicago
d. Karl Schmidt.
e. Ich spiele (play) Tennis.
f. Nicht gut.
g. Am Montag.
h. Zwei Monate.
i. Aus Bonn.
j. Ich gehe ins Konzert.
k. Am fünfzehnten Mai.
l. Nach Frankfurt.
m. Drei.

C.　Übung

Übersetzen Sie! Translate.

Beispiel:　What are you doing tonight?
Example: Was machen Sie heute abend?

1. How are you?
2. How much does this cost?

*Check unfamiliar words in the chapter vocabulary *(Wortschatz)* on page 13.

3.   What's your name?
4.   What are you doing tonight?
5.   Where do you live?
6.   Where are you from?   Fragen Sie...
7.   May I introduce...   (ask)
8.   Where are you going?
9.   My name is...
10.   I am from...(come from)
11.   I live in...   Sagen Sie...
12.   Many thanks.   (say)
13.   You are welcome.
14.   I am going to Munich.

Grammar

1.   The definite articles—der, die, das

Every German noun has a grammatical gender which is indicated by the definite article. English has only *one* definite article—*the*. German has three: **der, die, das**.

<u>der</u> words (masculine)
der Bus   *the bus*
der Mann   *the man*
der Tag   *the day*

<u>die</u> words (feminine)
die Frage   *the question*
die Antwort   *the answer*
die Frau   *the woman*

<u>das</u> words (neuter)
das Jahr   *the year*
das Konzert   *the concert*
das Kind   *the child*

The gender for all *plurals* is **die**.

Always learn a noun with its article!

> In German a young lady (das Mädchen) has no sex, while a turnip (die Rübe) has. Think what overwrought reverence that shows for the turnip, and what callous disrespect for the girl.
> Mark Twain

<u>der</u> words*   <u>die</u> words*
der Herr   die Dame
der Mann   die Frau   Gender and sex some-
der Student   die Studentin   times coincide...
der Vater   die Mutter

*If you don't recognize the English meaning of these nouns, look them up in the chapter vocabulary (*Wortschatz*) on page 13.

der words	**die** words	**das** words
der Tisch	die Gabel	das Messer
der Kalender	die Lampe	das Radio
der Computer	die Butter	das Haus
der Apfel	die Milch	das Geld

and sometimes not..

Nouns you want to use right away

	die Amerikanerin	die Eltern
	der Amerikaner	der Vater
	der Deutsche	die Mutter
	die Deutsche	die Tochter
	das Mädchen	FAMILY	der Sohn
PEOPLE	das Kind	der Bruder
	der Arzt	die Schwester
	der Kollege	
	die Kollegin	
	der Polizist	das Auto
		der Bus
	das Haus	die Straßenbahn
	die Wohnung	TRAVEL and	der Flughafen
HOME and	der Tisch	TRANSPORTATION	das Flugzeug
FURNISHINGS	die Lampe	der Zug
	das Telefon	der Bahnhof
	der Stuhl	das Taxi
	das Bett	der Paß
	das Radio	die Stadt
	der Fernseher	die Straße

A.   *Übung*

Write the *German* equivalent of the English definitions.

Beispiel: A person who heals the sick = der Arzt, die Ärztin

1. My father and mother are *meine* ....
2. You need this if you want to buy something ....

DON'T FORGET
THE ARTICLE...
(unless a pronoun
is given)

3. Items of transportation which are spelled the same in German and English
    .... or ....
4. Person who directs traffic ....
5. My parents' other son is *mein* ....
6. My parents' other daughter is *meine* ....
7. If you have one, you can talk long distance ....
8. A white beverage ....
9. You need these to eat your food .... and ....
10. I use this to watch the news ....

2.   Subject pronouns

A *pronoun* is a word that replaces a *noun*. The nominative case is the case of the subject. The subject is the person or thing performing the action. Look at these examples.

Was ist Karl?	Er ist Student.
Was ist Helga?	Sie ist Studentin.
Wie ist das Wetter?	Es ist schlecht.
Wie heißen die Kinder?	Sie heißen Hans und Karin.
Wo wohnen Sie?	Ich wohne in Chicago.

SINGULAR		**PLURAL**	
ich*	I	wir	we
er, sie, es	he, she, it	sie	they
Sie	you *(formal)*	Sie	you *(formal)*
du	you** (familiar)	ihr**	you *(familiar)*

The formal *Sie* is used when speaking to strangers and persons you would normally address as Herr (Mr., Sir), Frau (Mrs.), or Fräulein (Miss). The familiar *du* and *ihr* are used when speaking to relatives, close friends, children, animals, and generally among younger people and students. As a rule of thumb, use *du* and *ihr* with people whom you would call by their first name.

When to use du or Sie...

Customs regarding the use of *Sie* and *du* vary from place to place and change with time. If in doubt, you will always be correct to use *Sie* until you become certain that you may use *du*.

If in doubt... Sie!

A.   Übung

Supply the German pronoun suggested by the English cue.

Beispiel: ......Wir........ lernen Deutsch.   *We*

1. .... wohnt in New York.   *He*
2. .... tanzen oft.   *We*
3. .... fahren nach Deutschland.   *They*
4. .... lernt Deutsch.   *She*
5. .... spiele heute Tennis.   *I*
6. .... sind aus Hamburg.   *You*
7. .... ist kalt.   *It*
8. .... fahre nach Hause.   *I*
9. .... studiert Biologie.   *She*
10. .... arbeiten in New York.   *They*

> *Man* is a subject pronoun, corresponding to English one, people, you (but NEVER to English man). Hier trinkt man viel Bier. *One drinks a lot of beer here.*

---

*Unlike English *I*, German *ich* is not capitalized unless it begins a sentence. German *Sie* (you, formal) is always capitalized.

**There are three subject pronouns corresponding to English *you:* *du* (familiar sing.) *ihr* (familiar plural) and *Sie* (formal singular and plural). Since you will mostly encounter the *Sie* form, we will concentrate on the *Sie* form.

3. The gender of third-person pronouns

Pronouns must have the same gender as the nouns they replace. The corresponding pronouns for nouns if used as subject in a sentence are:

der = er   die = sie   das = es
plural die = sie

Herr Smith lernt Deutsch.	**Er** lernt Deutsch.
Mr. Smith is learning German.	*He is learning German.*
Frau Klein fährt nach Amerika.	**Sie** fährt nach Amerika.
Mrs. Klein is going to America.	*She is going to America.*
Der Tisch ist groß.	**Er** ist groß.
The table is large.	*It is large.*
Die Lampe ist teuer.	**Sie** ist teuer.
The lamp is expensive.	*It is expensive.*
Das Radio kostet zu viel.	**Es** kostet zu viel.
The radio costs too much.	*It costs too much.*

A.   *Übung*

Answer yes, replacing the *noun* with the appropriate *pronoun*.

Beispiel: Ist die Frage schwer? Ja, *sie* ist schwer.
Is the question difficult? Yes, it is difficult.

1. Fährt der Bus alle 15 Minuten? Ja, ... fährt alle 15 Minuten.
2. Ist das Konzert heute? Ja, ... ist heute.
3. Heißt die Dame Frau König? Ja, ... heißt Frau König.
4. Studiert Karl Medizin? Ja, ... studiert Medizin.
5. Ist das Auto neu? Ja, ... ist neu.
6. Kostet das Radio zu viel? Ja, ... kostet zu viel.
7. Ist der Tisch alt? Ja, ... ist alt.
8. Ist die Luisenstraße weit von hier? Ja, ... ist weit von hier.
9. Sind deutsche Autos gut? Ja, ... sind gut.
10. Sind John und Tim Amerikaner? Ja, ... sind Amerikaner.

4. The present tense form of verbs

The basic form of a German verb is the infinitive. Most German infinitives end in *en;* a few end in *n*. Dictionaries list verbs under the infinitive form.

Beispiel: kaufen = to buy

You will need these verbs right away.

for traveling and residing					
	kommen	*to come*		kosten	*to cost*
	gehen	*to go*	for shopping	kaufen	*to buy*
	fahren	*to drive, ride*		zahlen	*to pay*
	bleiben	*to remain*			
	wohnen	*to live*			
	reisen	*to travel*			
for having fun	tanzen	*to dance*	and other verbs we can't do without	haben	*to have*
	schwimmen	*to swim*		sein	*to be*
	spielen	*to play*		machen	*to do, make*

trinken	*to drink*	antworten	*to answer*
singen	*to sing*	lernen	*to learn*
heißen	*to be called*	arbeiten	*to work*

SINGULAR		PLURAL	
ich	kaufe	wir	kaufen
er		Sie	kaufen
sie }	kauft	sie	kaufen
es		ihr	kauft
du	kauf**st**		

A. Übung

Complete the sentences with the correct verb form.

Beispiel: Ich ...... frage .... viel.   *fragen*

1. Wie .... Sie?   *heißen*
2. Wo .... er?   *wohnen*
3. Woher .... sie (she)?   *kommen*
4. Ich .... eine Lampe.   *kaufen*
5. Was .... Hans?   *studieren*
6. Wo .... Frau Braun?   *arbeiten**
7. Ich .... viel.   *fragen*
8. Wir .... immer.   *antworten**

arbeiten	du arbeit**est**	er arbeit**et**	ihr arbeit**et**
finden	du find**est**	er find**et**	ihr find**et**
antworten	du antwort**est**	er antwort**et**	ihr antwort**et**

The most common way of saying in German that you like doing something is to use **gern** with a verb.

Ich trinke *gern* Orangensaft.
I like to drink orange juice.
Hans schwimmt gern.
Hans likes to swim.

If you don't like doing something, use **nicht** (not) between the verb and gern.

Ich trinke *nicht* gern Orangensaft.
Hans schwimmt *nicht* gern.

B. Übung

Say that the following people like doing certain activities.

Beispiel: Annie likes to sing.
Annie singt gern.

*When the verb stem ends in **-d** or **-t**, a linking **-e-** is inserted between the stem and the ending in order to facilitate pronunciation of the **du-**, **er-**, and **ihr-**forms.

1.   Hans likes to dance.
2.   We like to learn German.
3.   I like to drink coffee. (Kaffee)
4.   They like to work.
5.   Karin likes to swim.
6.   I like to play tennis.
7.   You like to travel.
8.   They like to sing.
9.   He likes to hike.
10.   We like to live in Florida.

If you were a native speaker of German learning English, you would have to learn three forms to express present time in English. Fortunately, German has only one.

regular present	*We save money.*	
progressive present	*We are saving money.*	Wir sparen Geld.
emphatic present	*We do save money.*	

In order to describe someone or something, you need to know some adjectives and adverbs. Learn these and you will be able to say a lot more.

ADJECTIVES		ADVERBS	
billig, teuer	*cheap, expensive*	immer, nie	*always, never*
gut, schlecht	*good, bad*	oft, selten	*often, seldom*
krank, gesund	*sick, healthy*	viel, wenig	*much, little*
intelligent, dumm	*intelligent, dumb*	hier, dort	*here, there*
kurz, lang	*short, long*	wieder	*again*
alt, jung	*old, young*		
alt, neu	*old, new*		
kalt, heiß	*cold, hot*		
warm, kühl	*warm, cool*		
groß, klein	*big, small*		
fleißig, faul	*busy, lazy*		

5.   Present tense of sein and haben

Sein *(to be)* and **haben** *(to have)* are key verbs because they are used so often. Their forms must be memorized and practiced.

	SINGULAR		*sein = to be*	PLURAL	
ich	bin	I am		wir sind	we are
er		he		Sie sind	you are *(formal)*
sie	ist	she	is	sie sind	they are
es		it			
du	bist	you are *(familiar)*		ihr seid	you are *(familiar)*

SINGULAR			*haben = to have*	PLURAL	
ich	habe	I have		wir haben	we have
er		he		Sie haben	you have *(formal)*
sie	hat	she	has	sie haben	they have
es		it			
du	hast	you have *(familiar)*		ihr habt	you have *(familiar)*

A. Übung

Supply the correct form of **sein**.

> Beispiel: Wir ......sind........ fleißig.

1. Herr Braun .... Amerikaner.
2. In Deutschland .... Bier billig.
3. Heute .... ich krank.
4. Franz .... intelligent.
5. Wir .... müde.
6. Der Koffer (suitcase) .... klein.
7. Die Leute (people) .... fleißig.
8. Wir .... aus der Schweiz.
9. .... Sie Amerikaner, Herr Brown?
10. Karin .... wieder gesund.

B. Übung

Say that the cued subjects have something.

> Beispiel: .....Haben....... Sie ein Radio?

1. Wir .... viel Zeit.
2. Hans .... ein teures Auto.
3. Ich .... ein neues Haus.
4. Karin .... einen Freund.
5. Das Kind .... einen Ball.
6. .... du ein Radio?
7. .... er Zeit?
8. .... Herr und Frau Schmidt Kinder?

C. Übung

Now translate all sentences of A and B into English.

> Beispiel: Die Leute sind fleißig. = *The people are busy (or industrious).*

D. Übung

Wer sind Sie?
Say something about yourself by replacing the underlined word with one or more
of the cued expressions that apply to you.

Ich bin *Student*—Studentin, Hausfrau, Amerikaner, Sportlerin, Geschäftsmann (businessman), Beamtin (civil servant), Manager.

Ich bin *charmant*—fit, jung, alt, nett, intelligent, fleißig.

Ich spiele gern *Tennis*—Fußball, Gitarre, Basketball, Golf, Klavier (piano).

Ich habe *Zeit*—Geld, Humor, Kinder, ein Auto, ein Haus, ein Boot, ein Motorrad.

Ich trinke gern *Milch*—Wasser, Kaffee, Tee, Wein, Bier, Apfelsaft, Cola.

Ich *spiele* gern—tanze, arbeite, trinke, wandere, reise, lerne, lese, schreibe, schwimme.

E.   Übung

Now say something about a friend.

> Beispiel: er/sie ist.... Er ist nett.
>
> er/sie ist...
>
> er/sie hat...
>
> er/sie spielt gern...
>
> er/sie trinkt gern...

6.   Verbs with vowel changes*

A number of common German verbs change their stem vowel in the *er/sie/es* and *du-forms* in the present tense. There are no rules; you must memorize them.

sprechen	er/sie/es	spricht	*to speak*
	du	sprichst	
sehen	er/sie/es	sieht	*to see*
	du	siehst	
lesen	er/sie/es	liest	*to read*
	du	liest	
essen	er/sie/es	ißt	*to eat*
	du	ißt	
fahren	er/sie/es	fährt	*to drive*
	du	fährst	
schlafen	er/sie/es	schläft	*to sleep*
	du	schläfst	

Wiederholung (Review)

A.   How would you greet a person at...

Beispiel: 2 p.m. = Guten Tag.

1.   at 12 noon.
2.   at 8 a.m.

*This vowel change is always indicated in the vocabulary in this manner: sprechen (spricht)... lesen (liest)...

3. at 7 p.m.
4. at 3 p.m.
5. at 10 a.m.

B.   Ask questions which would elicit the answers below.

Beispiel: Wo…? Sie ist jetzt in Österreich.
              Wo ist sie jetzt?

1. Wann…?   Herr Schmidt arbeitet heute.
2. Was…?   Er kauft Briefmarken.
3. Wie…?   Das Wetter ist schön.
4. Wieviel…?   Es kostet DM 15,30.
5. Wo…?   Frau Müller wohnt in Frankfurt.

C.   Say in German.

1. I like to travel.
2. What is your name?
3. How much does the radio cost?
4. We like to play Tennis.
5. They don't have time.
6. She lives in Munich.
7. Excuse me, please.
8. Where are you going now?

D.   Respond to:

1. Sind Sie Amerikaner?
2. Wohin fahren Sie?
3. Wo wohnen Sie?
4. Reisen Sie gern?
5. Wie lange bleiben Sie hier?

Wortschatz

Nouns

der Abschied, -e*   farewell, say goodbye

der Amerikaner, -   American, male

die Amerikanerin, -nen   American, female

der Angestellte, -n   male or female employee (clerk)

der Apfel, ¨   apple

der Apfelsaft, ¨e   apple cider

der Bahnhof, ¨e   train station

der Ball, ¨e   ball

die Banane, -n   banana

der Beamte, -n   civil servant

die Begrüßung, -en   greeting

das Beispiel, -e   example

das Bier, -e   beer

die Biologie   biology

das Boot, -e   boat

der Bruder, ¨   brother

der Bus, -se   bus

die Butter   butter

das Cola, -s   Cola (coke)

der Computer, -   computer

die Dame, -n   lady

(das) Deutsch   German

der Flughafen, ¨   airport

*letter(s) after comma indicate plural forms

die Frage, -n   question
die Frau, -en   woman
der Freund, -e   friend
die Freundin, -nen   friend, female
das Fußballspiel, -e   soccer (game)
die Gabel, -n   fork
das Geld, -er   money
die Geschäftsfrau, -en   businesswoman
der Geschäftsmann   businessman
die Geschäftsleute   business people
das Glas, ¨er   glass
das Haus, ¨er   house
  zu Haus(e)   at home
  nach Haus(e)   home
die Hausfrau, -en   housewife
der Herr, -en   gentleman
der Humor   humor (sense of humor)
das Jahr, -e   year
der Kaffee   coffee
der Kalender, -   calendar
das Kind, -er   child
das Klavier, -e   piano
der Koffer, -   suitcase
das Konzert, -e   concert
die Lampe, -n   lamp
der Löffel, -   spoon
der Manager, -   manager, male
die Managerin, -nen   manager, female

der Mann, ¨er   man
die Mark   German mark
die Medizin   medicine
das Messer, -   knife
die Minute, -n   minute
der Monat, -e   month
der Montag, -e   Monday
die Mutter, ¨   mother
der Orangensaft, ¨e   orange juice
das Radio, -s   radio
der Sohn, ¨e   son
die Schwester, -n   sister
der Sportler, -   sportsman
der Student, -en   student, male
die Studentin, -nen   student, female
der Tag, -e   day
der Tee, -s   tea
das Tennis   tennis
das Telefon, -e   telephone
der Tisch, -e   table
die Tochter, ¨   daughter

der Vater, ¨   father
das Wasser   water
das Wetter   weather
die Woche, -n   week
die Zeit, -en   time

Verbs

antworten   to answer
arbeiten   to work
bleiben   to remain, stay
fahren (fährt)   to drive, go
fragen   to ask
gehen   to go
heißen   to be called
kaufen   to buy
kommen   to come
kosten   to cost
lernen   to learn
machen   to make, to do
reisen   to travel
schwimmen   to swim
spielen   to play
tanzen   to dance
trinken   to drink
wandern   to hike
wohnen   to live, reside

Other Words

alle   all, every, everyone
alt   old
aus   out of, from
billig   cheap, inexpensive
braun   brown
dort   there
drei   three
faul   lazy
fleißig   busy, diligent
gern haben   to like
gesund   healthy
groß   large, big
haben   to have, possess
heiß   hot
hier   here
heute   today
heute abend   tonight
heute morgen   this morning
immer   always
intelligent   intelligent
jetzt   now

jung young
kalt cold
kühl cool
kurz short
lang long
links left
müde tired
nach to
nächst- next
nah(e) near
nett nice
neu new
nicht not
nie never
oft often
schlecht bad
teuer expensive
viel(e) much, many
von from
wann when
warm warm
warum why
was what
weit far
wenig few
wieder again
wie lang(e) how long
wie oft how often
wieviel(e) how much, how many

wo where
woher where from
wohin where to

Idiomatic Expressions

Auf Wiedersehen! Good-bye!
Bis bald. Till then.
Bis später. Until later.
Bitte schön. You are welcome.
Danke (schön). Thank you. Thanks.
Darf ich bekannt machen? May I introduce…
…eine Frage stellen …to ask a question
Entschuldigen Sie, bitte. Excuse me, please.
Freut mich! My pleasure!
Gern geschehen! You are welcome!
Grüß Gott! Good day! (Austrian)
Guten Abend! Good evening!
Guten Morgen! Good morning!
Gute Nacht! Good night!
Guten Tag! Good day!
Tschüß! Bye now!
Verzeihung! Excuse me!
Vielen Dank! Many thanks!
Wie geht es Ihnen? How are you?
Wie geht's? How are you?

Kapitel 2

Numbers

Culture Notes

When it comes to the chores of simple arithmetic, Europeans and Americans do it pretty much the same way nowadays: most of them use a calculator.

But the metric system—although officially adopted by the Congress of the United States in December 1975 as the system of measurements for the future—is still a bit strange to many Americans, especially when travelling in Europe.

This conversion table may be helpful.

Measures, Weights and Temperature

American Measures and the Metrical System

Lengths

1 mm	=	0.039 in	1 in	=	2.54 cm
1 cm	=	0.394 ft	1 ft	=	30.48 cm
1 m	=	1.094 yds	1 yd	=	91.44 cm
1 km	=	0.621 mile	1 mile	=	1.609 km

Areas or Surfaces

1 sq mm	=	0.002 sq in	1 sq in	=	6.45 sq cm
1 sq cm	=	0.155 sq in	1 sq ft	=	929.03 sq cm
1 sq m	=	1.196 sq yds	1 sq yd	=	0.836 sq m
1 ha	=	2.471 acres	1 acre	=	4047 sq m
1 sq km	=	0.386 sq miles	1 sq mile	=	2.59 sq km
	=	247.11 acres		=	259 ha

Weights

1 mg	=	0.015 grain	1 grain	=	0.065 g
1 g	=	15.432 grains	1 oz	=	28.35 g
1 kg	=	2.205 lb	1 lb	=	453.59 g
1 t	=	2205 lb	1 net cwt	=	45.34 kg
	=	1.102 net t	1 net t	=	907.185 kg
				=	0.907 t

Capacities

1 l	=	2.114 liquid pt	1 liquid pt	=	0.473 l
	=	1.057 liquid qt	1 liquid qt	=	0.946 l
	=	0.264 liquid gal	1 liquid gal	=	3.785 l
1 hl	=	26.418 liquid gal	1 bu	=	35.238 l

mm = millimeter, cm = centimeter, m = meter, km = kilometer; sq mm = square millimeter, sq cm = square centimeter, sq m = square meter, sq km = square kilometer, ha = hectare; mg = milligram, g = gram, kg = kilogram, t = ton (metric); l = liter, hl = hectoliter.

Conversion formula for temperature

°Fahrenheit (F)   ° Celsius (C)

$$°F = \frac{18C}{10} + 32 \qquad °C = \frac{10(F - 32)}{18}$$

inches

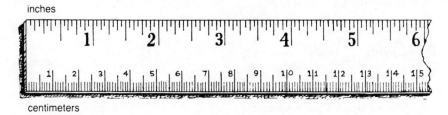

centimeters

The following points of reference and examples may bring the metric system a bit closer to home.

$$1 \text{ Liter} = \text{ca. a quart}$$
$$20°\ C = 68 \text{ Fahrenheit (fever begins at } 37.5 \text{ C)}$$
$$100 \text{ km} = 62 \text{ miles}$$
$$3000 \text{ Meter} = \text{ca. } 10,000 \text{ feet}$$
$$1000 \text{ m}^2 = \text{ca. } 0.25 \text{ acres}$$
$$1,65 \text{ m groß} = 5 \text{ feet, } 6 \text{ inches tall.}$$

Cardinal Numbers

Cardinal numbers (one, two, three, and so on) are used in *counting*. Ordinal numbers (first, second, third, and so on) show the *rank* of an item in a series.

0 null	14 vierzehn	70 siebzig
1 eins	15 fünfzehn	80 achtzig
2 zwei	16 sechzehn	90 neunzig
3 drei	17 siebzehn	100 hundert
4 vier	18 achtzehn	101 hunderteins
5 fünf	19 neunzehn	102 hundertzwei
6 sechs	20 zwanzig	103 hundertdrei
7 sieben	21 einundzwanzig	145 hundertfünfundvierzig
8 acht	22 zweiundzwanzig	200 zweihundert
9 neun	23 dreiundzwanzig	300 dreihundert
10 zehn	30 dreißig	600 sechshundert
11 elf	40 vierzig	700 siebenhundert
12 zwölf	50 fünfzig	1000 tausend
13 dreizehn	60 sechzig	

Note an essential difference when using numbers in English and German:

DEUTSCH (GERMAN)	*ENGLISCH (ENGLISH)*
26 = sechsundzwanzig	26 = twenty-six
48 = achtundvierzig	48 = forty-eight
53 = dreiundfünfzig	53 = fifty-three

German compound numbers are always written as one word. And here is another difference:

eine Million = one million
eine Milliarde = one billion
eine Billion = one trillion

A.   *Übung*

°to count   1. Zählen° Sie von null bis 20.

2. Zählen Sie von 40 bis 60.

°uneven   3. Sagen Sie alle ungeraden° Zahlen von 81 bis 101.

B.   *Übung*

Antworten Sie auf deutsch!

°your   1. Was ist Ihre° Telefonnummer?

2. Was ist Ihre Zimmernummer?

3. Was ist Ihre Hausnummer?

4. Wieviele Kilometer ist es von New York nach Los Angeles?

What about expressing "...times," something that is done or occurs more than once?

einmal = once
zweimal = twice
dreimal = three times
viermal = four times
zehnmal = ten times
hundertmal = hundred times

°to calculate   *Wie rechnen° die Deutschen?*

$8 + 7 = 15$	acht plus sieben ist fünfzehn
$26 - 9 = 17$	sechsundzwanzig minus neun ist siebzehn
$4 \times 6 = 24$	viermal sechs ist vierundzwanzig
$63 \div 7 = 9$	dreiundsechzig durch sieben ist neun

C.   *Übung*

Nun rechnen Sie—auf deutsch, bitte. Sagen Sie es laut.

1.	$33 + 14 = 47$	6.	$5 \times 7 = 35$
2.	$87 - 13 = 74$	7.	$42 - 8 = 34$
3.	$7 \times 3 = 21$	8.	$50 \div 10 = 5$
4.	$40 \div 8 = 5$	9.	$12 + 9 = 21$
5.	$17 + 6 = 23$	10.	$25 - 6 = 19$

---

a. **eins** has an **-s** when it stands alone as a cardinal number, but has no **-s** in compounds.

b. **dreißig** is spelled with an **ß**, not z.

c. **sechs** is pronounced /zeks/, but in **sechzehn** and **sechzig**, the **ch** sound is the same as in **ich**.

d. the **-en** in **sieben** is dropped in **siebzehn** and **siebzig**.

D. *Übung*

Antworten Sie auf deutsch, bitte!

1. Wie hoch ist Mt. McKinley?
2. Wie groß sind Sie?
3. Wieviel Mark bekommt man heute für den Dollar?
4. Wieviele Brüder und Schwestern haben Sie?
5. Wie alt sind Sie?

DIALOGE	*DIALOGS*
A. Die Äpfel hier—wieviel kosten sie?	These apples, how much are they?
B. Zwei Mark fünfzig das Kilo.	Two marks fifty a kilo.
A. Drei Kilo, bitte.	Three kilos, please.
B. Dreimal zwei fünfzig—das macht sieben Mark fünfzig.	Three times two fifty—that is seven marks fifty.

A. Wie weit ist es von Salzburg nach München?	How far is it from Salzburg to Munich?
B. Ungefähr 170 Kilometer.	Approximately 170 Kilometers.
A. Und wie lange fährt man?	And how long does it take?
B. Ungefähr zwei bis zweieinhalb Stunden.	Approximately two to two-and-a-half hours.

A. Wie warm ist es heute?	How warm is it today?
B. Ich glaube etwa fünfundzwanzig Grad.	I think about twenty-five degrees.
A. Nein, so warm ist es nicht.	No, it can't be that warm.
B. Oh doch, ich trage heute keinen Pullover.	O yes, I am not wearing a sweater today.

A. Wie lange bleibst du in Europa?	How long are you staying in Europe?
B. Zwei bis drei Wochen.	Two to three weeks.
A. Nicht länger?	Not longer?
B. Nein, ich habe leider kein Geld mehr.	No, unfortunately I don't have any more money.

Grammar

---

1. **A few rules about basic word order**

   a. *Subject-Verb (S-V)*

   When a sentence in German consists only of a main clause, the *subject-verb* word order is usually used.

	SUBJECT	VERB	
	Sie	fahren	nach Österreich.
°stops Beispiele:	Der Bus	hält°	hier.
	Es	ist	heute warm.

b.   *Verb-Subject (V-S)*

In questions without question words, the *verb-subject* (V-S) word order is used and the voice is raised at the end of the question.

	VERB	SUBJECT	
	Fahren	Sie	nach Österreich.
Beispiele:	Hält	der Bus	hier?
	Ist	es	heute warm?

A.   Übung

Change these statements into questions:

Beispiel: Familie Roberts kommt nach Salzburg.
          Kommt Familie Roberts nach Salzburg?

1.   Wir haben eine Wohnung.
2.   Hans hat ein Haus.
3.   Es ist weit von Berlin nach Wien.
4.   Wir bleiben zwei Wochen in Europa.
5.   Inge hat drei Brüder.
6.   Herr Braun hat viel Geld.

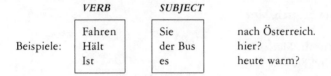

c.   *Question Word-Verb-Subject (Qu-V-S)*

Questions in which question words (interrogatives) are used, show the *question word-verb-subject* (Qu-V-S) word order.

	QUESTION WORD	VERB	SUBJECT
	Wann	kommt	die Straßenbahn?
Beispiele:	Wohin	fährt	der Bus?
	Wieviel	kostet	das Haus?

B.   Übung

Use the correct question word.

1.	.... ist hier das Telefon?	*Where*
2.	.... kommt der Bus?	*When*
3.	.... fahren Sie?	*Where (to)*
4.	.... ist die Studentin?	*Who*
5.	.... geht es Ihnen?	*How*
6.	.... glauben Sie das nicht?	*Why*
7.	.... kostet das?	*How much*
8.	.... kommen Sie?	*Where (from)*
9.	.... machen Sie heute abend?	*What*
10.	.... bleibt Maria in Österreich?	*How long*

C. *Übung*

Sie fragen…

> Beispiel: Do you have five marks?
>   Haben Sie fünf Mark?

1. How much does it cost?
2. Do they have children?
3. Does she stay three days or four days?
4. Does it cost 38 shillings or 83 shillings?
5. How far is it from here?
6. Does she need money?

D. *Übung*

Sagen Sie…

> Beispiel: It takes (one drives) four hours.
>   Man fährt vier Stunden.

1. It costs 15 marks.
2. I have two brothers and three sisters.
3. He buys the radio.
4. It is 12 degrees today.
5. You get the money tomorrow.
6. I don't have enough time.

These nouns are often used without an article:

(das) Geld	Haben Sie Geld?	*Do you have any money?*
(die) Zeit	Haben wir Zeit?	*Do we have time?*
(der) Hunger	Hat er Hunger?	*Is he hungry?*
(der) Durst	Hat sie Durst?	*Is she thirsty?*
(die) Mark	Haben Sie D-Mark?	*Do you have marks?*
(der) Schilling	Haben Sie Schillinge?	*Do you have shillings?*
(der) Franken	Hast du Schweizer Franken?	*Do you have Swiss francs?*
(der) Amerikaner	Ist er Amerikaner?	*Is he an American?*
(die) Schweizerin	Ist Maria Schweizerin?	*Is Maria Swiss?*

Ordinal Numbers

der, die, das			
	erste	elfte	zwanzigste
	zweite	zwölfte	einundzwanzigste
	dritte	dreizehnte	zweiundzwanzigste
	vierte	vierzehnte	dreißigste
	fünfte	usw.	vierzigste
	sechste		hundertste
	siebte		tausendste
	achte		zehntausendste
	neunte		millionste
	zehnte		

2.   Ordinal numbers

Ordinal numbers rank an item in a series. The definite article is always used.

note

from 2–19   = cardinal number + t + ending =
zweite, fünfte, dreizehnte

from 20–... = cardinal number + st + ending =
zwanzigste, achtunddreißigste

with
der, die, das
-te-

Note the ending when you use *ordinal numbers.*

Heute ist der sechs*te* Mai.

Morgen ist der dreizehn*te* Oktober.

but if you use
am (on the) =
-ten-

Hans kommt am vierundzwanzig*sten** Mai.

Inge heiratet am dreißig*sten* Juni.

Ordinal numbers are used to express the date.

Januar
Februar = Winter
März

April
Mai = Frühling
Juni

Here are the months
of the year and the
seasons

Juli
August = Sommer
September

Oktober
November = Herbst
Dezember

Both the months and the seasons have masculine gender. *Der* Januar, *der* Februar, *der* Winter, *der* Frühling, usw. (etc.)

How do you ask what day it is?	
Welcher Tag ist heute?	*What day is today?*
or Der wievielte (Tag) ist heute?	*What is today's date?*

A.   Übung

Antworten Sie bitte. Use *am* in your answer and add the ending *-ten* to the stem of the ordinal number.

Beispiel: Wann ist Ihr Geburtstag?   *When is your birthday?*
Mein Geburtstag ist am zwölften Juli.
or just   ...am zwölften Juli.

°Christmas   1.   Wann ist Weihnachten?°

°national holiday   2.   Wann ist der Nationalfeiertag° der USA?

*It's "am vierundzwanzigsten" because ordinals are declined like adjective endings. "Am = an dem" signals dative case which requires the -en ending. (see chapter 4)

3. Wann ist Silvester?°   °New Year's Eve
4. Wann ist Neujahr?
5. Wann fliegen° Sie nach Europa?   °fly
6. Wann fahren Sie nach Deutschland?
7. Wann haben Sie Geburtstag?
8. Wann fahren Sie nach Hause?

3. What about fractions?

Fractions in German are treated like neuter nouns. From *Drittel* on, they are
formed by adding the ending -el to the ordinal number.

$^1/_2$ ein halb-(*or* die Hälfte) $^1/_{10}$ ein Zehntel
$^1/_3$ ein Drittel $1^1/_2$ eineinhalb
$^1/_4$ ein Viertel $2^2/_3$ zweizweidrittel
$^3/_4$ Dreiviertel $^1/_{100}$ ein Hundertstel

A. *Übung*

Say: $^5/_8$; $^3/_5$; $^1/_9$; $^2/_3$; $^1/_5$
Complete the sentence with the cued fraction.

1. ($^1/_2$) Ein Pfund ist die . . . . von einem Kilo.
2. ($^1/_4$) Ich bleibe noch eine . . . . Stunde.°   °hour
3. ($^1/_8$) Er trinkt noch ein . . . . Wein.
4. ($^7/_{10}$) Liebfrauenmilch kommt in . . . . Flaschen.
5. ($^3/_4$) . . . . des Jahres lebe ich in Amerika.

DIALOGE (ORDINALZAHLEN)

A. Wann fliegen Sie nach Wien?	When are you flying to Vienna?
B. Im Juni.	In June.
A. Am wievielten?	What date?
B. Am vierzehnten.	On the fourteenth.

A. Wann hat Inge Geburtstag?	When is Inge's birthday?
B. Ich glaube am fünfundzwanzigsten Mai.	I believe on the 25th of May.
A. Und Paul?	And Paul's?
B. Am sechzehnten Juli.	On the 16th.

A. Ist das Ihre erste oder zweite Reise nach Deutschland?	Is this your first or your second trip to Germany?
B. Oh nein, das ist schon meine vierte.	O no, this is already my fourth.
A. Und wann fahren Sie wieder nach Amerika?	And when are you going back to America?
B. Am siebzehnten Februar.	On the 17th of February.

A. Herr Ober, ein Glas Wein, bitte.	Waiter, a glass of wine, please.
B. Ein Viertel oder ein Achtel?	A quarter or an eighth?
A. Ein Viertel, bitte.	A quarter, please.

A.   *Übung*

Sie fragen...

> Beispiel: Is he going to Chicago on the sixth?*
>   Fährt er am sechsten nach Chicago?

1.   Is she flying to Berlin on the 20th?
2.   Is Hans getting married on the 17th of June?
3.   Which day is today?
4.   Are you coming on the 14th?
5.   Is the 23rd a Monday?

B.   *Übung*

Sie sagen...

> Beispiel: I am here on the seventh.
>   Ich bin am siebten hier.

1.   She is here on the 21st.
2.   The 5th is a Saturday.
3.   He is coming on the 30th.
4.   We are flying to Germany on the 18th.
5.   I am buying a house on the 10th of May.

DIE WOCHENTAGE	THE DAYS OF THE WEEK
Montag	Monday
Dienstag	Tuesday
Mittwoch	Wednesday
Donnerstag	Thursday
Freitag	Friday
Samstag (or: Sonnabend)	Saturday
Sonntag	Sunday

The word for day is *der Tag*
The contraction of *an dem = am* is used with days and dates.

Hans kommt am Freitag.	*Hans is coming on Friday.*
Wir fahren am Mittwoch.	*We are driving (or: going) on Wednesday.*
Ich arbeite nicht am Samstag.	*I don't work on Saturday.*

4.   Formation of noun plurals

It is best to learn the plurals of nouns along with the singular. One cannot accurately predict what the plural form of a noun might be. However, there are some guidelines:

das Kind	die Kinder	add-*er*
das Buch	die Bücher	add Umlaut and-*er*
das Haus	die Häuser	add Umlaut and-*er*
die Frage	die Fragen	add-*n*

*For unfamiliar words, see chapter *Wortschatz* or the glossary.

die Frau	die Frauen	add-*en*
der Koffer	die Koffer	
der Löffel	die Löffel	no change
das Messer	die Messer	
der Bruder	die Brüder	add Umlaut
der Apfel	die Äpfel	
das Beispiel	die Beispiele	add-*e*
das Radio	die Radios	add-*s* (usually foreign words)

5. The accusative case

The *accusative* is the case of the direct object; the direct object is the recipient of the action.

Ask: **Whom?**   or   **What?**

NOMINATIVE	ACCUSATIVE
wer *who*	**wen** *whom*

Wen suchen Sie?	*For whom are you looking?*
Ich suche **den** Kellner.	*I am looking for the waiter.*
Ich suche **die** Kellnerin.	*I am looking for the waitress.*
Ich suche **das** Kind.	*I am looking for the child.*
Was bringt er? **Den** Wein.	*What is he bringing? The wine.*
Was kauft sie? **Die** Karte.	*What is she buying? The ticket.*
Was suchen Sie? **Das** Auto.	*What are you looking for? The car.*

Only the *masculine* changes

6. The indefinite article

As you know, the definite articles are **der, die, das.** The *indefinite* article for *der* and *das* is **ein;** for *die* it is **eine. Ein** and **eine** correspond to English *a* or *an*. As with the definite article, only the *masculine* changes in the accusative case.

Ich suche **einen** Kellner.	*I am looking for a waiter.*
Ich suche **eine** Kellnerin.	*I am looking for a waitress.*
Ich suche **ein** Kind.	*I am looking for a child.*

	NOMINATIVE	ACCUSATIVE
Masculine	der/ein/kein	**den**/einen/keinen
Feminine	die/eine/keine	die/eine/keine
Neuter	das/ein/kein	das/ein/kein
Plural	die/keine	die/keine

A.   *Übung*

Restate the sentence by replacing the definite article with the *indefinite* article.

Beispiel: Ich kaufe das Haus.	*I am buying the house.*
Ich kaufe ein Haus.	*I am buying a house.*

1.   Ich nehme den Zug.
2.   Wir kennen das Restaurant.

3. Hans sucht das Buch.
4. Brauchen Sie die Wohnung?
5. Kennt sie die Journalistin?
6. Maria kauft den Pullover.

Kein = not, not a, not any, no. It is the negative of **ein**. It follows the same pattern.

kein is
like *ein*...

Ich habe ein Auto.	Ich habe **kein** Auto.
Sie hat eine Wohnung.	Ich habe **keine** Wohnung.
Sie haben ein Zimmer.	Ich habe **kein** Zimmer.

Note: As you learned on page 21, German often uses nouns without the article (Zeit, Geld, Hunger, etc.). But know the gender of such nouns if you use them with *kein*.

B.   Übung

Answer in the negative.

Beispiel: Haben Sie heute Zeit?   *Do you have time today?*
          Nein, ich habe heute   *No, I don't have time*
          keine Zeit.   *today.*

1. Haben Sie ein Auto? Nein, ich habe . . . .
2. Haben Sie Geld? Nein, ich habe . . . .
3. Kaufen Sie eine Lederhose? Nein, ich kaufe . . . .
4. Trinken Sie ein Bier? Nein, ich trinke . . . .
5. Sehen Sie den Bus? Nein, ich sehe . . . .
6. Nehmen Sie Pillen? Nein, ich nehme . . . .
7. Haben Sie Kinder? Nein, ich habe . . . .

C.   Übung

More negations with *kein*. Put into the negative.

Beispiel: Spricht Ihre Frau Deutsch?   *Does your wife speak*
          Nein, sie spricht kein   *German? No, she doesn't*
          Deutsch.   *speak German.*

1. Gibt es hier ein Restaurant? Nein, hier gibt es . . . .
2. Gibt es hier einen Bahnhof? Nein, hier gibt es . . . .
3. Ist Fräulein Müller Journalistin? Nein, sie ist . . . .
4. Ist Herr Mayer Journalist? Nein, er ist . . . .
5. Fährt hier eine Straßenbahn? Nein, hier fährt . . . .
6. Hat er einen Paß? Nein, er hat . . . .

Accusative in action
Look at these examples:

A.   Wen heiratet Hans?   eine Freundin.
       Er heiratet...   ein Mädchen aus Deutschland.
          eine Deutsche.
          eine Österreicherin.

B. Es regnet. Was brauche   einen Regenschirm.
   ich? Ich brauche...   ein Taxi.
                                eine Tasse Tee.

C. Sie haben Durst.   ein Coca Cola.
    Sie trinken...   eine Flasche Bier.
                                ein Glas Wein
                                einen Liter Wasser.
                                ein Glas Orangensaft.

D. Was trinkt Maria nicht?   keinen Wein.
    Sie trinkt...   kein Bier.
                                keinen Alkohol.
                                keine Milch.

E. Was verstehe ich nicht?   den Computer nicht.
    Ich verstehe...   das metrische System nicht.
                                  die Frage nicht.
                                den Text nicht.
                                das Problem nicht.

F. Wen sehen Sie dort?   den Kellner.
    Ich sehe...   die Kellnerin.
                                  den Professor.
                                die Professorin.
                                die Leute.

G. Wen heiratet Erika?   einen Freund.
    Sie heiratet...   einen Mann aus Amerika.
                                einen Schweizer.
                                einen jungen Professor.

H. Sie sind krank. Was brauchen Sie? einen Arzt.
    Ich brauche...   eine Ärztin.
                                eine Pille.
                                einen Tee.

I. Was kaufen wir heute?   ein Auto.
    Wir kaufen...   einen Computer.
                                eine Lederhose.
                                ein Sofa.
                                einen Pullover.

7. The accusative of personal pronouns

Pronouns, like articles, change their form to show case.

Ich kenne Herrn Müller.	*I know Mr. Müller.*
Ich kenne **ihn.**	*I know him.*
Ich frage Frau Schmidt.	*I am asking Mrs. Schmidt.*
Ich frage **sie.**	*I am asking her.*
Ich sehe das Auto.	*I see the car.*
Ich sehe **es.**	*I see it.*

	SINGULAR					**PLURAL**			
NOMINATIVE	ich	du	er	sie	es	wir	ihr	sie	Sie
ACCUSATIVE	mich	dich	ihn	sie	es	uns	euch	sie	Sie

A.   *Übung*

Complete each sentence using the accusative form of the personal pronoun in the cue.

Beispiele: (er) Ich frage *ihn*.   *(he) I ask him.*
          (wir) Sie kennen *uns*.   *(we) They know us.*

1. Kennen Sie ....?   *ich*
2. Wir fragen ....   *sie (her)*
3. Besuchen Sie ....?   *wir*
4. Sehen Sie ....?   *er*
5. Versteht sie ....?   *du*
6. Ich frage ....   *Sie*
7. Fragen Sie ....?   *sie (them)*
8. Sie kennen ....   *ich*

As you know, personal pronouns often take the place of nouns. The gender of a personal pronoun is the same as that of the noun. Its case, however, is determined by its function in the sentence (subject, object).

Beispiele: Wie heißt der Kellner?   Er heißt Erich.   Kennen Sie *ihn*?
              Wer sind die Leute?   Sie sind Deutsche.   Kennen Sie *sie*?
              Wie heißt die Frau?   Sie heißt Maria Kuhn.   Kennen Sie *sie*?
              Wie heißt das Hotel?   Es heißt „Imperial."   Kennen Sie es?

A.   *Übung*

Complete each sentence with a personal pronoun standing for the cue in italics.

Beispiel: .....*Er*.............ist gut und ich trinke.....*ihn*..........   *der Wein*

1. ....ist neu und ich fahre........gern.   *das Auto*
2. ....fährt alle 15 Minuten und ich nehme ....täglich.°   *die Straßen-bahn*
3. ....hält hier und ich sehe........schon.   *der Bus*
4. ....ist ausverkauft. Wir hören........nicht.   *das Konzert*
5. ....ist billig und ich trinke........gern.   *das Bier*
6. ....heißt Müller und ich kenne........   *der Arzt*
7. ....heißt Mayer und ich sehe........oft.   *die Ärztin*
8. ....ist Österreicher und ich frage........   *der Mann*

°daily

8. Prepositions requiring the accusative case

A preposition is a word that shows the relationship of a noun or pronoun to other elements in the sentence. A number of prepositions always requires the use of the accusative case. These are the most frequently used:

durch	*through*	Wir fahren durch die (eine) Stadt.
für	*for*	Ich bin für ihn.
gegen	*against*	Wir sind gegen den (einen) Krieg.°	°war
ohne	*without*	Er kommt ohne den (einen) Freund.
um	*around*	Sie laufen um das (ein) Haus.

In every day speech, *durch, für, um* are contracted with the definite article *das*

durch das = durchs	Er geht durchs Zimmer.
für das = fürs	Ich brauche es fürs Auto.
um das = ums	Wir laufen ums Haus.

A. Übung

Complete the sentence as suggested by the cue, using the accusative case.

Beispiel: (der Bahnhof) Wir gehen durch....................
Wir gehen durch .. den Bahnhof....

1. Ich reise nie ohne....................   *ein Regenschirm*
2. Wir gehen oft durch....................   *der Park*
3. Ich fahre durch....................   *die Stadt*
4. Inge kauft ein Sofa für....................   *das Haus*
5. Wir fahren um....................   *der Zoo*
6. Wir sitzen um....................   *der Tisch*
7. Es geht heute nicht ohne....................   *das metrische System*
8. Sie spricht für....................   *die Frauen*

9. Negation with nicht

Nicht means "not." Its position in a German sentence is quite flexible. There are some rules on the word order with **nicht,** but also many exceptions. At the risk of oversimplification, look at these examples and consider them as guidelines to where **nicht** should be placed.

Nicht goes at the end when it negates the verb or the entire sentence.

Wir wissen es **nicht.**	*We don't know it.*
Ich kenne ihn **nicht.**	*I don't know him.*
Verstehen Sie das **nicht?**	*Don't you understand that?*

Nicht follows expressions of time.

Er kommt heute **nicht.**	*He is not coming today.*
Ich arbeite abends **nicht.**	*I don't work at night.*
Wir kommen morgen **nicht.**	*We are not coming tomorrow.*

But nicht often precedes adverbs, adjectives and expressions of place.

Das ist **nicht** wahr.	*That's not true.*
Fahren Sie **nicht** so schnell.	*Don't drive so fast.*
Es ist **nicht** zu spät.	*It's not too late.*
Wir sind noch **nicht** in Köln.	*We are not yet in Cologne.*

A.   *Übung*

Now apply the given guidelines. Answer these questions by negating them with *nicht*.

> Beispiele: Kennen Sie mich?
> Nein, ich kenne Sie nicht.
>
> Fährt Hans nach Wien?
> Nein, er fährt nicht nach Wien.
>
> Arbeiten Sie morgen?
> Nein, ich arbeite morgen nicht.

1. Wohnen Sie im Hotel? Nein, ich wohne . . . .
2. Sehen Sie es? Nein, ich sehe . . . .
3. Schreibt Thomas oft? Nein, er schreibt . . . .
4. Kommen Sie morgen? Nein, ich komme . . . .
5. Fahren Sie schnell? Nein, ich fahre . . . .
6. Sehe ich Sie heute abend? Nein, ich sehe Sie . . . .

B.   *Übung*

Sie fragen. . . .

> Beispiel: Don't you know her?
> Kennen Sie sie nicht?

1. Isn't he coming today?
2. Why aren't you going home?
3. Isn't he working tonight?
4. Don't you need that?
5. Why doesn't she stay here?

C.   *Übung*

> Beispiel: Hans isn't coming tomorrow.
> Hans kommt morgen nicht.

1. She doesn't walk fast.
2. You aren't speaking too fast.
3. He doesn't work in the evening.
4. She doesn't pay the bill.
5. We don't eat much.

10.   The function and use of adverbs

Adverbs modify or communicate further information about a verb. There are:

adverbs of time:	heute, morgen, jetzt, abends, usw.
adverbs of manner:	gern, gut, leider, oft, usw.
adverbs of place:	zu Hause, hier, dort, usw.

When a sentence contains more than one adverb, the sequence of adverbs in German is:

TIME = T   MANNER = M   PLACE = P

        T   M   P

Wir fahren im Sommer gern nach Hause.

We like to go home in the summer.   Compare!

        T   M   P

Ich bleibe am Wochenende oft zu Hause.

I often stay home on the weekend.

      T   M   P

Er fährt morgen mit dem Bus in die Stadt.

Tomorrow he is going downtown by bus.

Vocabulary Notes: Here are some adjectives and adverbs which you will need
right away.*

	warm		nie
temperatures	heiß		oft
and the	windig		selten
weather...	nebelig	how often...	täglich
	kühl		stündlich
	kalt		immer
			manchmal
	jetzt		
	morgen		dort
when...	heute	where...	hier
	heute abend		da
	sofort		drüben
	später		

A. Übung

Arrange the adverbs in an appropriate order and complete each sentence.

> Beispiel: ins Büro/krank/heute/Er geht...
> Er geht heute krank ins Büro.

1. in die Stadt/nie/allein/Inge geht...
2. allein/am fünften Mai/nach Hause/Ich fahre...
3. immer/in die Schule/pünktlich/Erich kommt...
4. leider/nicht/zu Hause/morgen/Er ist...
5. in die Stadt/alle 30 Minuten/Ein Bus fährt...

B. Übung

Sie fragen...

> Beispiel: Does he always come into the office on time?
> Kommt er immer pünktlich ins Büro?

1. Are you alone tonight?
2. Are we on time today?
3. Is he ill again?
4. Does the bus go every 15 minutes?

*For translations, see the chapter *Wortschatz* or the glossary.

C. *Übung*

Sie sagen...

> Beispiel: I gladly stay home today.
>   Ich bleibe heute gern zu Hause.

1. Mr. Schulz comes to the hotel on time.
2. She is not home today.
3. They are staying here until tomorrow.
4. Hans is flying home tomorrow.
5. We travel to Austria on the seventh.

Wiederholung

A.   Respond to each question using the cue in your answer.

> Beispiel: Was verstehen Sie nicht? (die Antwort)
>   Ich verstehe die Antwort nicht.

1. Was trinken Sie?   *Milch*
2. Wer ist krank?   *mein Freund*
3. Wen sehen Sie dort?   *eine Freundin*
4. Wieviel Geld brauchen Sie?   *100 Mark*
5. Wann kommt Fritz?   *am 17. März*
6. Wohin fahren Sie heute?   *nach Hamburg*
7. Woher kommen Sie?   *aus Texas*
8. Wie lange bleiben Sie hier?   *bis zum 8. Mai*

B.   Supply **kein, nicht,** or **nichts.** Watch endings for **kein.**

> Beispiel: Morgen fahre ich **nicht** nach Hause.

1. Haben Sie.................... Geld?
2. Bitte, fragen Sie....................
3. Ich trinke.................... Wein.
4. Wir haben.................... Arzt.
5. Sie hat.................... Zeit.
6. Ich kenne ihn....................
7. Hans versteht das....................
8. Heute kaufe ich....................

C.   Complete each sentence with a suitable antonym (opposite) for the italicized word.

> Beispiel: Im Januar ist es hier *kalt,*
>   aber im Juli ist es hier warm.

1. Ist die Wohnung *groß?* Nein, sie ist....................
2. Ist er *fleißig?* Nein, er ist....................
3. Der Bus hält *hier.* Nein, er hält....................
4. Das Bier ist *teuer.* Nein, es ist....................
5. Paul hat *nie* Zeit. Nein, er hat.................... Zeit.

6. Fahren Sie *heute* nach Frankfurt? Nein, ich fahre ....
7. Ist der Professor *jung?* Nein, er ist ....
8. Ist der Wein *gut?* Nein, er ist ....

D. Say in German:

1. 68 degrees Fahrenheit is 20 degrees Celsius.
2. Three times four is twelve.
3. Does the bus stop here?
4. I am thirsty.
5. Is she hungry?
6. Hans and Inge are getting married (marry) in spring.
7. What day is today?
8. I don't ask him.
9. We are buying a computer.
10. They are not against her.

E. Ask another person, using the *Sie* form.

Beispiel: When are you coming tomorrow?
Wann kommen Sie morgen?

1. Where are you going on the 26th?
2. How much does that cost?
3. What are you looking for?
4. Do you drink beer?
5. Is there a restaurant here?
6. Do you need a room?
7. Is Otto getting married in the fall?
8. Are you sick today?

Wortschatz

Nouns

das Achtel, - eighth
der Alkohol alcohol
der April April
der Arzt, ̈e physician, male
die Ärztin, -nen physician, female
der August August
das Auto, -s car
die Billion, -en trillion
das Buch, ̈er book
(das) Deutschland Germany
der Dezember December
das Drittel, - third
der Durst thirst
(das) Europa Europe
der Februar February
die Flasche, -n bottle

der Franken, - Swiss franc
der Frühling, -e spring
der Geburtstag, -e birthday
der Grad, -e degree
die Hälfte, -n half
die Hausnummer, -n house number
der Herbst, -e autumn, fall
das Hundertstel hundreth
der Hunger hunger
der Januar January
der Journalist, -en journalist, male
die Journalistin, -nen journalist, female
der Juli July
der Juni June
der Kellner, - waiter

die **Kellnerin, -nen**   waitress
das **Kilo, -s**   kilogram
der **Kilometer, -**   kilometer
die **Leute**   people
die **Lederhose, -n**   leather pants
das **Mädchen, -**   girl
der **Mai**   May
der **März**   March
die **Milliarde, -n**   billion
die **Million, -en**   million
der **Nationalfeiertag, -e**   national holiday
das **Neujahr**   New Year's Day
der **November**   November
der **Ober, -**   waiter, head waiter
der **Oktober**   October
der **Österreicher, -**   Austrian, male
die **Österreicherin, -nen**   Austrian, female
der **Park, -s**   park
der **Paß, ̈sse**   passport
das **Pfund, -e**   pound
der **Pullover, -**   pullover
der **Regenschirm, -e**   umbrella
die **Reise, -n**   trip, journey
das **Restaurant, -s**   restaurant
der **Schilling, -e**   shilling, currency of Austria
der **September**   September
der **Silvester**   New Year's Eve
das **Sofa, -s**   couch, sofa
der **Sommer, -**   summer
die **Stadt, ̈e**   city
die **Straßenbahn, -en**   streetcar
die **Stunde, -n**   hour
das **System, -e**   system
das **metrische System**   metric system
die **Telefonnummer, -n**   telephone number
das **Viertel, -**   fourth
(das) **Weihnachten**   Christmas
der **Wein, -e**   wine
der **Winter, -**   winter
die **Wohnung, -en**   apartment
die **Zahl, -en**   number
das **Zehntel, -**   tenth
die **Zeitung, -en**   newspaper
das **Zimmer, -**   room
die **Zimmernummer, -n**   room number

der **Zoo, -s**   zoo
der **Zug, ̈e**   train

Verbs

besuchen   to visit
brauchen   to need
fliegen   to fly
geben (gibt)   to give
  es gibt   there is
halten (hält)   to stop
hören   to hear
heiraten   to marry, get married
kennen   to know, be acquainted
nehmen (nimmt)   to take
rechnen   to calculate, figure
sehen (sieht)   to see
sitzen   to sit
sprechen (spricht)   to speak
suchen   to look for
verstehen   to understand
zählen   to count

Other Words

allein   alone
ausverkauft   sold out
da, dort, drüben   there, over there
durch   through
ein halb   one half
einmal   once
etwa   about, approximately
für   for
gegen   against
hoch   high
kein   no, not a
laut   loud
leider   unfortunately
manchmal   sometimes
mehr   more
mein   mine
minus   minus, less
morgen   tomorrow
nebelig   foggy
nichts   nothing
null   zero
ohne   without
plus   plus
pünktlich   punctually
schnell   quick, fast

schon   already
selten   seldom
sofort   immediately
spät   late
   später   later
stündlich   every hour
täglich   daily
ungerade   uneven
um   around
ungefähr   approximately
welcher   which

wieder   again
windig   windy
zu + adjective, adverb   too

Idiomatic Expressions

Das ist nicht wahr.   That isn't true.
Der wievielte (Tag) ist heute?   What
   is today's date?
Haben Sie Durst?   Are you thirsty?
Haben Sie Hunger?   Are you hungry?

Kapitel 3

Restaurants, Eating, Foods

Culture Notes

In the German-speaking countries, many restaurants post their menus and prices outside the establishment. A quick glance can be informative and may save you disappointment and "pocketbook aches."

Some restaurants serve hot meals only during certain hours, usually from 11:30 a.m. to 2 p.m. and from 5 p.m. to 8 p.m. Snacks are available, however, during all business hours. Many people in Germany, Austria, and Switzerland still prefer to eat their main hot meal during noon hours and a smaller meal in the evening. But changing work hours and greater commuting distances, especially in urban areas, are making it more and more difficult to uphold this German tradition of a big noon-time meal (Mittagessen).

Except for expensive and fancy restaurants, do not wait to be seated. Find yourself a free table and sit down. If all tables are taken, you may join others at a larger table if there is still room. Simply ask:

"Entschuldigen Sie bitte, ist hier noch frei?" Excuse me please, is this place still available?

or

"Entschuldigen Sie bitte, ist hier noch Platz?"

The prices listed on the menu include about ten to fifteen percent for the tip and the value-added tax (Mehrwertsteuer). Therefore, just round up the sum quoted and give it to the waiter or waitress as you pay. Do not leave a tip on the table. It is customary to pay the person who served you, not the cashier. To pay, just say "Herr Ober, bitte zahlen" (waiter), or "Fräulein, bitte zahlen" (waitress). Many waiters in Germany are guest workers (Gastarbeiter) from other countries. Their German may not be much better than yours.

Familiarize yourself with signs like these:

Heute Ruhetag. This is our day off.

Wegen Betriebsferien von… bis…geschlossen.		Closed for vacation from… to…
Geöffnet von… bis…		Open from… to…
Geschlossen ab…		Closed from…
Parkplatz hinter dem Restaurant.		Parking behind the restaurant.
Schöner, schattiger Gastgarten.		Nice, shady yard.
Wegen Renovierung geschlossen.		Closed for renovation.

Wir sind hungrig. Wo ist.…
(We are hungry. Where is.…)

For a regular, square meal look for…	ein Hotel	*hotel*
	ein Restaurant	*restaurant*
	ein Gasthaus	*inn*
	eine Gaststätte	*restaurant*
	eine Raststätte*	*restaurant*
For a quick snack there is…	ein Schnellimbiß	*snack bar*
	eine Milchbar	*dairy bar*
	eine Jausenstation	*Austrian snack bar*
	eine Weinstube	*place for snacks and beverages*
Sie fragen: Wo ist hier…	ein gutes/billiges/preiswertes Restaurant?	
	eine gute/billige/preiswerte Gaststätte?	
	ein gutes/billiges/preiswertes Hotel?	
	eine Bushaltestelle/Straßenbahnhaltestelle?	
	eine Bank?	
	ein Telefon, Taxi?	
	ein Postamt oder die Post?	

Grammar

1. Asking indirect questions

When you use question words to introduce *indirect* questions (I don't know *where* he lives), the verb last (V-L) word order applies. (Very much like in English.)

> Beispiele: Wissen Sie, wieviel das kostet?
> Do you know how much that costs?
>
> Er weiß nicht, wo das Hotel ist.
> He doesn't know where the hotel is.

A. *Übung*

Make *indirect* questions from the direct questions.

> Beispiel: Wo ist hier das Telefon?
> Wissen Sie, *wo hier das Telefon ist?*

1. Wann kommt der Bus?
   Wissen Sie,………………?
2. Wohin fährt diese Straßenbahn?
   Wissen Sie,………………?

*You will find *Raststätten* mostly on the *Autobahn* (freeways).

3. Wo ist hier der Ober?
    Wissen Sie, ... ?
4. Wie teuer ist das?
    Wissen Sie, ... ?
5. Wen frage ich dort?
    Wissen Sie, ... ?
6. Warum ist die Suppe kalt?
    Wissen Sie, ... ?
7. Wie heißt der Herr?
    Wissen Sie, ... ?
8. Wann fährt Herr Schmidt nach Hause?
    Wissen Sie, ... ?

B.   *Übung*

Form questions from these statements.

> Beispiel: Sie reservieren den Tisch.
>   Reservieren Sie den Tisch?

1. Sie suchen eine Milchbar.
2. Er fährt mit dem Bus.
3. Inge nimmt ein Taxi.
4. Du kommst ins Hotel.
5. Ihr seht das Taxi.
6. Ich finde das Restaurant.
7. Sie wartet auf die Straßenbahn.
8. Er bestellt das Menü.
9. Hans geht zum Schnellimbiß.
10. Das Auto steht vor dem Hotel.

2.   The conjugation of wissen (to know)

As a number of other verbs, *wissen* is an irregular verb and its conjugation must be memorized.

SINGULAR		WISSEN	PLURAL
ich	weiß		wir wissen
er			Sie wissen
sie	weiß		sie wissen
es			
man			
du	weißt		ihr wißt

A.   *Übung*

Fill in the blanks with the correct form of *wissen*.

> Beispiel: . . . . . .Weiß. . . . . . . .er, wo das Restaurant ist?

1. Ich ...., wann er kommt.
2. Wir ...., wieviel die Zeitung kostet.
3. Hans .... nicht, wie der Herr heißt.
4. Karin und Bärbel ...., wie gut das Restaurant ist.
5. .... die Kinder, wo die Eltern sind?
6. Herr Schmidt .... alles.
7. Ich .... nicht, warum er eine Milchbar sucht.
8. .... du, wer die Rechnung bezahlt?

B. *Übung*

Auf deutsch, bitte. (In German, please.)

> Beispiel: Why does she ask?
>   Warum fragt sie?

1. Where is a restaurant?
2. Does Hans know where the bus stops?
3. How much does the newspaper cost?
4. Do you (Sie) know why she is going home?
5. I don't know when the streetcar comes.
6. We know how inexpensive the inn is.
7. Do you (du) know where I live?
8. Whom do I ask?

DIALOG: WAS SUCHT MR. SMITH?*

Mr. Smith:	Entschuldigen Sie, bitte. Wo ist hier ein Hotel oder ein Gasthaus?
passer-by A:	Ein Hotel? Ein Gasthaus?—Es tut mir leid. Das weiß ich nicht. Ich bin nicht von hier.
Mr. Smith to passer-by B:	Bitte, gibt es hier ein Hotel oder ein Gasthaus?
passer-by B:	Was suchen Sie? Ein Hotel? Nein, hier gibt es kein Hotel.
passer-by C:	Aber ein Gasthaus. Gut und preiswert. Gar nicht weit von hier.
Mr. Smith:	Wie weit von hier?
passer-by C:	Sehen Sie die Ampel dort?
Mr. Smith:	Ja, ich sehe sie.
passer-by C:	Gehen Sie bis zur Ampel; und dann rechts um die Ecke.
passer-by B:	Und von dort geradeaus bis zum Marktplatz. Dort ist das Gasthaus „Zum Adler."
Mr. Smith:	Und wo finde ich ein Hotel?
passer-by D:	Fahren Sie mit dem Bus zur Bahnhofstraße. Dort ist das „Park Hotel."
passer-by C:	Oder nehmen Sie ein Taxi.
Mr. Smith:	Wieviel kostet das?
passer-by C:	Ich glaube sieben Mark.
Mr. Smith:	Vielen Dank.

This dialog provides some basic questions and answers which a traveller may encounter looking for a restaurant or a hotel. Besides questions with or without question words, it also introduces another important feature of "Survival German":

*Check answers on page 159 for translation.

3.   Giving orders the polite way

Formal commands and requests are very easy in German. Just use the infinitive of the verb + Sie (Subject-Verb word order).

Fahren Sie!	*go*	Warten Sie!	*wait*
Kommen Sie!	*come*	Fragen Sie!	*ask*
Gehen Sie!	*walk, go*	Nehmen Sie!	*take*
Bringen Sie!	*bring*	Sehen Sie!	*look*
Wählen Sie!	*choose*	Versuchen Sie!	*try*
Essen Sie!	*eat*	Suchen Sie!	*look for*
Zahlen Sie!	*pay*	Bestellen Sie!	*order*

As you can see, there is no difference between the "polite" imperative form and the question form (when no question word is used) except for intonation: In commands the voice goes down. Commands are also followed by an.exclamation mark. In questions the voice rises toward the end, and of course a question mark follows. Compare and say out loud:

COMMAND	*QUESTION*
Fahren Sie nach Berlin!	Fahren Sie nach Berlin?
Bestellen Sie jetzt!	Bestellen Sie jetzt?

A.   *Übung*

Give a command using the words indicated:

Beispiel: Essen/nicht so viel
~~Essen Sie nicht so viel!~~

1.   Bringen/ein Glas Wein
2.   Versuchen/diese Nachspeise
3.   Kochen/ohne Salz
4.   Warten/auf den nächsten Bus
5.   Kommen/heute abend
6.   Gehen/zur Ecke
7.   Wählen/das Beefsteak
8.   Fragen/den Ober
9.   Nehmen/wenig Pfeffer
10.   Fahren/mit einem Taxi

In giving directions, the polite imperative may be used like this:

	geradeaus	*straight ahead*
	nach rechts	*to the right*
	nach links	*to the left*
	bis zur Ecke	*to the corner*
Gehen Sie...	bis zum Platz	*to the square*
	bis zur Ampel	*to the traffic light*
	bis zur Brücke	*to the bridge*

	über die Brücke	*over the bridge*
	bis zum Schild	*to the sign*
	bis zur Haltestelle	*to the bus, streetcar stop*

DIALOGE		*DIALOGS*
Gast:	Servieren Sie jetzt Mittagessen?	Do you serve lunch now?
Ober:	Ja, schon seit 11 Uhr.	Yes, since 11 o'clock.
Gast:	Einen Tisch für vier, bitte.	A table for four, please
Ober:	Hier in der Ecke, bitte.	Here in the corner, please.

Gast:	Herr Ober, die Speisekarte bitte.	Waiter, the menu please.
Ober:	Bitte schön.	Here it is.
Gast:	Was können Sie empfehlen?	What can you recommend?
Ober:	Das Menü* ist heute sehr gut.	The special of the day is very good.
Ober:	Möchten Sie bestellen?	Would you like to order?
Gast:	Ja bitte—eine Kraftbrühe mit Ei, Gulasch mit Reis und grünen Bohnen.	Yes please—beef consomme with egg, goulash with rice and green beans.
Ober:	Möchten Sie auch einen Salat?	Would you like a Salad, too?
Gast:	Nein, danke.	No, thank you.

Gast:	Fräulein, bitte zahlen.	Miss, check please.
Frl.:	Ja, sofort.	Yes, right away.
	War alles in Ordnung?	Was everything alright?
Gast:	Ja, ausgezeichnet.	Yes, excellent.
Frl.:	Kommen Sie bald wieder.	Come back soon.
Gast:	Auf Wiedersehen!	Good-bye!
Frl.:	Auf Wiedersehen!	Good-bye!

Karin:	Willst du heute abend ins Kino gehen?	Do you want to go to the movie tonight?
Elke:	Nein, ich kann leider nicht.	No, unfortunately I can't.
Karin:	Was willst du denn machen?	What do you want to do?
Elke:	Ich muß wieder arbeiten.	I have to work again.

4. The function of modals (modal auxiliaries)

German, like English, has a small group of verbs that help us to express feelings, attitudes or desires. These verbs are known as *modal auxiliaries* or simply *modals*. They are usually used together with another verb which has to be in the infinitive form.

Beispiele: *Müssen* Sie schon *gehen?*	Must you go already?
	Do you have to go already?
Ich will jetzt *bestellen?*	I want to order now.
Hier *dürfen* Sie nicht *rauchen.*	You are not allowed to smoke here.

*Watch out—*Menü* is not the menu but the special dish of the day.

The meaning of modals.

Modal +
infinitive

infinitive

modal

Infinitive to the end!

dürfen	*may, to be allowed (to)*
können	*can, to be able (to)*
mögen	*to like (to), to prefer*
müssen	*must, to have (to)*
sollen	*ought (to), to be supposed (to)*
wollen	*to want (to)*

	dürfen	können	müssen	sollen	wollen
ich	darf	kann	muß	soll	will
er, sie, es	darf	kann	muß	soll	will
wir	dürfen	können	müssen	sollen	wollen
sie, Sie	dürfen	können	müssen	sollen	wollen
du	darfst	kannst	mußt	sollst	willst
ihr	dürft	könnt	müßt	sollt	wollt

Note: Except for **sollen**, each modal has a stem vowel change in all singular forms. The vowel of the plural forms is the same as that of the infinitive.

A. Übung

Complete the sentence with the modal in parentheses.

Beispiel: Ich.....*muß*.........jetzt essen.   *müssen*

1. Wir...............ins Restaurant gehen.   *können*
2. Der Geschäftsmann..................nach Amerika fahren.   *wollen*
3. ....Sie auch das Menü bestellen?   *wollen*
4. Wo..................ich ein billiges Gasthaus finden?   *können*
5. Kinder..................keinen Alkohol trinken.   *sollen*
6. Der Arzt..................jetzt einen Patienten besuchen. *müssen*
7. In diesem Restaurant..................man nicht rauchen. *dürfen*
8. Herr.Weber,..................Sie ein Taxi nehmen?   *können*
9. Was..................die Kinder trinken?   *dürfen*
10. Was..................du jetzt sehen?   *wollen*

Note: Sometimes modals are used without the infinitive. In such cases the
infinitive is implied or understood.
Ich kann Deutsch. (*sprechen*)
Herr Braun will nach Hause. (*gehen, fahren*)
Wir dürfen das nicht. (*tun, machen*)
Ich möchte eine Tasse Kaffee. (*haben*)

5. ***Möchten*** means "would like"—an expression you will need.

ich	möcht - e	I would like
er, sie, es		he, she, it would like
wir		we would like
Sie	möcht - en	you would like (formal)
sie		they would like
du	möcht - est	you would like (fam. singular)
ihr	möcht - et	you would like (fam. plural)

A. *Übung*

Say the subject would like to do whatever the cue says. Use the correct form of "möchten."

> Beispiel: Ich...................   *einen Tisch bestellen*
>   Ich möchte einen Tisch bestellen.

1. Kurt...................   *eine Tasse Kaffe*
2. Ich...................   *eine Tasse Tee trinken*
3. Ingrid...................   *jetzt essen*
4. Wo.................Sie...................?   *wohnen*
5. Er...................   *etwas Leichtes essen*
6. Wir...................   *zahlen, bitte*
7. Was.................du...................?   *trinken*
8. Herr Mayer...................   *einen Tisch bestellen*
9. Er...................   *ein Gasthaus finden*
10. Wohin.................Sie...................?   *fahren*

In the Restaurant: Initial Questions and Responses

Sie fragen oder sagen:

Servieren Sie jetzt Mittagessen/Abendessen?	*Do you serve lunch/dinner now?*
Gibt es noch etwas Warmes zu essen?	*Do you still serve hot meals?*
Einen Tisch für zwei/drei/vier, bitte.	*A table for two/three/four, please.*
Die Speisekarte, bitte.	*The menu, please.*

The waiter may ask you:

Was möchten Sie essen?	*What would you like to eat?*
Was möchten Sie bestellen?	*What would you like to order?*

B. *Übung*

Was möchten Sie tun? (besides eating)
Ich möchte...................

	Was möchten Sie trinken?	*What would you like to drink?*
	ein kleines/großes Bier	*a small/large beer*
	einen Apfelsaft (gespritzt)	*apple cider (with mineral water)*
Sie sagen:	einen Orangensaft	*orange juice*
Bringen Sie	ein Mineralwasser	*mineral water*
mir...	ein Coca Cola	*coke*

ein Glas Wein	*a glass of wine*
einen Gespritzten...	*a glass of wine with mineral water*
ein Glas Milch	*a glass of milk*
einen Cocktail**	*a cocktail*

What's on the menu *(die Speisekarte)?*

Major sections of the "Speisekarte" consist of:

	Vorspeisen	*appetizers*
	Suppen	*soups*
	Hauptgerichte	*main courses*
Was möchten	Beilagen	*potatoes, rice, noodles, etc.*
Sie essen oder	Gemüse	*vegetables*
trinken...	Salate	*salads*
	Nachspeisen	*desserts*
	Getränke	*beverages*
	Tagesmenü	*special of the day*

VORSPEISEN	**APPETIZERS**
die Austern	*oysters*
die Fleischpastete	*pastry filled with meat*
der Hering/Räucherhering	*herring/smoked herring*
der Hummer	*lobster*
die Krabben	*shrimp*
die Pilze	*mushrooms*
Russische Eier	*deviled eggs*
der Schinken	*ham*
die Spargelspitzen	*asparagus tips*
der Thunfisch	*tuna*
die Wurst/Wurstplatte	*sausage/assorted cold cuts*

SUPPEN	**SOUPS**
Bohnensuppe	*bean soup*
Bouillon (mit Ei.)	*clear bouillon (with egg)*
Fischsuppe	*fish soup*
*Frittatensuppe	*broth with pancake strips*
Frühlingssuppe	*spring vegetable soup*
*Grießnockerlsuppe	*cream of wheat dumpling soup*
Gulaschsuppe	*stewed beef soup (spicy)*
Kartoffelsuppe	*potato soup*
Königinsuppe	*beef, sour cream and almond soup*
Kraftbrühe (mit Ei)	*beef consommé (with egg)*
*Leberknödelsuppe	*liver-dumpling soup*
Linsensuppe	*lentil soup*
Nudelsuppe	*noodle soup*

Don't forget:
SUPPE takes *die*

**Many restaurants do not serve the typical American hard drinks before or with the meal. If that's what you want, you may have to go to the bar.

*Note: Soups marked with an * are typically Austrian.

Obstsuppe   *fruit soup (chilled)*
Ochsenschwanzsuppe   *oxtail soup*
Tomatensuppe   *tomato soup*
(Französische) Zwiebelsuppe   *(French) onion soup*

C. *Übung*

Now apply what you have learned about *questions, "möchte,"* and the *polite imperative.*

Beispiele: Nein, danke, ich......esse........keine Suppe.   *eat*
Was...möchten.....Sie...bestellen......?   *would like to order*

1.   Herr Ober,...................die Speisekarte.   *bring*
2.   Ich...................ein Glas Wein.   *would like*
3.   ....ein Coca Cola?   *would you like*
4.   ....eine Vorspeise...................?   *can you recommend*
5.   ....ist heute das Menü?   *How*
6.   ....Pilze?   *Do you have*
7.   ....der Hummer heute?   *How expensive is*
8.   Ich...................keine Austern.   *wouldn't like*
9.   Ich weiß, Sie...................Bier gern.   *drink*
10. Wissen Sie,...................das kostet?   *how much*

6.   More about word order

Before you can learn how to order a full course meal, you must learn more about German word order.

a.   Subject-Verb Word Order

You are already familiar with *S-V* word order. The sentence or clause begins with the subject and the verb follows.

Beispiele: 1. Ich möchte ein preiswertes Zimmer.
2. Wir essen gern Salat.
3. Herr Klein bestellt etwas Warmes.

b.   Verb-Subject Word Order

You have also learned that in questions V-S word order is used.

Beispiele: Möchten Sie eine Tasse Kaffee?
Servieren Sie jetzt Abendessen?
Ist das Menü teuer?

V-S word order is also used for formal commands.

Beispiele: Bringen Sie bitte die Speisekarte!
Rauchen Sie bitte nicht!
Schreiben Sie eine Postkarte!

c.   V-S word order is also used when the main verb is preceded by an element that is *not* the subject. This element may consist of a single word, a phrase, or a dependent clause. In questions, it is the question word.

Beispiele: Heute essen wir im Gasthaus.
Am Wochenende fahre ich nach Wien.
Wo wohnen Sie in Amerika?

d. Verb-last Word order

Verb-last word order is one of the most striking features of German. Mark Twain once quipped that he had read a German novel 257 pages long, yet had no idea what the action was until he came to the last page, where he found all the verbs.

Verb-last word order is used in dependent clauses. A dependent clause is one that does not make sense by itself, but depends on a main clause for its meaning. Dependent clauses frequently begin with *daß* (that), *weil* (because), or *wenn* (whenever, if). These words are known as subordinating conjunctions.

Beispiele: Ich esse viel Salat, weil das gesund *ist.*
I eat a lot of salad because it is healthy.
Hans trinkt nie Alkohol, wenn er Auto *fährt.*
Hans never drinks alcohol when he drives.
Wir wissen nicht, ob das Restaurant teuer *ist.*
We don't know, whether the restaurant is expensive.

The most common subordinating conjunctions are:

als	*when, as*	**obwohl**	*although, even though*
bevor	*before*	**seit, seitdem**	*since* (temporal)
bis	*until*	**sobald**	*as soon as*
da	*since* (casual), *because*	**solange**	*as long as*
damit	*so that*	**während**	*while, whereas*
daß	*that*	**weil**	*because*
ob	*whether*	**wenn**	*it, whenever*

A. Übung

Complete as suggested by the cue, using V-L word order.

Beispiel: (Wir haben Geld) Wir fliegen nach Deutschland, sobald . wir Geld haben. .

1. (Die Restaurants sind zu teuer)
   Wir essen zu Hause, weil . . . .
2. (Er fährt mit einem Taxi)
   Ich frage meinen Freund, ob . . . .
3. (Das Essen ist billig)
   Meine Familie ißt gern im Hotel Stern, weil . . . .
4. (Es gibt ein preiswertes Hotel)
   Wissen Sie, wo . . . .
5. (Ich habe wenig Geld)
   Ich esse im Restaurant, obwohl . . . .
6. (Das Wetter ist kalt)
   Herr und Frau Schmidt fahren nach Florida, wenn . . . .

B. Übung

Combine the clauses with the German equivalent of the cue conjunction.

Beispiel: Hans fragt mich. Ich trinke gern Wein.   *whether*
          Hans fragt mich, ob ich gern Wein trinke.

1. Ich bin glücklich. Ich bin jetzt in Deutschland.   *because*
2. Wir zahlen jetzt. Wir können nach Hause gehen.   *so that*
3. Der Kellner empfiehlt das Menü. Es ist nicht gut.   *even though*
4. Meine Frau bleibt in Europa. Ich arbeite hier.   *while*
5. Ich weiß nicht. Die Obstsuppe ist kalt.   *whether*
6. Der Kellner gibt uns einen Tisch am Fenster. Er kennt uns.   *because*
7. Herr König fährt oft mit dem Auto. Das Benzin ist teuer.   *even though*
8. Wissen Sie.... Der Bus fährt.   *how often*

If you start a sentence with the *dependent clause,* the main clause has verb-subject   Please note...
word order because the first (dependent) clause is considered the first element in
the sentence, and, as you know, the *verb* has to be the second.

>   Beispiele: Wenn ich eine Suppe esse, *bestelle* ich keinen Salat.
>   Sobald ich nach Hause komme, *lese* ich die Zeitung.
>   Obwohl Dr. Heinze Arzt ist, *hat* er kein Geld.

If you use a modal and another verb in a *dependent clause,* the modal must go to the
end of the clause.

>   Beispiele: Wissen Sie, daß man hier mit Dollar bezahlen *muß.*
>   Hans sagt, daß er gern ein Glas Bier bestellen *möchte.*
>   Ich fliege morgen nach Deutschland, weil ich meinen Onkel besuchen will.

C. *Übung*

Übersetzen Sie.

>   Beispiel: Do you know whether Georg has to work?
>   Wissen Sie, ob Georg arbeiten muß?

1. I would like mushrooms if they are not too expensive.
2. We are staying in the Hotel Dresden until we buy a house.
3. He is supposed to come home because he doesn't have any money.
4. I want to see you even though I am sick.
5. My friend is looking for the waitress so that he can pay.
6. They won't go home until you come.
7. Fritz orders an appetizer whenever he eats in a restaurant.
8. You (Sie) can travel when you have time.

Now let's continue talking about foods....

HAUPTGERICHTE MIT BEILAGEN (MAIN COURSE WITH...)*

The most common "Beilagen" are:

Kartoffel	*potatoes*
Bratkartoffel	*hashed browns*
geröstete Kartoffel	*fried potatoes*
Kartoffelbrei	*mashed potatoes*
Pommes frites	*French fries*
Salzkartoffel	*peeled, boiled potatoes*
Reis, der	*rice*
Nudeln, die	*noodles*
Knödel, die	*dumplings*

Welche Beilagen
essen Sie?

*In some restaurants the "Beilagen" are included in the price; in others they are charged as extras.
Check the "Speisekarte" or ask the waiter/waitress.

FLEISCHSPEISEN	MEAT DISHES
(deutsches) Beefsteak, das	*(German) hamburger steak*
Bierwurst	*beer sausage*
Blutwurst } die	*black pudding (blood) sausage*
Bockwurst	*large frankfurter*
Eisbein, das	*pig's knuckle*
Faschierte, das	*minced meat (hamburger)*
Filetsteak, das	*beef steak*
Frikadellen, die	*croquettes*
Gulasch, das	*goulash (beef stewed in gravy)*
Hackbraten, der	*meat loaf*
Kasseler Rippen, die (pl.)	*smoked pork*
Leber, die/Leberkäse, der	*liver/special meatloaf*
Rippensteak, das	*rib steak*
Rouladen, die (pl.)	*slices of beef or veal filled, rolled and braised*
Schinken, der	*ham*
Schnitzel, das	*cutlet, usually veal*
Naturschnitzel	*cutlet served with mushrooms*
Wiener Schnitzel	*breaded veal cutlet*
Speck, der	*bacon*

Welche Fleisch-speisen bestellen Sie?

Und wie möchten Sie Ihr Fleisch? How would you like your meat?

nicht durchgebraten, fast roh	*rare*
halb durchgebraten	*medium*
durchgebraten	*well-done*

Also be familiar with these terms:

gebacken	~~baked~~
gebraten	*roasted*
gekocht	*boiled*
gegrillt	*grilled*
gedämpft/gedünstet	*steamed*
gefüllt	*stuffed*
vom Rost	*broiled*
geschmort	*braised*

Sie haben die Wahl!
You have a choice.

D.   *Übung*

Sagen oder schreiben Sie auf deutsch, bitte.

> Beispiel: I know she would like lentil soup.
> Ich weiß, daß sie Linsensuppe möchte.

1.   I take goulash with dumplings.
2.   Do you eat oysters?
3.   Today I recommend asparagus tips, or breaded veal cutlet with rice.
4.   I would like the meat well done.
5.   Please bring me the pork roast with mashed potatoes.
6.   He would like tomato soup.
7.   Would you like your rib steak from the grill?
8.   How much is the ham?

GEMÜSE UND SALATE	VEGETABLES AND SALADS	
GEMÜSE UND SALATE	*VEGETABLES AND SALADS*	
Blumenkohl/Karfiol, der	*cauliflower*	
Bohnen, die (pl.)	*beans*	
Broccoli, der	*broccoli*	
Erbsen, die (pl.)	*peas*	
Karotten, die (pl.)	*carrots*	
Kohl, der	*cabbage*	
Weißkohl, der	*white cabbage*	
Rotkohl, der, Blaukraut, das	*red cabbage*	
Kürbis, der	*pumpkin*	Wenige Kalorien
Mais, der	*maize, corn*	und gesund!!
Meerrettich, der	*horseradish*	
Pilze, die (pl.)	*mushrooms*	
Radieschen, die (pl.)	*radishes*	
Rosenkohl, der	*brussels sprouts*	
Salat, der	*salad*	
gemischte Salat, der	*mixed salad*	
Bohnensalat	*bean salad*	
Gurkensalat	*cucumber salad*	
Kartoffelsalat	*potato salad*	
Spargel, der	*asparagus*	
Spinat, der	*spinach*	
Tomaten, die (pl.)	*tomatoes*	
Zwiebeln, die (pl.)	*onions*	

OBST	FRUIT
OBST	*FRUIT*
Ananas, die, -	*pineapple*
Banane, die, -n	*banana*
Birne, die, -n	*pear*
Erdbeere, die, -n	*strawberry*
Kirsche, die, -n	*cherry*
Melone, die, -n	*melon*
Orange, die, -n	*orange*
Pampelmuse, die, -n	*grapefruit*
Pflaume, die, -n	*plum*
Traube, die, -n	*grape*
Zitrone, die, -n	*lemon*
Apfel, der, ⁻	*apple*
Pfirsich, der, -e	*peach*

E. *Übung*

Wie möchten Sie Ihr Fleisch oder Gemüse? Wie möchten andere Leute ihr Fleisch?

Complete each sentence with the correct form of "möchten."

Beispiel: Ich.................mein Fleisch durchgebraten.
      Ich möchte mein Fleisch durchgebraten.

1. Erika.................ihr Fleisch gegrillt.
2. Meine Frau und ich.................unser Fleisch halb durchgebraten.
3. ....du dein Fleisch immer durchgebraten?

4. Wir . . . . unser Fleisch fast roh.
5. . . . . ihr euer Fleisch durchgebraten?
6. Ich weiß, Sie . . . . Ihr Fleisch immer durchgebraten.

F.   Übung

Make a suitable choice from the list below. More than one answer may be possible.

1. Ich habe Gemüse gern . . . .
2. Ich möchte mein Faschiertes . . . .
3. Er möchte das Rippensteak . . . .
4. Ist der Leberkäse . . . . oder . . . .
5. Sind die Rouladen . . . . ?
6. Servieren Sie den Hackbraten . . . . oder . . . . ?
7. Wir möchten unser Steak . . . .

gedämpft	gefüllt
gekocht	vom Rost
gebacken	gegrillt
geschmort	gebraten

G.   Übung

Which word doesn't fit here? Cross it out.

1. Nudeln	Frikadellen	Reis	Knödel
2. Erbsen	Pilze	Äpfel	Radieschen
3. Eisbein	Kasseler Rippen	Schinken	Spargel
4. Zwiebel	Pfirsiche	Birnen	Ananas
5. Hackbraten	Schnitzel	Rouladen	Pommes frites
6. Gurken	Trauben	Spinat	Rotkohl

H.   Übung

Sagen oder schreiben Sie auf deutsch.

1. Do you have stuffed tomatoes?
2. I would like my steak well-done.
3. Please steam the carrots.
4. I don't like fruit.
5. Karin always orders salad.
6. Would you like to eat in a (im) restaurant or at home?
7. I would like to recommend the "Menü."
8. Please bring me meatloaf and mashed potatoes.

DIALOG

Kellner:	Möchten Sie noch eine Nach- speise?	Would you like dessert?
Gast:	Ja, was gibt es?	Yes, what do you have?
Kellner:	Wie wär's mit...	How about?
Gast:	Was können Sie zum Nachtisch empfehlen?	What can you recommend for dessert?

Kellner:	Nun, möchten Sie etwas Leichtes oder einen Kuchen?	Well, do you want something light or cake?
Gast:	Etwas mit wenig Kalorien.	Something with few calories.
Kellner:	Dann nehmen Sie doch ein Kompott?	Why don't you take some stewed fruit?

NACHSPEISEN / DESSERTS

NACHSPEISEN	DESSERTS	
Apfelstrudel, der	*apple strudle*	
Berliner, der	*filled doughnuts*	
Bienenstich, der	*honey almond cake*	
Gugelhupf, der	*molded cake with raisins*	
Kaiserschmarren, der	*shredded pancake filled with marmelade (Austrian)*	gut—aber nicht für die "schlanke Linie"*
Käsekuchen, der	*cheese cake*	
Mohrenkopf, der	*chocolate meringue*	
Pudding, der	*pudding*	
Windbeutel, der	*cream puffs*	
Cremeschnitte, die	*cream tarts* (Bismarck)	
Sachertorte, die	*Viennese cake with layers of marmelade*	
Schwarzwälderkirschtorte, die	*Blackforest—with black cherries, whipped cream*	
Käse, der	*cheese*	
Kompott, das	*stewed fruit (sauce)*	
Apfelkompott, das	*apple sauce*	

With any dessert you will often hear:

mit Schlag**? mit Sahne?	*with whipped cream*
ohne Schlag? ohne Sahne?	*without whipped cream?*

EIS / ICE CREAM/SHERBET

EIS	ICE CREAM/SHERBET
Erdbeereis, das	*strawberry ice cream*
Fruchteis, das	*mixed fruit sherbet*
Schokoladeneis, das	*chocolate ice cream*
Vanilleeis, das	*vanilla ice cream*
Zitroneneis, das	*lemon sherbet*

A. *Übung*

1. Was hat mehr Kalorien? (you may want to review the dessert list)
   a) eine Portion Eis
   b) ein Windbeutel ohne Schlag
   c) ein Stück Sachertorte mit Schlag
2. Wer viel Kuchen ißt, soll viel
   a) schlafen
   b) laufen
   c) zahlen

"Man ist, was man ißt" (a quote by the German philosopher *Feuerbach*)

*schlanke Linie = waist line
**Schlag = Austrian

B.   *Übung*

You are at a bus stop. You ask a person who is also waiting:

1. where the bus goes,
2. if the bus will come soon,
3. how much it costs.

C.   *Übung*

You are arriving at a hotel after 9 p.m. and you ask or say to the person at the desk...

1. Do you still serve hot meals?
2. I would like something light.
3. I would like a room too.
4. How much does the room cost?

D.   *Übung*

You have joined some Germans at a large table in a Gasthaus. You strike up a conversation and they ask you these questions. How would you respond?

1. Sind Sie Amerikaner oder Engländer?
    Sind Sie Amerikanerin oder Engländerin?
2. Wohnen Sie hier im Hotel (Gasthof)?
3. Wohin fahren Sie von hier?

E.   *Übung*

Sie essen gern Obst, aber nicht Gemüse.
Der Kellner bringt... Was wählen Sie, was nicht?

a)	Spinat	e)	Äpfel
b)	Erbsen	f)	Gurken
c)	Kirschen	g)	Pilze
d)	Tomaten	h)	Ananas

Other things you want to know or say at a restaurant

wo ist hier ein Telefon?	*Where is a telephone, please?*
wo ist die Toilette?	*Where is the restroom, please?*
wo ist das Gastzimmer?	*Where is the guest room?*
wo ist die Bar?	*Where is the bar, please?*
wo ist der Ober?	*Where is the waiter, please?*

Bitte,

noch ein Glas Milch.	*Another glass of milk, please.*
noch ein Glas Bier.	*Another beer, please.*
noch eine Tasse Kaffee.	*Another cup of coffee, please.*
haben Sie eine Zeitung?	*Do you have a newspaper, please?*
haben Sie ein Adreßbuch?	*Do you have an address book, please?*
haben Sie ein Telefonbuch?	*Do you have a telephone book, please?*

And before you leave the restaurant...

Bitte, zahlen.	*I would like to pay, please.*
Die Rechnung bitte.	*The bill, please.*

And if you want to praise them a little bit:

Es hat geschmeckt.	*It tasted good. The meal was good.*
Es war sehr gut.	*It was very good.*
Wir waren zufrieden.	*We were satisfied/pleased.*
Wir kommen wieder.	*We will come again.*

Auf Wiedersehen!

F. *Übung*

How to complain—if you have to...
Ich möchte mich beschweren!!!
Match the German statements with their English equivalents.

1. Ich möchte mich beschweren.
2. Das habe ich nicht bestellt.
3. Die Suppe ist kalt.
4. Das Bier ist warm.
5. Das Fleisch ist zäh.
6. Das schmeckt nicht gut.
7. Das Fleisch ist zu fett.
8. Bitte bringen Sie etwas anderes.
9. Das ist versalzen.
10. Wir warten schon lange.
11. Der Löffel ist schmutzig.
12. Wann kommt das Essen?
13. Das Tischtuch ist nicht sauber.

a) We have been waiting for a long time.
b) I would like to complain.
c) I didn't order that.
d) That doesn't taste good.
e) The meat is too tough.
f) The soup is cold.
g) Please bring me something else.
h) That has too much salt.
i) The meat is too fatty.
j) The beer is warm.
k) The tablecloth is not clean.
l) When is the food being served?
m) The spoon is dirty.

Situationen

Was sagen oder fragen Sie? Auf deutsch, natürlich!
Try to handle these situations with your acquired "Survival German" skills.

1. You are a bit hungry, but not ready for a big meal.
2. You ask a passer-by where there is a snack bar or dairy bar.
3. You want to know if it is far from here.
4. Finally, you ask if you (should) take a streetcar or bus.

7. Compound nouns

Many German nouns consist of two or more words joined together; the compound nouns are written as one word. While English has similar compound nouns, the parts often continue to be written separately, even though they are pronounced as a single word. In German, compound nouns take their gender from that of the *final* component.

das Auto   die Bahn = **die** Autobahn

das Auto   die Bahn   das Restaurant = **das** Autobahnrestaurant

In some cases, a linking -s-, -es-, or -n-is inserted between the components.

die Zitrone   das Eis = das Zitroneneis

A.   *Übung*

Sagen oder schreiben Sie "compounds."

1. die Leber / der Käse
2. die Natur / das Schnitzel
3. der Käse / der Kuchen
4. das Obst / die Torte
5. der Gast / das Haus
6. der Spargel / die Spitzen
7. die Frucht / das Eis

B.   *Übung*

Combine and match the words on the left with an appropriate one from the right. We did the first one for you.

Beispiel: .... Auto - die Bahn = die Autobahn

1.	................Straße...................	a. das Haus
2.	................Gast...................	b. die Bahn
3.	................Bus...................	c. der Kuchen
4.	................Käse...................	d. die Haltestelle
5.	................Stadt...................	e. der Plan
6.	................Haus...................	f. der Portier
7.	................Hotel...................	g. die Frau

Wiederholung*

A.   Telling, asking, complaining...
How would you tell a person

1. to go (drive) ...straight ahead/to the left/to the right
2. to walk...to the corner/to the sign/over the bridge
3. to take...the bus/the streetcar/a taxi
4. to bring...the menu/the newspaper/the telephone book

B.   How would you ask the waiter

1. to bring you...a coke/a glass of milk/the menu
2. to have your meat cooked...rare/well done
3. to have your vegetables steamed
4. to have your dessert with whipped cream/without cream

*Don't forget to check your answers with the answers on page 163.

C. How would you complain that

1. you have been waiting for a long time
2. the soup is cold
3. the beer is warm
4. this is too salty
5. the table cloth is not clean
6. the meat is tough

D. How would you ask anyone

1. where there is a telephone
2. for another glass of wine/cup of coffee/ice cream
3. whether this place is taken/still free
4. whether they still serve hot meals/lunch/dinner

E. How would you say

1. you want to pay/it was good/we are coming again
2. we were satisfied
3. excuse me, please
4. good-bye!

F. Was ist das? Indicate whether the following dishes are:

a. eine Vorspeise	*an appetizer*
b. ein Getränk	*a beverage*
c. eine Nachspeise	*a dessert*
d. Fleisch	*meat*
e. eine Suppe	*a soup*
f. ein Gemüse	*a vegetable*

1. Pilze . . . .
2. Eisbein . . . .
3. Erbsen . . . .
4. Wiener Schnitzel . . . .
5. Leberknödelsuppe . . . .
6. Faschiertes . . . .
7. Kaltschale . . . .
8. Bienenstich . . . .
9. Bohnen . . . .
10. Sachertorte . . . .
11. Spinat . . . .
12. Kaiserschmarren . . . .
13. Hackbraten . . . .
14. Cremeschnitte . . . .
15. Schweinebraten . . . .
16. Milch . . . .

Wortschatz*

Nouns

das Abendessen, - dinner
der Adler, - eagle
die Ampel, -n traffic light
die Bank, -en bank
das Benzin gasoline
die Brücke, -n bridge
die Bushaltestelle, -n bus stop
die Ecke, -n corner
der Engländer, - inhabitant of England, male
die Engländerin, -nen inhabitant of England, female
das Essen, - meal
das Fenster, - window
das Fräulein, - Miss; here: waitress
der Gastgarten, ⸚ outdoor sitting area of a restaurant
das Gasthaus, ⸚er inn
die Gaststätte, -n restaurant
das Gemüse, - vegetable
das Getränk, -e beverage
das Hotel, -s hotel
der Hotelportier, -s desk clerk, concierge
die Jausenstation, -en (Austrian) snack bar
der Kuchen, - cake
der Marktplatz, ⸚e market place
die Milchbar, -s dairy bar
das Mittagessen, - lunch
die Nachspeise, -n dessert
das Obst fruit
der Onkel, - uncle
der Parkplatz, ⸚e parking place
die Postkarte, -n postcard
die Raststätte, -n restaurant (at the Autobahn)
die Rechnung, -en bill, invoice
die Renovierung, -en renovation
der Ruhetag, -e day off
der Salat, -e salad
das Salz salt
das Schild, -er sign
der Schnellimbiß, -sse snack bar
der Stadtplan, ⸚e city map

die Straßenbahnhaltestelle, -n streetcar stop
die Suppe, -n soup
das Tagesmenü, -s special of the day
die Tasse, -n cup
das Tischtuch, ⸚er table cloth
die Uhr, -en clock, watch
   um 11 Uhr at 11 o'clock
die Vorspeise, -n appetizer
die Weinstube, -n wine tavern
das Wochenende, - weekend

Verbs

sich beschweren to complain
bestellen to order
bringen to bring
dämpfen to steam
dürfen (darf) may, to be allowed (to)
empfehlen (empfiehlt) to recommend
essen (ißt) to eat
kochen to cook
können (kann) can, to be able (to)
mögen (mag) to like
rauchen to smoke
reservieren to reserve
schlafen (schläft) to sleep
schmecken (dat.) to taste good
sollen ought (to), to be supposed (to)
stehen to stand
versuchen to choose, try
warten to wait
wissen (weiß) to know
wollen (will) to want
zahlen to pay

Other Words

aber but
alles everything
als when
ausgezeichnet excellent
bis as far as
bevor before
damit so that
daß that

*Vocabulary items pertaining to food and meals are listed on p. 47–51.

durchgebraten well done
fett fat
gar nicht not at all
gebacken baked
gebraten roasted
gedämpft steamed
gefüllt filled, stuffed
gegrillt grilled
gekocht cooked
geöffnet open
geradeaus straight ahead
geräuchert smoked
geschlossen closed
geschmort braised
glücklich happy
halb durchgebraten medium well
hinter behind
leicht light, easy
ob whether, if
obwohl although
oder or
preiswert low-priced, reasonably priced
rechts right

roh rare, raw
sauber clean
schattig shady
schmutzig dirty
schön beautiful, pretty
seit since
sobald as soon as
solange as long as
versalzen salted too much
vom Rost broiled
von...bis from...til (to)
während while, whereas
wegen because
weil because
wen whom
wenn if, whenever
wieviel how much
zäh tough
zur (= zu der) to the

Idiomatic Expressions

Alles in Ordnung? Everything o.k.?
Es tut mir leid. I am sorry.

Kapitel 4

Overnight Accommodations

Culture Notes

You are travelling in a German speaking country and need a place to stay overnight. Since you haven't made any reservations in advance, you might look for a:

(das) Hotel	*hotel*
(der) Gasthof	*inn (restaurant and rooms)*
(das) Gasthaus	*restaurant, often with rooms*
(die) Pension	*boarding house*
(das) Fremdenzimmer	*room for rent*
(die) Jugendherberge	*youth hostel*

If you arrive by plane or train, most larger cities have a counter at the airport or train station called

Zimmernachweis, Hotelnachweis oder Information
(room information, hotel information or information)

If you are travelling by car, the same help may be available at the outskirts of a city, especially on the *Autobahn.*

Hotel prices differ according to the *Kategorie* under which they are listed - A, B, C, D, or I. II., etc. Prices are usually higher in metropolitan areas.

Zimmer mit Bad means a room with a bath tub, sink, and toilet (W.C.), while *Zimmer mit Dusche* includes only a shower, with W.C. across or down the hall. A *Zimmer ohne Bad und Dusche* may still be a nice, clean room, but bath, shower and W.C. are somewhere else.

Note that the price of a double room is often listed *pro Person.* If it says *DM 35.00 pro Person,* that double room will cost DM 70.00 for two.

The price for lodging usually includes a standard breakfast consisting of coffee, tea, or hot chocolate; rolls or bread with butter, cheese, jam or honey.

Telephone calls from your hotel room cost thirty to a hundred percent more than a call from a pay phone or the post office.

Tips for the maid are included in the price. But tip the person who carries your luggage to your room.

All travellers must register, even if it is only for one night. It's the law.

Hotels near railroad stations are often more expensive than hotels in the inner city or in the suburbs. Travelling by car gives you the chance to find less expensive and often charming overnight accommodations outside the city.

European (Euroscheck) and American credit cards are accepted in most higher priced hotels. Smaller establishments, especially in the countryside, are not used to "plastic money." Not yet!

An alternative to hotels is lodging in a place with the sign: *Zimmer frei*. This is the German equivalent to "bed and breakfast." These are private homes (farms) renting out rooms. It's an economical way to stay overnight. Most of these places are nice and clean, and often provide contact with a family.

Then there is the inexpensive *Jugendherberge,* the youth hostel, which is popular with young people. Families can use them too. *Jugendherbergen* have mostly *Schlafsäle* (large rooms with several single beds) and no private bath, shower, etc. Some also stick to a *Sperrstunde*—you must be in at a stated hour. *Jugendherbergen* differ in quality and location. There you can also meet interesting people from all over the world.

DIALOGE

Gast:	Haben Sie noch ein Zimmer frei?	Do you still have a vacant room?
Portier:	Nein, es tut mir leid, wir sind besetzt.	No, I am sorry. We have no vacancy.
Gast:	Und morgen?	And tomorrow?
Portier:	Einen Augenblick, ich sehe nach. Ja, morgen können Sie ein Einzel- oder Doppelzimmer mit Dusche bekommen.	Just a moment, I will see. Yes, tomorrow you can have a single or double with shower.
Gast:	Wieviel kostet es?	How much does it cost?
Portier:	Das Einzelzimmer kostet 75 Mark, das Doppelzimmer 110.	The single is 75 marks and the double is 110.
Gast:	Gut, ich nehme das Doppelzimmer.	Good. I will take the double.

Portier:	Entschuldigen Sie, gehört Ihnen dieser Koffer?	Excuse me, is this your suitcase?
Gast:	Ja, er gehört mir, und diese Tasche auch.	Yes, that's mine, and this bag belongs to me too.
Portier:	(to the porter) Hans, bitte helfen Sie der Dame mit dem Gepäck. (porter to lady)	Hans, please help the lady with her luggage.
Träger:	Bitte folgen Sie mir.	Please follow me.

Herr S.:	Wohin fahren Sie in Urlaub?	Where are you going for your vacation?
Herr H.:	Diesmal in die Schweiz, nach Grindelwald.	This time we are going to Switzerland, to Grindelwald.

Herr S.:	Und wer fährt mit?	And who all is going?
Herr H.:	Die ganze Familie, meine Frau, unser Sohn und unsere Tochter.	The whole family, my wife, our son and our daughter.
Herr S.:	Wie schön. Haben Sie schon Quartier?	How nice. Do you already have a place?
Herr H.:	Ja, wir mieten eine Ferienwohnung. Drei Zimmer mit Küche und Balkon.	Yes, we are renting a vacation home. Three rooms with kitchen and balcony.
Herr S.:	Und wie kommen Sie hin?	And how are you getting there?
Herr H.:	Wir fliegen bis Zürich und von dort fahren wir mit dem Zug bis Grindelwald.	We are flying to Zurich and from there we are going by train to Grindelwald.

Frau K.:	Und wer wohnt neben uns?	And who is living next to us?
Frau L.:	Wo? Links oder rechts von Ihnen?	Where? To the left or right from you?
Frau K.:	Links von uns.	To the left.
Frau L.:	Das ist Familie Gruber. Herr Gruber ist Manager von einem großen Geschäft und Frau Gruber arbeitet als Wirtschaftsprüferin für die Stadt.	That is the Gruber family. Mr. Gruber is the manager of a large store, and Mrs. Gruber works as an accountant for the city.
Frau K.:	Nette Leute?	Nice people?
Frau L.:	Oh ja, ich hoffe, Sie lernen sie bald kennen.	O, yes, I hope you will meet them soon.

Grammar

1.   The dative case

The dative is the case of the *indirect object,* answering the question *wem?* (to whom? or for whom?). Basically, the dative case is used to identify the person or thing for whom an action is carried out.

Wem gehört das Auto?	*To whom does the car belong?*
Es gehört dem Mann dort.	*It belongs to the man over there.*
Wem geben Sie das Geld?	*To whom are you giving the money?*
Ich gebe es der Frau.	*I am giving it to the woman.*
Wem erzählst du die Geschichte?	*To whom are you telling the story?*
Ich erzähle sie den Kindern.	*I am telling it to the children.*

	MASCULINE	*FEMININE*	*NEUTER*	*PLURAL*
NOMINATIVE	der	die	das	die
	ein	eine	ein	keine
DATIVE	dem	der	dem	den
	einem	einer	einem	keinen
ACCUSATIVE	den	die	das	die
	einen	eine	ein	keine

Beispiele:

Wir schreiben den Kindern.	*We are writing to the children.*
Sagen Sie es der Ärztin.	*Tell (it to) the doctor.*
Geben Sie dem Kellner die Rechnung.	*Give the bill to the waiter.*
Ich zeige den Touristen die Stadt.	*I am showing the tourists the city.*
Die Mutter kauft dem Kind eine Limonade.	*The mother is buying the child a lemonade.*

A.   Übung

In each of the following sentences an indirect object is used. The dative case is in italics. Restate the sentence with the cued noun in the dative.

> Beispiel: Ich zeige *dem Mann* das Buch.   *die Frau*
>   Ich zeige *der Frau* das Buch.

1. Ich zeige .... das Buch.   *die Freunde*
2. Ich zeige .... das Buch.   *der Arzt*
3. Ich zeige .... das Buch.   *das Kind*
4. Ich zeige .... das Buch.   *der Professor*
5. Ich zeige .... das Buch.   *das Mädchen*
6. Ich zeige .... das Buch.   *die Managerin*

2.   Dative ending for a few masculine nouns in the singular

While most German nouns do not change their form in the dative case singular, a few add -*en* in all cases, except the nominative. Here are some of these nouns.

NOMINATIVE	DATIVE	ACCUSATIVE
der Herr	dem Herrn	den Herren
der Tourist	dem Touristen	den Touristen
der Junge	dem Jungen	den Jungen
der Student	dem Studenten	den Studenten

3.   Dative endings for nouns in the plural

a.   Almost all nouns end in -*(e)n* in the dative plural.

> Wir geben den Kinder*n* das Geld.   *We give the money to the children.*
> Ich zeige den Gäste*n* das Haus.   *I am showing the guests the house.*

b.   There are also some exceptions. Words that form their plural by adding *s* (mostly foreign words) keep that *s* in the dative case plural too.

> Wir sprechen von den Auto*s*.*   *We are speaking about the cars.*
> Mit den Foto*s* habe ich viel Spaß.*   *I have a lot of fun with the pictures.*

A.   Übung

Complete using the cued expression.

> Beispiel: Geben Sie .... das Geld.   *die Kinder*
>   Geben Sie *den Kindern* das Geld.

1. Sagen Sie es ....   *der Herr*
2. Erzählen Sie es ....   *die Kinder*

*mit and *von* are dative prepositions. See p. 62.

3. Geben Sie es ....   *die Studenten*
4. Zeigen Sie es ....   *der Freund*
5. Sagen Sie es ....   *die Freunde*
6. Zeigen Sie es ....   *der Tourist*
7. Zeigen Sie es ....   *die Touristen*

B.   Übung

Übersetzen Sie.

> Beispiel: Say it to the student [male].
> Sagen Sie es dem Studenten.

1. Give it to the tourists.
2. We show it to mother.
3. I am saying it to the teacher.
4. Karl writes to the businessman.
5. I am telling it to the people.

4.   Dative prepositions

The following prepositions always require the use of the *dative* case.

aus	*out of, from*	nach	*after, toward, according to*
außer	*except for*	seit	*since, for (referring to time)*
bei	*near, at*	von	*from*
mit	*with*	zu	*to, at*

> Beispiele: Hans wohnt bei seinen Eltern.   *Hans lives with his parents.*
> Erika kommt aus der Bibliothek.   *Erika is coming out of the library.*

A.   Übung

Complete the sentence as suggested, using the dative.

> Beispiel: Gehen wir jetzt zu .. dem Bahnhof...   *der Bahnhof*
> or: zum Bahnhof

1. Ich fahre nicht gern mit ....   *der Bus*
2. Fritz kommt aus ....   *das Geschäft*
3. Was hörst du von ....   *die Freunde*
4. Seit .... rauche ich nicht mehr.   *ein Monat*
5. Nach .... gehe ich nach Hause.   *das Konzert*

5.   The dative case of personal pronouns

Nominative:	ich *(I)*	er *(he)*	sie *(she)*	wir *(we)*	Sie *(you)*
Dative:	mir *(to me)*	ihm *(to him)*	ihr *(to her)*	uns *(to us)*	Ihnen *(to you)*
Accusative:	mich *(me)*	ihn *(him)*	sie *(her)*	uns *(us)*	Sie *(you)*

Note: here are the forms for the *du* and *ihr* forms:

du *(you)*	dir *(to you)*	dich *(you)*
ihr *(you)*	euch *(to you)*	euch *(you)*

Here are a few examples in which only the *dative* of personal pronouns are used:

Dieser Koffer gehört nicht uns.	*This suitcase does not belong to us.*
Bitte schreiben Sie mir.	*Please write to me.*
Was gebe ich ihr?	*What do I give her?*
Gehört Ihnen dieser Koffer?	*Does this suitcase belong to you?*

And here are *dative* pronouns with a *direct object:*

Sie gibt ihm das Geld.	*She gives him the money.*
Wir kaufen ihr ein Auto.	*We are buying her a car.*
Ein Freund zeigt uns die Stadt.	*A friend is showing us the city.*
Er verkauft ihnen das Haus.	*He is selling the house to them.*

A. *Übung*

Apply the personal pronoun of the *dative* case in context. Complete the command with the appropriate pronoun.

Beispiel: Ich brauche ein Taxi. Bitte rufen Sie *mir* ein Taxi.

1. Fritz sucht eine Wohnung. Finden Sie .... eine Wohnung.
2. Wir haben kein Zimmer. Geben Sie .... ein Zimmer.
3. Maria möchte die Zeitung. Bringen Sie .... die Zeitung.
4. Ich habe keine D-Mark. Bitte geben Sie .... D-Mark.
5. Die Touristen möchten die Stadt sehen. Bitte zeigen Sie ....
   die Stadt.
6. Was, du hast keinen Regenschirm, Hans? Ich kaufe .... einen
   Regenschirm.

6. Verbs which require the dative case

If you use these verbs, you must always use the *dative* case:

antworten	*to answer*	helfen (hilft)	*to help*
danken	*to thank*	leid tun	*to be sorry*
gefallen (gefällt)	*to like*	passen	*to suit*
gehören	*to belong*	scheinen	*to seem*
glauben	*to believe*	schmecken	*to taste*

Dieses Auto gefällt meinem Vater.	*My father likes this car.*
Ich danke der Frau.	*I thank the woman.*
Bitte antworten Sie mir.	*Please answer me.*
Es tut ihr leid.	*She is sorry.*
Gehört das Ihnen?	*Does that belong to you?*
Wir glauben Ihnen nicht!	*We don't believe you.*
Hans hilft dem alten Mann.	*Hans is helping the old man.*
Wie schmeckt dir das?	*How does this taste? (to you)*
Freitag abend? Ja, das paßt uns.	*Friday night? Yes, that suits us.*

A. *Übung*

Restate each sentence replacing the italicized noun with a suitable pronoun.

Beispiel: Das Wiener Schnitzel schmeckt dem Jungen.
Das Wiener Schnitzel schmeckt ihm.

1. Das tut *der Amerikanerin* leid.
2. Antworten Sie *dem Mann.*
3. Ich glaube *den Leuten.*
4. Das paßt *den Kindern.*
5. Wie gefällt *dem Vater* das Haus?
6. Die Wohnung gehört *Frau Müller.*
7. Wir danken *dem Schweizer.*
8. Können Sie *Ingrid* helfen?

B.   *Übung*

Now restate each sentence replacing the *dative* pronoun with the *dative* case of the noun in italics.

Beispiel: Das Eis schmeckt ihm.   *der Junge*
Das Eis schmeckt *dem Jungen.*

1. Bitte helfen Sie ihr.	*die Frau*
2. Glaubt er ihm nicht?	*der Amerikaner*
3. Das paßt uns nicht.	*die Österreicher*
4. Wir danken ihnen.	*die Deutschen*
5. Diese Wohnung gefällt mir.	*die Studentin*
6. Das Haus gehört uns.	*die Firma*
7. Schmeckt es Ihnen?	*die Gäste*
8. Es tut mir leid, daß Sie ihm	
nicht helfen können.	*das Kind*

7.   Separable prefix verbs

Many German (and English) verbs consist of two parts: a *prefix* and a *stem*.

Beispiele:
prefix	*stem*	
an	kommen	*to arrive*
ab	fahren	*to depart*

an·fangen*	*to begin*	zurück·fliegen	*to fly back*
an·rufen	*to call*	an·schauen	*to look at*
ein·ziehen	*to move in*	ein·steigen	*to board, get in*
um·ziehen	*to move*	aus·steigen	*to get off*
aus·ziehen	*to move out*	zu·machen	*to close*
mit·nehmen	*to take along*	auf·machen	*to open*
auf·stehen	*to get up*	mit·gehen	*to go along*

Note: In *separable* prefix verbs, the *stress* is on the prefix. The *prefix* is separated from the verb...

a)   in a main clause (present and past tense)
Der Bus *kommt* um neun Uhr *an.*   *The bus arrives at 9 o'clock.*

b)   in a command
Rufen Sie mich morgen *an!*   *Call me tomorrow.*

*Separable prefix verbs are listed in dictionaries in this manner: ab·fahren, an·rufen, mit·nehmen, etc.

c) in a question
   Ziehen Sie im Sommer *um?*   *Are you moving in the summer?*

A. Übung

Complete the statement or question with the correct German equivalent of the English verb.

> Beispiel: Wann.................. der Zug ....?   *to arrive*
>   Wann kommt der Zug an?

1. Wann.................. Maria in die neue
    Wohnung......?   *to move*
2. Bitte.................. Sie das Buch......   *to take along*
3. Herr Braun.................. Sie morgen......   *to call*
4. Bitte.................. Sie das Fenster......   *to close*
5. Wann.................. Sie nach Amerika......   *to fly back*
6. Der Zug.................. um 16 Uhr 40......   *to depart*
7. Herr Richter.................. am Freitag......   *to arrive*
8. Wann.................. das Konzert?......   *to begin*

A separable prefix *does not* separate...

a) when it is used as an infinitive:
    Ich muß um 7 Uhr aufstehen.   *I have to get up at 7 o'clock.*
b) when used in a dependent clause:
    Ich weiß nicht, ob Hans anruft.   *I don't know if Hans is going to call.*

B. Übung

Complete the sentence with the cued statement.

> Beispiel: Karl fährt morgen ab.
>   Ich weiß nicht, ob...
>   Ich weiß nicht, ob Karl morgen abfährt.

1. Maria fliegt am Mittwoch zurück.
    Ich glaube, daß...
2. Ernst zieht im Sommer um.
    Ich möchte wissen, warum...
3. Das Spiel fängt um 19 Uhr an.
    Wissen Sie, ob...
4. Ingrid kommt nach Österreich mit.
    Ich freue mich, wenn...
5. Er fährt am Sonntag ab.
    Wir besuchen Fritz heute, weil...
6. Karin steigt dort immer aus.
    Fragen Sie Karin, warum sie...

8. Word order of direct and indirect objects
What are the rules for word order when you encounter both a direct and indirect object in a sentence or clause?

a)   The indirect object usually *precedes* the direct object.

	INDIRECT OBJECT	DIRECT OBJECT
Ich gebe	der Frau	den Schlüssel.
I give	*the woman*	*the key.*
Sie zeigt	dem Mann	die Wohnung.
She shows	*the man*	*the apartment.*
Wir kaufen	den Kindern	die Bücher.
We buy	*the children*	*the books.*

b)   All pronouns *precede* nouns.

	INDIRECT OBJECT	DIRECT OBJECT
Ich gebe	ihr	den Schlüssel.
I give	*her*	*the key.*
Sie zeigt	ihm	die Wohnung.
She shows	*him*	*the apartment.*
Wir kaufen	ihnen	die Bücher.
We buy	*them*	*the books.*

	DIRECT OBJECT	INDIRECT OBJECT
Ich zeige	es	dem Gast.
I show	*it*	*to the guest.*
Wir kaufen	sie	den Kindern.
We buy	*them*	*for the children.*

c)   But when both the direct and indirect objects are pronouns, the direct object *precedes* the indirect object. Needless to say, such sentences make sense only in context.

	INDIRECT OBJECT	DIRECT OBJECT
Ich gebe	ihn	ihr.
I give	*it*	*to her.*
Sie zeigt	sie	ihm.
She shows	*it*	*to him.*
Wir kaufen	sie	ihnen.
We buy	*them*	*for them.*

A.   Übung

Restate, replacing the italicized word(s) with the appropriate direct or indirect object pronoun. Watch word order.

Beispiel: a)   Der Ober gibt *dem Gast* die Rechnung.
                         Der Ober gibt ihm die Rechnung.
                   b)   Der Ober gibt dem Gast *die Rechnung*.
                         Der Ober gibt sie dem Gast.
                   c)   Der Ober gibt *dem Gast die Rechnung*.
                         Der Ober gibt sie ihm.

1.   a)   Helmut bringt *Elke* den Koffer.
     b)   Helmut bringt Elke *den Koffer*.
     c)   Helmut bringt *Elke den Koffer*.

2. a) Wir verkaufen *den Amerikanern* ein Haus.
    b) Wir verkaufen den Amerikanern *ein Haus*.
    c) Wir verkaufen *den Amerikanern ein Haus*.
3. a) Ich zeige *den Freunden* die Stadt.
    b) Ich zeige den Freunden *die Stadt*.
    c) Ich zeige *den Freunden die Stadt*.

B. *Übung*

Form three sentences of your choice using any of the direct and indirect objects
listed.

Beispiel: Wir verkaufen dem Studenten einen Volkswagen.

	sie
	den Deutschen
	ihnen
	ein Auto
Wir zeigen...	dem Studenten
Ich bringe...	ihr
Er kauft...	einen Koffer
	es
	ihm
	den Österreichern

Kurzer Geschäftsbrief
Sehr geehrter Herr Müller!*
    Mein Kollege John Tyler und ich kommen am 23. Juni um 15 Uhr 30 mit
Lufthansaflug 79 aus Hamburg in Düsseldorf an. Holen Sie uns am Flughafen ab,
oder sollen wir direkt zum Hotel fahren? Wir freuen uns, wenn Sie uns abholen,
aber es ist nicht nötig.
    Bitte schreiben Sie uns, bevor wir hier abreisen.
Mit freundlichen Grüßen
Ihr...

9. Two-way prepositions
These nine prepositions require either the **accusative** or **dative** case.

an	*at the side of, at, on, to*
auf	*on top of, on, to*
hinter	*in back of, behind*
in	*inside of, in, into*
neben	*next to, beside*
über	*over, above, about*
unter	*under, among*
vor	*in front of, before*
zwischen	*between*

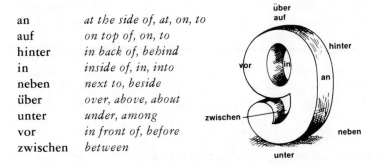

*Did you understand this letter? If not, consult answers on p. 165.

These prepositions take the *accusative* if there is motion from one place to another; in other words, if there is a change in location. They usually answer the question *wohin? where to?*

Wohin fahren Sie?   *Where are you going (to)?*
Ich fahre in die Stadt.   *I am driving into the city.*

But the same nine prepositions take the *dative* case when they express position in a place and when they answer the question *wo? where?*

Wo wohnen Sie?   *Where do you live?*
Ich wohne in der Stadt.   *I live in the city.*

These prepositions also take the *dative* case when the verb indicates action or motion *within* a place and thus also answers the question *wo? where?*

Wo arbeiten Sie?   *Where do you work?*
Ich arbeite in einem Büro.   *I work in an office.*

Contractions of the definite articles *dem, das* and some of the two-way prepositions are commonly used in everyday speech.

an + dem = am	über + dem = überm
hinter + dem = hinterm	unter + dem = unterm
in + dem = im	vor + dem = vorm

The same prepositions are often contracted with the definite article **das** when they occur in the accusative with a neuter singular noun: **ans, hinters, ins, übers, unters, vors.**

A. Übung

Dative or **accusative?** Complete using the cue in the **accusative** or the **dative** as appropriate. Hint: Do you ask wohin? or wo?

Beispiel: Wir ziehen morgen in ....   *die Wohnung*
          Wir ziehen morgen in die Wohnung.

1. Ich ziehe jetzt in....................   *die Stadt*
2. Wir warten vor..................auf Sie.   *das Hotel*
3. Die Kinder laufen hinter....................   *das Haus*
4. Sie sitzt neben....................   *ein Mann*
5. Die Rechnung liegt auf....................   *der Tisch*
6. Wir gehen heute auf....................   *ein Berg*
7. Ich bleibe oft in....................   *ein Gasthof*
8. Wir essen oft in....................   *das Gasthaus*
9. Der Hund liegt vor....................   *das Sofa*
10. Der Tourist geht an....................   *die Ecke*

B. Übung

Restate the sentence, contracting the preposition and the definite article.

Beispiel: Wann ziehen Sie in das Haus?
          Wann ziehen Sie ins Haus?

1. Wir sprechen über das Wetter.
2. Bitte gehen Sie an das Fenster.
3. Das Auto steht vor dem Geschäft.
4. Fahren Sie heute in das Büro?
5. Mein Paß ist in dem Koffer.
6. Die Katze liegt unter dem Tisch.

C. Übung

Restate the sentence with the cued verb.

> Beispiel: Hans wohnt in der Stadt.   *fahren*
>   Hans fährt in die Stadt.

1. Wir fahren ins Hotel.   *wohnen*
2. Schreiben Sie den Brief im Büro?   *bringen*
3. Ich gehe jetzt ins Geschäft.   *arbeiten*
4. Frau Müller lebt in der Schweiz.   *reisen*
5. Karin ißt in dem Gasthaus.   *gehen*

Wiederholung

A. Ask in German...

1. if there is still a room available.
2. whether it is a single room or a double room.
3. how much it costs.
4. if you can see the apartment.
5. when you can move in.
6. if there is a lease.
7. for how long one can rent the vacation apartment.
8. if dogs are allowed in the apartment.
9. how many rooms the apartment has.
10. when you should call.

B. Tell someone that...

1. you are moving to Zürich this summer.
2. Oskar is renting a vacation apartment in Austria.
3. the apartment has two rooms, a balcony, and a kitchen.
4. they like to stay in New York.
5. this suitcase does not belong to you.
6. you would like to make her acquaintance.

C. Give it...to whom?

> Beispiel: Geben Sie es .... (to me)
>   Geben Sie es mir.

1. Geben Sie es .... (to them)
2. Geben Sie es .... (to her)
3. Geben Sie es .... (to him)
4. Geben Sie es .... (to a student, male)

5. Geben Sie es .... (to the students)
6. Geben Sie es .... (to us)

D.   Delete the modal auxiliary in the following sentences. All the verbs used have *separable* prefixes. Check your English translation.

Beispiel: Ich muß um 6 Uhr aufstehen.   *I must get up at 6 o'clock.*
          Ich stehe um 6 Uhr auf.   *I get up at 6 o'clock.*

1. Wir wollen Franz am Wochenende abholen.
2. Ich soll am Sonntag anrufen.
3. Ich möchte ihn auf der Party kennenlernen.
4. Er kann den Koffer nicht mitnehmen.
5. Wo müssen wir aussteigen?
6. Wann darf ich dort einziehen?
7. Erika will am Freitag ankommen.
8. Das Konzert soll um 19 Uhr anfangen.

E.   Restate, replacing the italicized word(s) with the appropriate direct or indirect object pronoun. Watch word order.

Beispiel: Hans bringt dem Gast *das Gepäck.*
          Hans bringt es dem Gast.
          Wir zeigen *der Deutschen die Stadt.*
          Wir zeigen sie ihr.

1. Wir kaufen *dem Jungen* das Buch.
2. Ich schreibe *der Frau einen Brief.*
3. Fritz zeigt dem Gast *das Zimmer.*
4. Sie bringt *der Freundin einen Hund.*
5. Er gibt *dem Touristen* die Schlüssel.
6. Ich verkaufe *dem Studenten* das Auto.

F.   Sagen Sie auf deutsch bitte!

1. The apartment belongs to her.
2. When do you arrive in Frankfurt?
3. We are not pleased with the house. (use *gefallen*)
4. She is coming back on Wednesday.
5. Please show me the two-room apartment.
6. I want to become acquainted with her.
7. Get off (depart) at the main square.
8. The guest would like a room with a shower.
9. I must get up at 7 o'clock.
10. Please help the girl.

Wortschatz

Nouns

die Anzeige, -n advertisement, ad
der Balkon, -e balcony
die Beförderung, -en promotion
der Berg, -e mountain
die Bibliothek, -en library
das Büro, -s office
der Deutsche, -n German, male
die Deutsche, -n German, female
das Doppelzimmer, - double room
die Dusche, -n shower
das Einzelzimmer, - single room
die Eltern parents
die Familie, -n family
die Ferienwohnung, -en vacation apartment
die Firma, die Firmen firm, company
der Flughafen, - airport
der Gast, ⁻e guest
der Gasthof, ⁻e inn
das Gepäck luggage
das Geschäft, -e store, business
der Geschäftsbrief, -e business letter
Grindelwald town in Switzerland
der Gru†, ⁻e greetings
der Hauptplatz, ⁻e main square
der Hund, -e dog
der Junge, -n boy
die Kirche, -n church
die Katze, -n cat
der Kollege, -n colleague, male
die Kollegin, -nen colleague, female
das Krankenhaus, ⁻er hospital
die Küche, -n kitchen
der Lufthansaflug, ⁻e Lufthansa (airline) flight
der Manager, - manager, male
die Managerin, -nen manager, female
der Mietvertrag, ⁻e lease
der Name, -n name
der Österreicher, - Austrian (male)
die Österreicherin, -nen Austrian (female)
das Quartier, -e quarters, room
der Schlüssel, - key
die Schweiz Switzerland
der Schweizer, - Swiss, male

die Schweizerin, -nen Swiss, female
das Spiel, -e game
die Tasche, -n bag, purse
das Theater, - theater, playhouse
das Tier, -e animal
der Tourist, -en tourist, male
die Touristin, -nen tourist, female
der Träger, - porter
der Urlaub, -e vacation
der Wirtschaftsprüfer, - certified public accountant, male
die Wirtschaftsprüferin, -nen certified public accountant, female
das Zimmer, - room
Zürich city in Switzerland
die Zwei-Zimmerwohnung, -en two-room apartment.

Verbs

ab·fahren (fährt ab) to depart
ab·holen to pick up
ab·laufen (läuft ab) to expire, run out
an·fangen (fängt an) to begin, to start
an·rufen to phone, call
an·kommen to arrive
an·schauen to look at, watch
auf·hören to stop
auf·machen to open
auf·stehen to get up
aus·steigen to get off
aus·ziehen to move out
ein·steigen to get in, to board
ein·ziehen to move in
erlauben to allow, permit
folgen to follow
sich freuen to enjoy, to be glad
gefallen (gefällt) dat. to be pleased, to like
gehören dat. to belong
glauben dat. to believe
helfen, (hilft) dat. to help
hier·bleiben to remain, to stay
hin·kommen to get there
kaufen to buy

kennen·lernen   to meet, to become
  acquainted
leben   to live, reside
leid·tun   to be sorry, to regret
liegen   to lie
mieten   to rent
mit·fahren (fährt mit)   to drive along,
  come along
mit·gehen   to go along
nach·schauen   to look up, inquire
nach·sehen (sieht nach)   to check
passen dat.   to suit well, fit
rufen   to call
scheinen dat.   to seem
schreiben   to write
verkaufen   to sell
vermieten   to rent
versetzen   to transfer
um·ziehen   to move

vorbei·kommen   to stop by, visit
zeigen   to show
ziehen   to pull
zu·machen   to close
zurück·kommen   to return,
  come back

Other Words

auch   also, too
bald   soon
besetzt   occupied, taken
von...bis   from...to (until)
diesmal   this time
frei   free, vacant
ganz   whole, entire
neben   next to, beside

Idiomatic Expression

Wie schön!   How nice!

Kapitel 5

Telling Time

Culture Notes

Germans use two sets of time systems side by side. One is for everyday use and conversations, comparable to our a.m. and p.m. system. Another is for "official" purposes, the 24-hour system.

The 24-hour system is always used for official business, by radio and television stations, and by the Armed Forces. Bus, train, airline, movie and theater schedules are also listed in the 0-24 hour manner.

But for most other communications referring to time, the 0-12 hour system will suffice. Our a.m. and p.m. hours are mostly implied through context. If someone tells you *"Kommen Sie um 3 Uhr,"* it will hardly mean 3 a.m. but 3 p.m. If ambiguity could exist, adding *früh, vormittag, nachmittag, abend* will settle the matter; for instance, 9 Uhr vormittags as distinguished from *9 Uhr abends.*

Instead of *null Uhr* (zero hour), Germans say *um Mitternacht.* However, *ein Uhr* must become clear through context, since it could mean 1 a.m. or 1 p.m. in colloquial German.

If you want to be sure of the local time, call a certain number listed under *Zeitangabe.*

Sie sehen…	Sie sagen…
0:40	null Uhr vierzig
5:25	fünf Uhr fünfundzwanzig
11:17	elf Uhr siebzehn
13:50	dreizehn Uhr fünfzig
20:15	zwanzig Uhr fünfzehn
23:04	dreiundzwanzig Uhr vier

When expressing time, we have a number of options. For conversational use, the "quarter" and "half" hour method is a common way to specify time.

> 3:00 or 15:00 = Es ist drei Uhr.
> 3:15 or 15:15 = Es ist viertel nach drei (or: viertel vier*).
> 3:30 or 15:30 = Es ist halb vier.

*The expressions used in parentheses are often used in Southern Germany and Austria.

3:45 or 15:45 = Es ist viertel vor vier (or: dreiviertel
vier*).
4:00 or 16:00 = Es ist vier Uhr.

If you want to be precise, use the "minute" method.

4:05 or 16:05 = Es ist fünf nach vier.
4:25 or 16:25 = Es ist fünf vor halb fünf (or: vier Uhr
fünfundzwanzig)
4:40 or 16:40 = Es ist zwanzig vor fünf (or: vier Uhr
vierzig).

DIALOGE

Time tables govern the lives of people everywhere. Here are a few situations
in a German setting, using time expressions.

Im Hotel

Portier:	(ruft an) Guten Morgen, Herr Jones. Es ist halb sieben.	(calls) Good morning Mr. Jones It is half past six.
Jones:	Danke. Ab wann gibt es bei Ihnen Frühstück?	Thank you. When do you start serving breakfast?
Portier	Ab sieben Uhr. Im Frühstückssaal.	From seven o'clock on. In the breakfast room.
Jones:	Vielen Dank.	Thank you very much.

Bei der Bahnhofs-Information		At the train station information
Frau R.:	Guten Tag. Bitte, wann fährt ein Schnellzug von Wien nach Salzburg?	Hello. When does an express train go from Vienna to Salzburg?
Auskunft:	Wann wollen Sie fahren—morgens, mittags oder abends?	When do you want to go—in the morning, afternoon or in the evening?
Frau R.:	Am Vormittag.	In the late morning.
Herr K.:	Es gibt einen Schnellzug—Abfahrt um 10 Uhr 17 vom Westbahnhof.	There is an express train, departure at 10:17 from the West-train station.
Frau R.:	Und wann kommt dieser Zug in Salzburg an?	And when does this train arrive in Salzburg?
Herr K.:	Um 14 Uhr 52.	At 2:52 p.m.
Frau R.:	Fährt dieser Zug auch am Wochenende?	Does this train go on the weekend as well?
Herr K.:	Ja, er fährt täglich. Ich wünsche gute Fahrt.	Yes, it goes every day. Have a nice trip.
Frau R.:	Danke schön.	Thank you.

Eine Verabredung / *A meeting*

Herr T.:	Können wir uns heute nachmittag treffen?	Could we meet this afternoon?
Frl. S.:	Ja, vielleicht. Um wieviel Uhr?	Yes, perhaps. At what time?
Herr T.:	Um halb fünf.	At four thirty.

Frl. S.:	Das ist zu früh für mich. Unser Büro schließt erst um viertel nach fünf.	That's too early for me. Our office doesn't close til quarter after five.
Herr T.:	Sie arbeiten aber lange!	You sure work long (hours).
Frl. S.:	Ja, am Freitag sind es immer acht einhalb Stunden. Da komme ich schon um viertel vor neun ins Büro.	Yes, on Friday I work eight and a half hours. (Then) I arrive at the office at fifteen before nine.
Herr T.:	Sie sind sehr fleißig. Paßt Ihnen sechs Uhr? Ich warte vor dem Büro.	You are very busy. Is six o'clock o.k.? I'll wait in front of the office.
Frl. S.:	Einverstanden.	Agreed.

An der Universität

Rick:	Sag, weißt du, wann Professor Wilhelm sein Seminar hält?
Udo:	Ich glaube, Montag und Donnerstag von 16 bis 18 Uhr.
Rick:	Fängt er pünktlich an?
Udo:	Nein, es beginnt immer erst um viertel nach vier.
Rick:	Prima, dann komme ich nicht zu spät. Ich habe bis halb vier eine Tennisstunde.

At the university

Say, do you know when Professor Wilhelm holds his seminar?
I believe on Monday and Thursday from 4 til 6 p.m.
Does he start on time?
No, it (the seminar) never starts until a quarter after four.
Great, then I won't be late. I have a tennis lesson until three thirty.

Auf einer Party   Sie danken der Gastgeberin und wollen nach Hause gehen.

At a party   You thank the hostess and want to go home.

Frau K.:	Vielen Dank für die Einladung. Es war wirklich nett bei Ihnen.
Herr P.:	Was, Sie wollen schon gehen? Es ist doch erst elf.
Herr K.:	Ja, wir müssen noch packen. Wir fliegen morgen nach Zürich.
Frau P.:	Wann geht Ihr Flug?
Frau K.:	Leider schon um 6 Uhr 45. Und man muß eine halbe Stunde vor Abflug dort sein.
Frau P.:	Ja, ich weiß. Guten Flug.
Frau K.:	Danke. Auf Wiedersehen.
Herr P.:	Auf Wiedersehen.

Thank you for the invitation. It was really nice here.
What, you want to go already! It is only eleven o'clock.
Yes, we still have to pack. We are flying to Zurich tomorrow.

When does your flight leave?
Unfortunately, already at 6:45. And one has to be there a half hour before departure.

Yes, I know. Have a good flight.
Thank you. Good-bye.
Good-bye.

A. *Übung*

What's your time table? Fill in the appropriate time expression.

> Beispiel: Ich gehe um .... ins Kino.   *at half past seven*
> Ich gehe um halb acht ins Kino.

1. Ich stehe um .... auf.   *quarter past six*
2. Mein Freund und ich laufen eine ....   *half an hour*
   im Park.
3. Wir kommen um .... in Frankfurt an.   *at 9:35*
4. Treffen wir uns um .... am Flughafen?   *quarter of eight*
5. Um .... esse ich Mittag.   *one o'clock*
6. Um .... gehe ich nach Hause.   *quarter past five*
7. Ich gehe um .... ins Bett.   *half past ten*

B. Übung

Answer these questions with the given time cue. Provide only the time element in your answer.

> Beispiel: Wann kommen Sie zurück? (3:30)
> Um drei Uhr dreißig. (or: um halb vier)

1. Wann fährt der Zug ab? ....   *at 16:45*
2. Wie spät ist es? *11:15*
3. Um wieviel Uhr beginnt das Konzert? ....   *at 20:00*
4. Wie lange arbeiten Sie morgen? ....   *until 5:45*
5. Wieviele Stunden in der Woche arbeiten Sie? ....   *42 hours*
6. Wann spielt Inge Golf? ....   *at 4:30*

C. Übung

Übersetzen Sie!

1. We eat every day at quarter of six.
2. I'll come back at two thirty.
3. Please, call me at 10:30.
4. At what time is she leaving?
5. He calls me every half hour.
6. Can you visit us tomorrow?
7. I must be at the train station at 19:40.
8. We will be home in three hours.

Grammar

Present perfect tense

Any time we wish to describe an event in the past, we must use one of the past tenses.

Past tense:	Ich ging nach Hause.	*I went home.*
Present Perfect:	Ich bin nach Hause gegangen.	*I have gone home. (I went home.)*
Past Perfect:	Ich war nach Hause gegangen.	*I had gone home.*

In everyday life, Germans usually use the present perfect, especially in conversation. The present perfect in German, as in English, is a compound tense, formed with *an auxiliary verb* plus the *past participle of the verb.* The auxiliary verb can be either **haben** or **sein.** The auxiliary verb is the second element in a clause or sentence, the past participle goes to the end.

	auxiliary	+		past participle
Wir	haben	Tennis		gespielt.
Er	hat	bis 6 Uhr		gearbeitet.
Erika	hat	heute zu Hause		gegessen.
Ich	bin	nach Hause		gefahren.
Sie	sind	zu uns		gekommen.

While most German verbs use **haben** as the auxiliary in the present perfect, **sein** is used to denote either *a change of place* or *a change in condition*. Such verbs must also be intransitive, that is such verbs must never take a direct object.

Compare: Ich bin mit dem Zug gefahren.   *I went by train.*
       but Ich habe den Porsche gefahren.   *I drove the Porsche.*

How to form a past participle in German

1. **Regular (weak) verbs**

Prefix **ge** + stem + ending **t(et)**

INFINITIVE	PAST PARTICIPLE	
spielen	gespielt	*Ich habe Tennis gespielt.*
lernen	gelernt	*John hat Deutsch gelernt.*
hören	gehört	*Wir haben gute Musik gehört.*

2. **Irregular (strong) verbs**

Prefix **ge** + stem + ending **-en**

INFINITIVE	PAST PARTICIPLE	
kommen	gekommen	*Ist Erika gestern gekommen?*
finden	gefunden	*Wir haben ihn gefunden.*
schreiben	geschrieben	*Ich habe einen Brief geschrieben.*

Note: A vowel change occurs in the past participle of many verbs. This vowel change cannot be predicted. It must be learned by heart—just like foreigners learning English must memorize verbs like: go, went, gone; write, wrote, written, etc.

3. **Separable prefix verbs**

Separable Prefix **ge** + stem + ending

INFINITIVE	PAST PARTICIPLE	
mit·spielen	mitgespielt	*Haben Sie mitgespielt?*
an·rufen	angerufen	*Hans hat angerufen.*
ab·fahren	abgefahren	*Der Zug ist abgefahren.*

4. **Inseparable prefix verbs**

German verbs with inseparable prefixes (be-, emp-, ent-, er-. ver-, zer-,) *don't use ge-* in forming their past participle.

verkaufen   verkauft   *Wir haben das Haus verkauft.*

The same is true for verbs whose infinitive ends in *-ieren.*

studieren   studiert   *Inge hat Biologie studiert.*

5. **Irregular verbs using *haben***

Ich **habe** mit ihm gesprochen.	*I spoke with him.*
Er/sie **hat** mit ihm gesprochen.	*He/she spoke with him.*
Wir **haben** mit ihm gesprochen.	*We spoke with him.*
Sie **haben** mit ihm gesprochen.	*You spoke with him.*
Sie **haben** mit ihm gesprochen.	*They spoke with him.*
Du **hast** mit ihm gesprochen.	*You (fam. sing.) spoke with him.*
Ihr **habt** mit ihm gesprochen.	*You (fam.pl) spoke with him.*

6. **Irregular verbs using *sein***

Ich **bin** in die Stadt gefahren.	*I went downtown.*
Er/sie **ist** in die Stadt gefahren.	*He/she went downtown.*
Wir **sind** in die Stadt gefahren.	*We went downtown.*
Sie **sind** in die Stadt gefahren.	*You went downtown.*
Sie **sind** in die Stadt gefahren.	*They went downtown.*
Du **bist** in die Stadt gefahren.	*You (fam.sing.) went downtown.*
Ihr **seid** in die Stadt gefahren.	*You (fam.pl.) went downtown.*

7. **Regular verbs using *sein***

Ich **bin** viel gereist.	*I travelled a lot.*
Er/sie **ist** viel gereist.	*He/she travelled a lot.*
Wir **sind** viel gereist.	*We travelled a lot.*
Sie **sind** viel gereist.	*You travelled a lot.*
Sie **sind** viel gereist.	*They travelled a lot.*
Du **bist** viel gereist.	*You (fam.sing.) travelled a lot.*
Ihr **seid** viel gereist.	*You (fam.pl.) travelled a lot.*

Finally, German has a small group of *mixed verbs.* They combine both the characteristic irregular vowel change and the regular ending.

Ich **habe** das nicht **gewußt.**	*I didn't know that.*
Er/sie **hat** das nicht **gewußt.**	*He/she didn't know that.*
Wir **haben** das nicht **gewußt.**	*We didn't know that.*
Sie **haben** das nicht **gewußt.**	*You didn't know that.*
Sie **haben** das nicht **gewußt.**	*They didn't know that.*
Du **hast** das nicht **gewußt.**	*You (fam.sing.) didn't know that.*
Ihr **habt** das nicht **gewußt.**	*You (fam.pl.) didn't know that.*

Other verbs which follow this pattern are:

denken	gedacht	*to think*
bringen	gebracht	*to bring*
rennen	gerannt	*to run*
brennen	gebrannt	*to burn*

A. *Übung*

Complete with the past participle of the cue verb. For irregular verbs, the vowel change is indicated (nehmen, o). However, there may be other changes too.

> Beispiel: (nehmen, o) Haben Sie ein Zimmer ....?
>   Haben Sie ein Zimmer genommen?

1. John hat ein Jahr in der Schweiz ....   *wohnen*
2. Wir sind gestern abend im Kino ....   *sein, e*
3. Ich habe Erika eine Karte ....   *schreiben, ie*
4. Herr Müller hat um 9 Uhr ....   *an·rufen, u*
5. Wann ist das Team ....?   *ab·fliegen, o*
6. Haben Sie ein Zimmer ....?   *reservieren*
7. Wo haben Judy und Fritz ....?   *studieren*
8. Haben Sie diesen Regenschirm .... ?   *vergessen, e*

B. *Übung*

To talk about activities which have taken place, German speaking people will most likely use the present perfect tense to describe them. Pay attention to the auxiliary *haben* or *sein* and the form of the past participle.

> Beispiel: Das weiß ich nicht. Das habe ich nicht gewußt.
>   Er fährt nach Wien. Er ist nach Wien gefahren.

1. Ich arbeite gern in diesem Büro.
2. Wir bleiben zwei Tage in Hamburg.
3. Rufen Sie Frau Hödl an!
4. Otto ist nicht zu Hause.
5. Gehst du in den Zoo?
6. Die Amerikaner finden das Restaurant nicht.
7. Wohin laufen die Kinder?
8. Ich finde nie einen Parkplatz.

C. *Übung*

Respond with an answer of your choice.

> Beispiel: Was haben Sie gestern abend gemacht?
>   Ich habe einen Freund besucht.

Was haben Sie gestern abend gemacht? Ich habe...

- Karten gespielt.
- Tennis gespielt.
- Freunde besucht.
- ein gutes Buch gelesen.
- ferngesehen.
- meine Eltern angerufen.
- im Restaurant gegessen.
- Radio gehört.
- fleißig gearbeitet.
- die Zeitung gelesen.
- ein Auto gekauft.

Ich bin...	{	einkaufen gegangen.
		ins Kino gegangen.
		zu Hause geblieben.
		früh schlafen gegangen.
		auf einer Party gewesen.
		zu Freunden gefahren.

Was hat Inge heute morgen gemacht?

Sie ist.... { zwei Meilen gelaufen.
um 6 Uhr aufgestanden.
um 8 Uhr 30 ins Büro gegangen.
bis 7 Uhr im Bett geblieben.

Sie hat... { um 7 Uhr gefrühstückt.
um Viertel nach 10 telefoniert.
keinen Parkplatz bekommen.
die Zeitung gelesen.

Wir haben... { einen Ausflug gemacht.
eine Ausstellung gesehen.
Golf gespielt.
lange geschlafen.
zu viel gegessen.
Freunde besucht.

Was habt ihr am Wochenende gemacht?

Wir sind... { in die Berge gefahren.
nach Berlin geflogen.
zu Hause geblieben.
in die Stadt gegangen.
bei Freunden gewesen.

D. Übung

Complete each sentence with an appropriate verb. Choose one from the list below. More than one choice may be possible.

Beispiel: Wir haben ihn gestern auf der Party ....
gesehen, getroffen, gesprochen

1. Jedes Wochenende sind wir in die Berge ....
2. Haben Sie heute schon die Zeitung ....?
3. Wann ist der Bus ....?
4. Wo haben Sie das ....?
5. Warum ist Franz nach Schweden ....?
6. Wie hat Ihnen die Ausstellung ....?
7. Wir haben uns vor dem Bahnhof ....
8. Wie lange ist Frau Ebner in Österreich ....?
9. Ich bin heute vormittag in die Stadt ....
10. Wo haben Sie Ihren Freund ....

fahren	reisen	laufen
ab·fahren	lesen	sehen
an·kommen	gefallen	kaufen
finden	bleiben	hören
treffen	gehen	sein

DIALOGE

Read these four brief dialogs and see if you can understand them. If you are
having problems, check the chapter or end vocabulary.

Im Hotel beim Portier

Frau Miller:	Guten Tag, ich bin Frau Miller, Elisabeth Miller.
	Ich habe letzte Woche ein Zimmer bestellt.
Portier:	Haben Sie uns geschrieben oder haben Sie telefoniert?
Frau Miller:	Ich habe eine Postkarte aus Hamburg geschickt.
Portier:	Einen Augenblick, ich sehe gleich nach.
	Ja, wir haben Ihre Karte bekommen.
Frau Miller:	Und haben Sie ein Zimmer für mich reserviert?
Portier:	Ja, ein Einbettzimmer für zwei Nächte. Zimmer 7 im ersten Stock.

In einem Studentenheim

Karl:	Guten Morgen, John!
	Hast du gut geschlafen?
John:	Danke, sehr gut—und lange.
Karl:	Wann bist du heute aufgestanden?
John:	Erst um halb neun. Ich bin gestern sehr spät ins Bett gegangen.
Karl:	Bist du auf einer Party gewesen?
John:	Nein, ich bin nur sehr müde gewesen. Am Nachmittag habe ich Tennis gespielt und abends habe ich dann noch lange in der Bibliothek gelesen.

Gespräch auf einer Party

Karin:	Hab' ich richtig gehört? Sie sind im letzten Sommer in Amerika gewesen?
Klaus:	Ja, das stimmt. Wir haben unsere Verwandten in Chicago besucht.
Karin:	Wie lange haben Sie in den USA verbracht?
Klaus:	Fünf Wochen. Ich habe leider nicht mehr Urlaub gehabt.
Fritz:	Haben Sie außer Chicago noch anderes gesehen?
Klaus:	Ja, ein bißchen von New York. Dort sind wir beim Hinflug angekommen.
Fritz:	Und wie hat Ihnen Amerika gefallen?
Klaus:	Recht gut. Wir möchten wieder hin.

Anruf beim Flughafen

Herr Bieber:	Guten Abend. Bitte ist der Lufthansaflug 312 aus Köln schon angekommen?
Information:	Nein, Lufthansaflug 312 hat Verspätung. Er ist noch nicht von Köln abgeflogen.
Herr Bieber:	Und wann kommt er hier an?
Information:	Das kann ich Ihnen leider noch nicht sagen. Bitte rufen Sie in einer Stunde bei uns an.

...eine Stunde später...

Herr Bieber:	Guten Abend, ich habe vor einer Stunde mit Ihnen gesprochen. Wissen Sie jetzt schon, wann Lufthansaflug 312 hier ankommt?
Information:	Einen Augenblick, ich schaue mal auf unserem Computer nach.
	Ja, Lufthansaflug 312 ist um 17 Uhr 35 in Köln abgeflogen.
Herr Bieber:	Und ist der Flug schon gelandet?
Information:	Nein, noch nicht. Voraussichtliche Landezeit ist hier 19 Uhr 25.
Herr Bieber:	Vielen Dank.

8.   The genitive case

The last German case is the *genitive*. The genitive usually expresses possession or a relationship.

> Beispiele: Georgs Vater ist krank.
> *George's father is sick.*
> Ich verstehe die Reaktion des Lehrers nicht.
> *I don't understand the reaction of the teacher.*
> Fritz kommt am Ende des Monats.
> *Fritz is coming at the end of the month.*

Look at the chart and notice the genitive endings for the definite and indefinite articles.

	MASCULINE	FEMININE	NEUTER	PLURAL
NOMINATIVE	der ein	die eine	das ein	die keine
GENITIVE	des eines	der einer	des eines	der keiner

Also note that *masculine* and *neuter* nouns take an *-s* in the singular (*-es* if the noun has one syllable).

> Beispiele: das Auto des Vaters, des Freundes, des Onkels
> der Hund des Kindes, des Lehrers, des Mannes

Like in English, proper nouns add an *-s,* but not an apostrophe, unless the name already ends in an -s, then an apostrophe is added.

> Beispiele: Gerlindes Haus ist neu.
> *Gerlinde's house is new.*
> Achims Kinder sind noch klein.
> *Achim's children are still small.*
> Thomas' Mutter kommt heute.
> *Thomas' mother is coming today.*

A.   *Übung*

Übersetzen Sie!

> Beispiel: *I don't know the name of the town.*
> Ich weiß den Namen der Stadt nicht.

1.   Where is Karin's father?
2.   Is this Karl's room?
3.   Do you know the professor's name?
4.   I don't have the address of the restaurant.
5.   The children's parents have left.
6.   Would you like to see Heidi's photos?
7.   We can't buy John's car.

Wiederholung

A.   Was machen Sie um diese Zeit? What are you doing at that time? Make use of the expressions below.

Beispiel: 6:00 Ich stehe um sechs Uhr auf.   *oder*
           Um sechs Uhr stehe ich auf.

1.	7:00	9.	16:30
2.	7:45	10.	17:15
3.	8:15	11.	17:45
4.	9:30	12.	18:00
5.	10:30	13.	19:00
6.	12:30	14.	20:00
7.	13:45	15.	21:00
8.	15:00	16.	22:30

frühstücken	in den Park gehen	zu Abend essen
zur Arbeit fahren	ins Büro zurückgehen	die Nachrichten hören
im Büro ankommen	einen Kaffee trinken	einen Nachbarn besuchen
mit Kunden sprechen	mit dem Chef sprechen	fern-sehen
Briefe lesen und	zu Hause ankommen	ein Buch lesen
beantworten	nach Hause gehen	Klavier spielen
auf die Post gehen	die Zeitung lesen	ins Bett gehen
mittagessen gehen		

B. You are on a trip in Europe and you are writing a letter to a German friend. See if you can complete it by providing the correct auxiliaries **haben** or **sein** and verb forms. (Present Perfect Tense) The infinitives of the verbs are listed in order below.

                                    Berlin, den 2. Juli

Lieber Stefan!

Am 8. Mai .... ich um 18:15 in Berlin .... Vom Flughafen .... ich ein Taxi .... und ....
sofort zum Hotel .... Ich .... den Portier ....
........, ob er ein Zimmer für mich .... Ja, ich .... Glück .... Ich .... ein Zimmer für drei Tage .... Ich .... drei Tage in Berlin .... Ich .... einige deutsche Firmen ....
und ich .... auch öfters bei deutschen Kollegen ....
Herr Müller von der Firma Siemens .... mir auch eine neue Fabrik .... Am Wochenende .... wir einen Ausflug in den Grunewald .... An einem Abend .... ich ins Konzert .... Es .... mir sehr gut .... Die Berliner Philharmoniker .... Beethoven und Mozart ....
.....

Herzliche Grüße
Dein Michael

ankommen	haben	zeigen
nehmen	bekommen	machen
fahren	sein	gehen
fragen	besuchen	gefallen
reservieren	sein	spielen.

Wortschatz

Nouns

der Abend, -e evening
   am Abend in the evening
die Abfahrt, -en departure
der Abflug, ¨e flight departure
der Anruf, -e telephone call
der Ausflug, ¨e outing, trip
die Ausstellung, -en exhibit
das Bett, -en bed
der Brief, -e letter
der Chef, -s boss, male
die Chefin, -nen boss, female
das Einbettzimmer, - single room
der Einkauf, ¨e purchase, shopping
   trip
die Einladung, -en invitation
die Eltern parents
die Fahrt, -en trip, journey
der Flug, ¨e flight
das Frühstück, -e breakfast
die Gastgeberin, -nen hostess
das Gespräch, -e conversation
der Hinflug, ¨e flight to
die Karte, -n postcard
das Kino, -s movie
der Kunde, -n customer
die Landezeit, -en landing time,
   arrival time
der Nachmittag, -e afternoon
   am Nachmittag in the afternoon
der Nachbar, -n neighbor
die Nachricht, -en news
der Mittag, -e noon
   am Mittag at noon
die Nacht, ¨e night
der Portier, -s desk clerk (hotel)
der Schnellzug, ¨e express train
Schweden Sweden
das Seminar, -e seminar
der Stock, die Stockwerke floor
   im 1. Stock on the *second* floor
das Studentenheim, -e dormitory
die Tennisstunde, -n tennis lesson
die Verabredung, -en appointment,
   date
der Verwandte, -n relative
der Vormittag, -e time before noon
   am Vormittag in the morning

die Verspätung, -en delay
der Westbahnhof West-railway station

Verbs

ab·fliegen, ist abgeflogen to depart
   by plane, to fly off
an·fangen (fängt an), angefangen to
   begin, start
auf·stehen, ist aufgestanden to get up
fern·sehen (sieht fern), ferngesehen to
   watch television
frühstücken, gefrühstückt to have
   breakfast
gefallen (gefiel), gefallen (dat.) to
   like
halten (hält) gehalten to conduct, to
   hold
landen, ist gelandet to land
laufen (läuft), ist gelaufen to run
lesen (liest), gelesen to read
mit·spielen, mitgespielt to play, to take
   part in
nach·sehen (sieht nach), nachgesehen to
   check out, to look for
packen, gepackt to pack
schicken, geschickt to send, mail
schließen, geschlossen to close, shut
studieren, studiert to study
telefonieren, telefoniert to telephone
treffen (trifft), getroffen to meet
verbringen, verbracht to spend (time)
vergessen (vergißt), vergessen to forget
wünschen, gewünscht to wish

Other Words

abends in the evening
ander- other
bei with, at, near
bißchen a little bit
dann then
erst (um) not until
früh early
gleich right away, at once
halb half
heute today
heute nachmittag this afternoon

hin to (there)
letzt- last
mittags at noon
morgens in the morning
recht quite
  recht gut quite well
sehr very
viertel quarter

voraussichtlich probably, approximately.

Idiomatic Expressions

Ab wann? From what time on?
Das stimmt. That's correct.
Einverstanden! Agreed!
Um wieviel Uhr? At what time?

Kapitel 6

Health Care

Culture Notes

If you are in a German-speaking country for a long period of time, you will probably choose your physicians the same way you do it at home: through recommendations of friends or business associates, and through referrals.

But for emergencies abroad keep in mind that one does not have to go to a hospital. Many German, Swiss and Austrian cities maintain a medical emergency service at night, on weekends, and on holidays. Participating physicians take turns performing this service at their office, your home or even in hotels. These *Notdienst* (emergency) physicians who are on call are listed in the local newspapers. Their telephone numbers can also be obtained through special *Notruf* numbers listed in the phone book under: *Notdienst* or *Notruf,* or *Erste Hilfe.*

Since most Germans, Austrians and Swiss must carry health insurance, physicians and dentists receive most of their payments from health insurance companies. Thus, doctors and their office staff are well-versed in the ensuing *Papierkrieg* (the battles with paper work and bureaucracy). Advice to the traveler: bring your insurance forms along. In case of a health emergency they probably will be accepted and filled out by physicians in these countries.

If hospitalization is required, several *Klassen* (categories) of rooms are available. *Erste Klasse* or *Sonderklasse* means a private room. *Zweite Klasse:* you share the room with another person. *Dritte Klasse* could be a larger room with several people.

Learn to distinguish between a *Drogerie* (drug store) and an *Apotheke* (pharmacy). You can buy prescription drugs only in an *Apotheke.* If you need medicine during the night, you usually can find a *Nachtapotheke* open.

DIALOGE

Klaus:	Gehst du ins Museum mit?	Are you coming along to the museum?
Kurt:	Nein, ich fühle mich leider nicht wohl.	No, unfortunately, I don't feel well.
Klaus:	Was fehlt dir denn?	What's wrong with you?
Kurt:	Ich habe furchtbare Halsschmerzen.	I have a terrible sore throat.
Klaus:	Warst du schon beim Arzt?	Have you been to the doctor yet?
Kurt:	Nein, noch nicht. Ich wollte noch ein bißchen warten.	No, not yet. I wanted to wait a bit.

| Klaus: | Komm, ich fahre dich lieber zu Dr. Müscher. Er ist unser Hausarzt. | Come, I'll take you to Dr. Müscher. He is our family doctor. |
| Kurt: | Ja, das ist vielleicht das Beste. | Yes, that's perhaps the best. |

Frau S.:	Waren Sie schon einmal im Krankenhaus?	Have you ever been in a hospital?
Frau K.:	Ja, als ich Kind war. Warum?	Yes, when I was a child. Why?
Frau S.:	Mein Blinddarm muß raus.	I have to have my appendix removed.
Frau K.:	Wann?	When?
Frau S.:	Noch diese Woche.	This week still.
Frau K.:	Hatten Sie wenigstens Zeit, ein gutes Krankenhaus auszusuchen?	Did you at least have time to look for a good hospital?
Frau S.:	Mein Arzt empfahl mir das Universitätskrankenhaus.	My doctor recommended the University hospital.
Frau K.:	Da war meine Mutter, als man ihr einen Herzschrittmacher einsetzte.	That's where my mother was when they gave her a pacemaker.
Frau S.:	Wirklich? Das wußte ich nicht.	Really? I didn't know that.
Frau K.:	Ja, sie war sehr zufrieden.	Yes, she was very satisfied.
Frau S.:	Gut—dann gehe ich also ins Universitätskrankenhaus.	Good, then I will go to University hospital.

Karin:	Du siehst aber blaß aus.	You look really pale.
Elke:	Mir ist ganz schwindelig, und ich habe auch Fieber.	I am very dizzy, and I also have a temperature.
Karin:	Vielleicht hast du die Grippe.	Perhaps you have the flu.
Elke:	Ich glaube auch.	I believe so too.
Karin:	Hast du schon Aspirin genommen?	Did you already take aspirin?
Elke:	Ja, ich nahm vor einer Stunde wieder zwei.	Yes, I took two an hour ago.
Karin:	Hast du auch genug getrunken?	Did you drink enough?
Elke:	Natürlich. Ich trank seit gestern bestimmt zwei Liter Mineralwasser.	Of course. I probably drank five liters mineralwater since yesterday.
Karin:	Ich muß jetzt gehen.	I have to go now.
Elke:	Hoffentlich fühlst du dich bald besser.	I hope you will feel better soon.

Arzt:	Wo tut's denn weh?	Where does it hurt?
Patient:	Ich habe schreckliche Ohrenschmerzen.	I have a terrible earache.
Arzt:	Lassen Sie mich mal sehen…Ja, Sie haben eine schlimme Entzündung.	Let me see. Yes, you have a bad infection.
Patient:	Der Hals tut mir auch weh.	My throat hurts too.
Arzt:	Machen Sie den Mund weit auf. Sagen Sie A, A, A,	Open your mouth wide. Say A, A, A,

Patient:	A, A, A,	A, A, A,
Arzt:	Die Mandeln sind auch geschwollen.	The tonsils are swollen too.
Patient:	Was soll ich dagegen nehmen?	What should I take for it?
Arzt:	Ich verschreibe Ihnen ein Rezept.	I will write you a prescription.
	Nehmen Sie die Tabletten wie vorgeschrieben.	Take the tablets as prescribed.

Grammar

1.   The simple past tense

So far you have learned the preferred way of expressing past time situations—the conversational past (or present perfect tense). Another way of expressing past time in German is the simple past tense (also known as the narrative past). The simple past is used primarily when reporting past events.

> Beispiele: Mein Arzt *emfahl* mir das Universitätskrankenhaus.
> *My doctor recommended the University Hospital to me.*
> Ich *nahm* ein Aspirin.
> *I took an aspirin.*
> Hans *hatte* die Grippe.
> *Hans had the flu.*

German *regular* verbs form their past tense by adding a -*t*- plus ending to the stem.

	Present Tense		Past Tense		English Meaning
ich sag	e	ich	sag	te	I said
er/sie sag	t	er/sie	sag	te	he/she said
wir sag	en	wir	sag	ten	we said
Sie sag	en	Sie	sag	ten	they said
du sag	st	du	sag	test	you said
ihr sag	t	ihr	sag	tet	you said

When the stem of a regular verb ends in a *d* or *t*, a linking *e* is inserted between the stem and the ending.

> arbeiten = ich arbeitete   antworten = er antwortete

A.   *Übung*

Restate, changing the present tense to the *past tense*.

> Beispiel: Frau Klein spielt Golf.
> Frau Klein spielte Golf.

1.   Der Patient glaubt das nicht.
2.   Großvater hört nicht gut.
3.   Was fehlt Ihnen?
4.   Der Ausländer sagt nichts.
5.   Ich fühle mich nicht gut.
6.   Wir lernen Deutsch.

7. Wo arbeiten Sie?
8. Der Tourist fragt sehr viel.

Irregular verbs form their past tense by changing the stem vowel. The personal endings are slightly different. There is no ending in the *ich* and *er/sie* forms, and no *e* in the *du* and *ihr* forms.

	REGULAR VERB			IRREGULAR VERB	
glauben	*to believe*	fahren		*to drive*	
ich glaubte	*I believed*	ich	fuhr	*I drove*	
er/sie glaubte	*he/she believed*	er/sie	fuhr	*he/she drove*	
wir glaubten	*we believed*	wir	fuhren	*we drove*	
Sie glaubten	*you believed*	Sie	fuhren	*you drove*	
sie glaubten	*they believed*	sie	fuhren	*they drove*	
du (fam. sg.) glaubtest	*you believed*	du	fuhrst	*you drove*	
ihr (fam. pl.) glaubtet	*you believed*	ihr	fuhrt	*you drove*	

Note: A few irregular verbs change not only the stem vowel, but also the stem:

gehen	er ging	*to go*	*he went*
tun	er tat	*to do*	*he did*
stehen	er stand	*to stand*	*he stood*

Also, when the stem ends in *d* or *t*, a linking *e* is inserted between the stem and the ending in the *du* and *ihr* forms: finden - du fandest. As in English, the best way to learn the past tense of irregular verbs is *to memorize* them. Here is a list of a few: Check the appendix on pp.185–186 for others.

Infinitive	Past	Past Participle	English
fahren	fuhr	ist gefahren	*to drive*
kommen	kam	ist gekommen	*to come*
sehen	sah	gesehen	*to see*
trinken	trank	getrunken	*to drink*
essen	aß	gegessen	*to eat*
sein	war	ist gewesen	*to be*
nehmen	nahm	genommen	*to take*
tun	tat	getan	*to do*
schreiben	schrieb	geschrieben	*to write*
empfehlen	empfahl	empfohlen	*to recommend*
gehen	ging	ist gegangen	*to go*
anrufen	rief an	angerufen	*to call*
lesen	las	gelesen	*to read*

B. *Übung*

Restate the sentences in the past tense. Then translate them into English.

> Beispiel: Wir fahren oft nach Europa.
> Wir fuhren oft nach Europa.
> *We often went to Europe.*

1. Karin nimmt die Tabletten.
2. Der Arzt verschreibt Penicillin.
3. Wer bekommt oft Post?

4. In Deutschland trinkt man viel Bier.
5. Die Amerikaner essen viele Hamburger.
6. Die Touristen besuchen viele Museen.
7. Wir schreiben oft nach Hause.
8. Ich arbeite jeden Tag.
9. Frau Müller liest ein interessantes Buch.
10. Der Gast versteht die Leute nicht.

C.   *Übung*

Say what you did during the day. Use the simple past tense.

1. Um sieben Uhr...	*I got up*
°frühstückte 2. Dann...	*ate breakfast°*
3. Um 9 Uhr...	*I read a book*
4. Um 10 Uhr...	*I went shopping*
5. Später...	*I visited a friend*
6. Um 12 Uhr...	*we ate again*
7. Um 1 Uhr...	*I went home*
8. Am Nachmittag...	*I worked in the garden*
9. Abends...	*I saw a movie*
10. Spät abends...	*I called my mother*
11. Um Mitternacht...	*I went to bed*

D.   *Übung*

Hier sind einige Fragen zu den *Dialogen.* Beantworten Sie sie. Be sure to use *past tense.* You may need to read the *Dialoge* on pp. 87–88 again.

Beispiel: Wer empfahl das Krankenhaus?
          Der Arzt empfahl es.

DIALOG 1

1. Was tat Kurt weh?
2. Warum war er noch nicht beim Arzt?
3. Wie hieß der Hausarzt?
4. Wer fuhr Kurt zum Arzt?

DIALOG 2

1. Warum mußte Frau S. ins Krankenhaus gehen?
2. Welches Krankenhaus empfahl der Arzt?
3. Wer war auch im Universitätskrankenhaus?

DIALOG 3

1. Warum sah Elke blaß aus?
2. Wer besuchte sie?
3. Wann hat sie Aspirin genommen?
4. Wieviel Mineralwasser hat sie getrunken?
5. Was sagte Elke, als sie weg ging?

DIALOG 4

1. Warum ging der Patient zum Arzt?
2. Hatte er nur Ohrenschmerzen?
3. Was verschrieb der Arzt?

KRANKHEITSVOKABULAR

to catch an illness	sich an·stecken
to become unconscious, faint	bewußtlos werden
to get immunized	geimpft werden
to have a physical examination	sich untersuchen lassen
to hurt oneself	sich verletzen
to break an arm or a leg	sich einen Arm oder ein Bein brechen
to take one's blood pressure	den Blutdruck messen
to take a blood test	eine Blutprobe machen
to put on a cast	einen Gipsverband anlegen
to have a heart attack	einen Herzanfall haben
to have an operation	sich operieren lassen
to take (swallow) pills	Pillen schlucken
to feel one's pulse	den Puls fühlen
to use CPR (Cardiac Pulmonary Resuscitation)	Wiederbelebungsversuche machen
to take one's temperature	Fieber messen

ILLNESSES

KRANKHEITEN

asthma	das Asthma
appendicitis	die Blindarmentzündung
cold	die Erkältung
fever	das Fieber
veneral disease	die Geschlechtskrankheit
flu	die Grippe
cough	der Husten
cancer	der Krebs
pneumonia	die Lungenentzündung
stomach-, head-, throat-, ear-, back-, heart-, aches or pain	die Bauch- (Magen), Kopf-, Hals-, Ohren-, Rücken-, Herz-, schmerzen
cardiac pacemaker	der Herzschrittmacher
organ transplant	die Organverpflanzung

SPECIALISTS

FACHÄRZTE

eye doctor, opthalmologist	*der Augen-*
dermatologist	*der Haut-* ⎫ *arzt, ˙e*
pediatrician	*der Kinder-* ⎬ *ärztin, -nen, die*
gynecologist	*der Frauen-* ⎭
family doctor (general practitioner)	*Praktischer Arzt*
surgeon	*der Chirurg, -en*
internist	*der Internist, -en*
radiologist	*der Röntgenologe, -n*
midwife	*die Hebamme, -n*
nurse	*die Krankenschwester, -n*
(doctor's) receptionist	*die Sprechstundenhilfe, -n*
optician	*der Optiker, -*
thermometer	*der Fiebermesser, -*

A.   Übung

Was machten Sie in diesen Situationen? Choose from the answers below and mark a, b, or c. More than one answer may be correct. Check vocabulary list on p. 91 and p. 97–98 if necessary.

> Beispiel: Sie brauchten einen Herzschrittmacher.
>   Antwort: c. (Ich mußte ins Krankenhaus gehen.)

1. Sie wachten mit Kopfschmerzen auf. Antwort..................
2. Ihre Mandeln müssen raus. Antwort..................
3. Sie hatten furchtbare Bauchschmerzen. Antwort..................
4. Sie hatten die Grippe. Antwort..................
5. Sie hatten hohes Fieber. Antwort..................
6. Ihr Arzt wollte eine Blutprobe machen. Antwort..................
7. Sie hatten Lungenentzündung. Antwort..................
   a. Ich machte nichts.
   b. Ich blieb zu Hause and legte mich ins Bett.
   c. Ich mußte ins Krankenhaus gehen.
   d. Ich ging zum Arzt.

B.   Übung

Beantworten Sie diese Fragen. (See Krankheitsvokabular if necessary, p. 91)

> Beispiel: Wie oft gehen Sie zum Arzt?
>   Ich gehe nur, wenn ich krank bin.

1. Was machten Sie, als Sie die Grippe hatten?
2. Was tat Ihnen weh?
3. Bei welchen Krankheiten muß man ins Krankenhaus gehen?
4. Wann verschreibt ein Arzt Medikamente?
5. Was machten Sie, als Sie eine Erkältung hatten?
6. Haben Sie einen Hausarzt?
7. Warum haben viele Menschen Lungenkrebs?
8. Wie oft gehen Sie zum Arzt?
9. Bekommen Sie genug Schlaf?
10. Wie bleibt man gesund? (Was sollte man tun/nicht tun?)

DIALOGE

Herr B.:	Möchten Sie mit zum Fußball-spiel?	Would you like to go to the soccer game?
Herr K.:	Ja gerne. Ich interessiere mich sehr für Fußball.	Yes, gladly. I am very interested in soccer.
Herr B.:	Wir müssen uns aber beeilen.	But we have to hurry.
Herr K.:	Wir können gleich gehen.	We can go immediately.
	Ich ziehe mir nur noch einen Pullover an.	I just have to put on a sweater.

| Karl: | Warum hast du dich verspätet? | Why are you late? |
| Peter: | Mein Wecker hat nicht geklingelt. | My alarm clock did not ring. |

Karl:	Deshalb hast du dich nicht rasiert?	That's why you didn't shave?
Peter:	Ja, ich habe mich nur schnell geduscht.	Yes, I quickly took only a shower.
Karl:	Gehen wir jetzt.	Let's go.
Peter:	Ich kann mich nicht erinnern, wann wir uns mit Herrn König treffen.	I can't remember when we are meeting with Mr. König.

2.   Reflexive pronouns

Reflexive pronouns are used when the *subject* and the *object* are the same. Note that sometimes the object can be a *dative*, sometimes an *accusative*.

Fritz rasiert sich.	*Fritz is shaving (himself).*
Ich fühle mich gut.	*I feel fine.*
Du kämmst dir das Haar.	*You are combing your hair.*

You will note that the forms of the reflexive pronouns are the same as those for the accusative and dative of the personal pronouns, except in the third-person singular and plural, where the reflexive pronoun is *sich*.

PERSONAL PRONOUNS						REFLEXIVE PRONOUNS	
Nominative		Accusative		Dative		Accusative	Dative
ich	*(I)*	mich	*(me)*	mir	*(to me)*	mich	mir
du	*(you)*	dich	*(you)*	dir	*(to you)*	dich	dir
er	*(he)*	ihn	*(him)*	ihm	*(to him)*	*sich*	*sich*
sie	*(she)*	sie	*(her)*	ihr	*(to her)*	*sich*	*sich*
es	*(it)*	es	*(it)*	ihm	*(to it)*	*sich*	*sich*
wir	*(we)*	uns	*(us)*	uns	*(to us)*	uns	uns
ihr	*(you)*	euch	*(you)*	euch	*(to you)*	euch	euch
sie	*(they)*	sie	*(them)*	ihnen	*(to them)*	*sich*	*sich*
Sie	*(you)*	Sie	*(you)*	Ihnen	*(to you)*	*sich*	*sich*

Note: Although only the *ich* and *du* forms of the reflexive pronouns are different in the accusative and the dative, you still need to know when to use the accusative or the dative. If there is just one reflexive pronoun object referring back to the subject, use the *accusative*. If there is a direct object plus a reflexive pronoun, use the *dative* form of the pronoun.

Beispiele:

Hans fühlt *sich* nicht wohl.	*Hans doesn't feel well.*
Ich habe *mich* erkältet.	*I have caught a cold.*
Du kaufst *dir* ein Auto.	*You are buying yourself a car.*
Ich putze *mir* die Zähne.	*I am brushing my teeth.*

German has many verbs which can be used either reflexively or non-reflexively. Their English equivalent often is nonreflexive.

Beispiele: Ich interessiere mich für Sport.   reflexive
               I am interested in sports.

Der Sport interessiert ihn.   non-reflexive
Sports interest him.
Die Mutter zieht das Kind an.   non-reflexive
The mother is dressing the child.
Die Mutter zieht sich an.   reflexive
The mother is getting dressed.
    (is dressing herself)

A.   Übung

Fill in the blanks with the appropriate *reflexive pronoun.*

Beispiel: Ich habe . . . . erkältet.
          Ich habe mich erkältet.

1. Peter duscht . . . . jeden abend.
2. Karl rasiert . . . . nur morgens.
3. Maria kämmt . . . . oft.
4. Der Junge zieht . . . . die Schuhe an.
5. Ich kaufe . . . . ein neues Kleid.
6. Wir interessieren . . . . für Musik.
7. Aber Herr Schmidt interessiert . . . . für Sport.
8. Heute muß ich . . . . beeilen.
9. Ich kaufe . . . . einen Mantel.
10. Frau Braun, wie fühlen Sie . . . . ?

More reflexive verbs:

1.	*to take a shower*	sich duschen
2.	*to get dressed*	sich anziehen
3.	*to shave*	sich rasieren
4.	*to brush one's teeth*	sich die Zähne putzen
5.	*to comb one's hair*	sich das Haar kämmen
6.	*to be interested in something*	sich interessieren für
7.	*to be in a hurry*	sich beeilen
8.	*to remember something/someone*	sich erinnern an + acc.
9.	*to look forward to*	sich freuen auf + acc.
10.	*to be mistaken*	sich irren

Learn these useful expressions...

B.   Übung

Übersetzen Sie!

Beispiel: I am interested in golf.
          Ich interessiere mich für Golf.

1. We have to hurry.
2. Mr. Johnson did not shave. (watch tense)
3. Elke doesn't feel well.
4. I am buying myself a watch.
5. We are meeting at 10 with Dr. Blume.
6. I can't remember the name.
7. I brush my teeth.

8. Karl is getting dressed.
9. Linda, did you comb your hair? (watch tense and use familiar form)
10. I think you are mistaken.

3. Possessive adjectives (pronouns)

Possessive adjectives—*mein (my)*, *dein (your)*, *sein (his)*, etc.—are also called *ein words* because they take the same ending as the indefinite article *ein* and *kein*. Look at these examples.

Ich sehe einen Hund.	*I see a dog.*
Ich sehe meinen Hund.	*I see my dog.*
Ich sehe eine Katze.	*I see a cat.*
Ich sehe meine Katze.	*I see my cat.*
Ich gebe einem Kind das Buch.	*I give a child the book.*
Ich gebe meinem Kind das Buch.	*I give my child the book.*

As you can see, the ending of the possessive adjective, like that of *ein* and *kein*, is determined by the gender and case of the noun that follows it. Look at this chart and learn the possessive adjectives.

POSSESSIVE ADJECTIVES

Singular			*Plural*		
ich	= mein	*my*	wir	= unser	*our*
er	= sein	*his*	sie	= ihr	*their*
sie	= ihr	*her*			
es	= sein	*its*			
Sie	= Ihr	*your, polite, singular and plural*			
du	= dein	*your*	ihr	= euer	*your*

Remember that these possessive adjectives have the same endings as *ein* or *kein*. Watch case and gender in the following exercises.

A. *Übung*

Fill in the blanks with the correct German equivalent of the English possessive adjectives in parentheses.

> Beispiel: Geben Sie mir bitte .... Zeitung.   *your*
> Geben Sie mir bitte Ihre Zeitung.

1. Ich möchte mit .... Eltern sprechen.   *her*
2. Herr Braun braucht .... Koffer.   *his*
3. Wir haben .... Freunde lange nicht gesehen.   *her*
4. Fräulein Meyer konnte .... Fiebermesser nicht finden. *her*
5. Hans wollte .... Arzt anrufen.   *his*
6. .... Kind muß geimpft werden.   *my*
7. Haben Sie .... Museum schon besucht?   *our*
8. Herr Schmidt, was ist .... Telefonnummer?   *your*
9. Ute, iß .... Gemüse.   *your*
10. Frau und Herr Selke haben .... Enkel noch nie   *their*
    gesehen.

B. *Übung*

You are looking for an object or person and ask who has seen it or them.

Beispiele: *(his radio)* = Wer hat sein Radio gesehen?
(my watch) = Wer hat meine Uhr gesehen?

1. (our car keys) . . . . ?
2. (my umbrella) . . . . ?
3. (his suitcase) . . . . ?
4. (their car) . . . . ?
5. (her theater ticket) . . . . ?
6. (your, polite, book) . . . . ?
7. (his suit) . . . . ?
8. (my dictionary) . . . . ?
9. (our children) . . . . ?
10. (her sister) . . . . ?

4. The use of *als, wenn, wann.*

Als (when) describes or tells something about the past.
Als ich krank war, konnte ich dich nicht besuchen.
When I was sick, I could not visit you.
Als wir in Hamburg waren, hatten wir das schönste Wetter.
When we were in Hamburg, we had the nicest weather.

Wenn (whenever, if) usually signals an "if-situation" or a repeated event *(whenever)*.
Immer wenn Hans die Grippe hatte, trank er viel Orangensaft.
Whenever Hans had the flu, he drank a lot of orange juice.
Wenn ich in Deutschland bin, spreche ich immer Deutsch.
Whenever I am in Germany, I always speak German.
Wenn es morgen regnet, bleibe ich zu Hause.
If it rains tomorrow, I will stay home.

Wann (when) is always a question word. It can also be used in indirect questions or statements.
Wann gehen wir ins Kino?
When are we going to the movie?
Wann mußt du ins Krankenhaus gehen?
When do you have to go to the hospital?
Ich weiß nicht, *wann* ich ins Krankenhaus gehen muß.
I don't know when I have to go to the hospital.

A. *Übung*

Complete the sentence or question with *als, wenn,* or *wann.*

Beispiel: . . . . haben Sie Geburtstag?
Wann haben Sie Geburtstag?

1. . . . . wir in der Schweiz waren, sind wir oft gewandert.
2. Herr Braun fragt, ... die Post kommt?
3. Wissen Sie, ... der Zug ankommt?
4. . . . . Frau Schmidt krank ist, nimmt sie immer Aspirin.

5. ....ich viel Zeit habe, lese ich meistens.
6. Spielst du auch Tennis, ...es sehr kalt ist?
7. ....Hans studierte, war er sehr arm.
8. ....kommen Sie nach Amerika?
9. Fritz fragte mich, ...wir ins Kino gehen.
10. Sind Sie oft ins Ausland geflogen, ...Sie für Lufthansa arbeiteten?

Wiederholung

A. Schreiben Sie 1. infinitive, 2. simple past, and 3. participle. Indicate when *sein* should be used as the auxiliary.

Beispiel: *to depart*   abfahren, fuhr ab, ist abgefahren

	Infinitive	Simple Past	Participle
1.	*to go*		
2.	*to write*		
3.	*to eat*		
4.	*to drink*		
5.	*to drive*		
6.	*to arrive*		
7.	*to be*		
8.	*to have*		
9.	*to take*		
10.	*to give*		

B. Übersetzen Sie

1. Did you (singular familiar) buy yourself a suit case?
2. He shaves in the morning and at night.
3. Have you seen my brother?
4. I have taken an aspirin.
5. Perhaps she has the flu.
6. We have to go now.

C. Write a question replacing the italicized word(s).

Beispiel: *Hans* hat hohes Fieber.
          Wer hat hohes Fieber? (Hans hat hohes Fieber.)

1. *Gestern* war er im Kino....................................
2. Hans hat sich *ein neues Auto* gekauft........................
3. Wir sind gestern *krank* gewesen.............................
4. *Wir* bekommen nicht genug Schlaf............................
5. Gestern fuhr Herr Schwarz *nach Köln.*.......................

Wortschatz

Nouns

der Anzug, ¨-e suit
das Aspirin, -s aspirin
das Ausland   abroad, foreign country

der Ausländer, - foreigner, male
die Ausländerin, -nen foreigner, female

der Autoschlüssel, -   car key
der Blindarm, -e   appendix
die Blutprobe, -n   blood test
der Enkel, -   grandson
die Enkelin, -nen   granddaughter
die Entzündung, -en   inflammation
das Fieber, -   fever, temperature
der Fiebermesser, -   thermometer
die Grippe, -n   flu
das Haar, -e   hair
der Hals, ̈e   throat
die Halsschmerzen   sore throat
der Hausarzt, ̈e   family doctor, male
die Hausärztin, -nen   family doctor,
    female
der Herzschrittmacher, -   pacemaker
der Liter, -   liter
die Lungenentzündung, -en   pneu-
    monia
die Mandeln   tonsils
der Mantel, ̈   coat
das Medikament, -e   medicine
das Mineralwasser, -   mineral water
der Mund, ̈er   mouth
das Museum, die Museen   museum
die Musik   music
der Ohrenschmerz, -en   earache
der Patient, -en   patient
die Post, das Postamt, ̈er   post office
die Prüfung, -en   exam
das Rezept, -e   prescription
der Schirm, -e   umbrella
der Schmerz, -en   pain, ache
der Schuh, -e   shoe
der Sport   sport
die Sprechstunde, -n   office hour
die Tablette, -n   pill, tablet
die Theaterkarte, -n   theater ticket
das Universitätskrankenhaus, ̈er
    university hospital
der Wecker, -   alarm clock
das Wörterbuch, ̈er   dictionary
der Zahn, ̈e   tooth

Verbs

(sich) an·stecken   to catch an illness
sich an·ziehen, zog an, angezogen   to
    get dressed
auf·wachen   to wake up
*aus·sehen, (sieht aus), sah aus, aus-
    gesehen*   to look like

aus·suchen   to choose
sich beeilen   to hurry
brechen, (i) brach, gebrochen   to break
sich duschen   to take a shower
ein·setzen   to implant
sich erkälten   to catch a cold
sich erinnern   to remember
fehlen   to miss
    was fehlt Ihnen?   what's wrong with
    you?
(sich) fühlen   to feel
impfen   to immunize, to vaccinate
(sich) kämmen   to comb
klingeln   to ring (a bell)
lassen (läßt), ließ, gelassen   to let, per-
    mit
(sich) putzen   to clean, brush
(sich) rasieren   to shave
raus·müssen, muß raus, rausgemußt
    to get out, have to leave
regnen   to rain
schwellen, schwoll, geschwollen   to
    swell
stehen, stand, gestanden   to stand
tun (tut), tat, getan   to do, to make
untersuchen   to examine
    sich untersuchen lassen   to be ex-
    amined by (a physician)
verschreiben, verschrieb, verschrieben
    to prescribe
sich verspäten   to be late, to be delayed
weh·tun (tut weh), tat weh, wehgetan   to
    hurt

Other Words

also   therefore; well, so
best   best
bestimmt   certain(ly)
blaß   pale
deshalb   therefore, that's why
gestern   yesterday
furchtbar   terrible
genug   enough
hoffentlich   hopefully
interessant   interesting
jeder, jede, jedes   each
schlimm   bad
schwindelig   dizzy
wenigstens   at least
zufrieden   satisfied

Kapitel 7

Television and Radio

Culture Notes

Television and radio stations in Germany, Austria and Switzerland are owned by their federal governments. The law states that television and radio must be neutral politically. Independent boards, made up of people from all walks of life, are in charge of programming. Several television networks called "Programme" as well as local radio stations offer news, educational programs, sports, entertainment, etc.

Although television and radio is government supported in these countries, all owners of television and radio sets must pay a flat monthly fee usually collected by the post office.

There are no interruptions of programs by commercial advertisements. However, television ads are presented "en bloc" at specific times for about five to fifteen minutes two or three times daily.

Television broadcasting usually begins early in the afternoon and ends at midnight or shortly thereafter. Some radio stations broadcast around the clock.

DIALOGE

Frau M.:	Siehst du immer noch fern?	Are you still watching TV?
Herr M.:	Ja, das Fußballspiel ist noch nicht vorbei.	Yes, the soccer game isn't over yet.
Frau M.:	Ich möchte mir aber die Nachrichten ansehen.	But I would like to see the news.
Herr M.:	Das geht nicht. Ich schalte jetzt noch nicht um.	That's not possible. I am not going to change the channel now.
Frau M.:	Immer diese verrückten Sportprogramme!	Always these crazy sports programs.
Herr M.:	Naja. Ich habe meine verrückten Sportprogramme und du deine langweiligen Quiz-Shows.	Oh, well. I have my crazy sports programs and you your boring quiz-shows.

Karin:	Was gibt's heute abend im Fernsehen?	What's on TV tonight?
Elke:	(Liest das Fernsehprogramm) Nichts Besonderes. Im ersten	(reads the TV guide) Nothing special. On channel 1 they are showing a well-known

	Programm gibt es einen bekannten Krimi, im zweiten Programm eine alberne Unterhaltungssendung und im dritten Programm einen langweiligen Dokumentarfilm über Brasilien.	detective film, on channel 2 a silly entertainment show and on channel 3 a boring documentary about Brazil.
Karin:	Was sollen wir uns ansehen?	What should we watch?
Elke:	Nichts. Ich lese lieber den neuen *Spiegel** und höre mir etwas Schönes im Radio an.	Nothing. I would rather read the new *Spiegel* and listen to something nice on the radio.

Herr S.:	Was halten Sie vom amerikanischen Fernsehen?	What do you think of American television?
Herr J.:	Ich finde es ganz gut, nur stören mich die dummen Werbungen.	I think it's pretty good, only the stupid commercials bother me.
Herr S.:	Ja, Sie haben recht. In Deutschland gibt es keine Werbungen im Fernsehen.	Yes, you're right. In Germany there aren't any commercials on television.
Herr J.:	Doch. Aber nur zu bestimmten Zeiten zwei oder dreimal am Tag.	Yes, there are. But only at certain times two or three times a day.
Herr S.:	Aber nie während einer Sendung.	But never during a program.
Herr J.:	Das stimmt.	That's right.
Herr S.:	Das würde mir auch gefallen.	I would like that too.

Herr K.:	(Klopft an die Tür)	(knocks at the door)
Herr F.:	Herein.	Come in.
Herr K.:	Guten Tag, Herr Felder. Darf ich Sie stören, oder sind Sie sehr beschäftigt?	Hello, Mr. Felder. May I disturb you, or are you very busy?
Herr F.:	Ich höre mir ein interessantes Radioprogramm aus Deutschland an.	I am listening to an interesting radio program from Germany.
Herr K.:	Was, Sie bekommen die "Deutsche Welle?" Ist das eine politische Debatte aus Bonn?	What, you are getting the "German Short Wave?" Is that a political debate from Bonn?
Herr F.:	Ja, ich interessiere mich doch für deutsche Politik.	Yes, I am interested in German politics.
Herr K.:	Und deutschen Wein.	And German wine.
Herr F.:	Das auch.	That too.
Herr K.:	Hören Sie manchmal auch Opernübertragungen?	Do you sometimes listen to opera broadcasts?
Herr F.:	Nein, sie sind mir zu langweilig.	No, they are too boring for me.
Herr K.:	Schade. Sie wissen nicht, was Sie verpassen.	Too bad, you don't know what you are missing.
Herr F.:	Könnte sein.	Could be.

---

*The most important weekly magazine in Germany; similar to *Newsweek* or *Time* magazines.

Grammar

1. Adjectives—used as predicate adjectives

When adjectives follow nouns, they have no ending and remain unchanged. They are called *predicate adjectives* and often complete statements introduced by verbs like *sein* (to be), *werden* (to become) or *bleiben* (to remain).

Das Programm ist langweilig.	*The program is boring.*
Meine Eltern werden alt.	*My parents are getting old.*
Das Wetter bleibt schön.	*The weather remains nice.*

A. *Übung*

Let's review some adjectives. Give the opposites.

Beispiel: Hamburg ist groß, Siegburg ist .....klein.........

1. Meine Freundin ist gesund, ich bin...................
2. Meine Kinder sind faul, Ihre sind...................
3. Fritz steht immer früh auf, Ernst immer...................
4. Die Demokratie in Deutschland ist jung, in Amerika ist sie...................
5. Vater sagt: "Ich werde alt, aber Mutter bleibt immer...................
6. Das Essen in eurem Hotel war gut, aber in unserem war es...................
7. Dieses Jahr war der Sommer richtig heiß, aber letztes Jahr war er eigentlich ....
8. Dein Urlaub war sehr lang, meiner war leider zu...................
9. Ältere Leute spielen ihr Radio ziemlich leise, aber Teenagers spielen es meistens zu...................
10. Die Mathematikprüfung war schwer, aber die Englischprüfung war......... ....

2. Adjectives—attributive adjectives

Attributive (descriptive) adjectives describe the noun they modify. They almost always add an ending to show the noun's number, gender and case.

A. Adjectives which follow definite articles, (*der, die, das*), demonstratives (*dieser, solcher*), or interrogatives (*welcher*) have these endings:

	Masculine	Feminine	Neuter	Plural
Nominative	der klein*e* Tisch	die klein*e* Stadt	das klein*e* Zimmer	die klein*en* Kinder
Accusative	den klein*en* Tisch	die klein*e* Stadt	das klein*e* Zimmer	die klein*en* Kinder
Dative	dem klein*en* Tisch	der klein*en* Stadt	dem klein*en* Zimmer	den klein*en* Kindern

Beispiele:

Ich nehme dieses preiswert*e* Zimmer.	*I'll take this reasonable room.*
Wo haben Sie diesen billig*en* Flug bekommen?	*Where did you get this cheap flight?*
Diese interessant*e* Sendung gefällt mir.	*I like this interesting program.*

B.   Adjectives which follow indefinite articles (ein, eine), the negative kein(e), or the possessives (mein, dein, sein, etc.) take slightly different endings.

	Masculine	*Feminine*	*Neuter*	*Plural*
Nominative	ein klein*er* Tisch	eine klein*e* Stadt	ein klein*es* Zimmer	keine klein*en* Kinder
Accusative	einen klein*en* Tisch	eine klein*e* Stadt	ein klein*es* Zimmer	keine klein*en* Kinder
Dative	einem klein*en* Tisch	einer klein*en* Stadt	einem klein*en* Zimmer	keinen klein*en* Kinder*n*

Beispiele:

Ich konnte keine katholisch*e* Kirche finden.	*I couldn't find a Catholic church.*
Wir sahen gestern einen ausländisch*en* Film.	*We saw a foreign film yesterday.*
Kennen Sie meine deutsch*en* Verwandten?	*Do you know my German relatives?*

Note: All **datives** and **plurals** take the -en ending. You have to make a choice between endings in three instances:

masculine nominative singular	-e or -er
neuter nominative singular	-e or -es
neuter accusative singular	-e or -es

C.   Finally, unpreceded adjectives (no *ein* or *der* word) in most cases take the same ending as the *definitive articles*.

	Masculine	*Feminine*	*Neuter*	*Plural*
Nominative	kalten Wein	kalte Milch	kaltes Wasser	kalte Getränke
Accusative	kalten Wein	kalte Milch	kaltes Wasser	kalte Getränke
Dative	kaltem Wein	kalter Milch	kaltem Wasser	kalten Getränke

Beispiele:

Kalte Milch schmeckt gut. (nominative, feminine *die = e*)
Ich esse gern weißes Brot. (accusative, neuter *das = es*)
Wir servieren nur frischen Fisch. (accusative, masculine *den = en*)

Note: While adjective endings are important, you should remember that it takes time to learn them correctly. (Even Germans sometimes make mistakes with adjective endings.)

A.   Übung

Add the correct adjective ending. Watch whether the adjective is preceded by a *der word* or an *ein word,* or is unpreceded.

1.   Februar ist ein kurz........ Monat.
2.   Wann fährt der nächst......... Zug ab?
3.   Ich möchte eine billig........ und sauber........ Wohnung.
4.   Diese dumm........ Reklamen stören mich.

5. Das deutsch........ Fernsehen soll sehr gut sein.
6. Möchten Sie einen rot........ oder einen weiß........ Wein?
7. Wir essen nur frisch........ Fisch.
8. Im Sommer haben wir lang........ Ferien.
9. Wollen Sie wirklich diesen hoh........ Berg besteigen?
10. Meine krank........ Tochter geht heute nicht in die Schule.

B. *Übung*

Übersetzen Sie bitte.

Beispiel: I would like a big piece of cake.
Ich möchte ein großes Stück Kuchen.

1. You have pretty black hair.
2. I know a good doctor.
3. We are watching an interesting movie.
4. I like this small town.
5. German is an easy language.
6. Franz is a difficult child.
7. You should eat green vegetables often.
8. Do you have an inexpensive room?
9. They always go to expensive restaurants.
10. We are buying a new house.

3. Adjectives used as nouns

In German many adjectives are used as nouns. When used as nouns, they are always *capitalized and declined*—they have endings.

Beispiele:	ein reicher Mann	ein Reicher
	der reiche Mann	der Reiche
	eine arme Frau	eine Arme
	die arme Frau	die Arme
	reiche Leute	die Reichen
	die reichen Leute	die Reichen

A. *Übung*

Change the sentence by replacing the adjective with the appropriate noun.

Beispiel: Der fremde Mann spricht kein Deutsch.
Der.....Fremde......spricht kein Deutsch.

1. Mein ältester Sohn bekommt ein neues Auto.
.................bekommt ein neues Auto.
2. Der große Junge ist mein Sohn.
.................ist mein Sohn.
3. Ich kenne das kleine Mädchen nicht.
Ich kenne die.................nicht.
4. Meine jüngste Tochter ist Ärztin.
.................ist Ärztin.
5. Helfen Sie doch der kranken Frau.
Helfen Sie doch.................

6. In Amerika gibt es viele arme Menschen.
   In Amerika gibt es viele..................

7. Pele ist der beste Fußballspieler.
   Pele ist...................

Kleiner Fernsehquiz*

Mark the answers which apply to you.

1. Ich habe einen

   a. schwarz-weiß Fernseher.
   b. Farbfernseher.

2. Ich sehe gern

   a. Unterhaltungssendungen.
   b. Dokumentarfilme. ˙
   c. Nachrichten.
   d. Sportübertragungen.

3. Ich sehe

   a. so oft wie möglich fern.
   b. selten fern.
   c. fast nie fern.

4. Ich sehe gerne Programme, die

   a. mich unterhalten.
   b. mich informieren.

5. Am Wochenende

   a. gehe ich meistens ins Kino.
   b. sehe ich meistens fern.
   c. besuche ich Freunde.

6. Ich finde die amerikanischen Werbungen

   a. albern.
   b. interessant.
   c. störend.
   d. langweilig.

7. Das amerikanische Fernsehen zeigt zu viele

   a. Sportübertragungen.
   b. Unterhaltungssendungen.
   c. Dokumentarfilme.
   d. Nachrichten.

8. Ich finde das amerikanische Fernsehen

   a. interessant.
   b. langweilig.
   c. zu einseitig.

*If you don't know a word, look it up in the Wortschatz.

9.　Ich finde die amerikanischen Nachrichten

    a.　objektiv.

    b.　voreingenommen.

    c.　sachlich.

10.　Was sind Sie?

    a.　Ich bin vor allem Zeitungsleser.

    b.　Ich bin vor allem Radiohörer.

    c.　Ich sehe vor allem viel fern.

Lesestück

Read this Lesestück *and notice how adjectives are used almost excessively. Underline all adjectives and notice their endings. The vocabulary is "house" and "family" oriented.*

Das Wetter ist mild und warm; es ist ein schöner Sommertag, und die Sonne brennt nicht zu heiß. Der Vater, die Mutter und Onkel Fritz sitzen gemütlich im Garten. Der Vater trinkt starken schwarzen Kaffee, die Mutter Eistee und der Onkel kalte Limonade. Sie essen frisches Brot mit Butter und Marmelade. Das noch warme Brot duftet so stark, daß der Nachbar hungrig wird!

Die Eltern sprechen von dem Sohn; er ist ein lebendiges und manchmal lautes Kind. Er heißt Karl und ist acht Jahre alt. „Karl ist nicht dumm, er ist intelligent. In der Schule sollte er der Beste sein," sagt der Vater. „Ja, ja…" antwortet Onkel Fritz, gähnt ein bißchen und beißt wieder ins frische, duftende Brot.

Karl spielt im großen, frischgemähten Garten. Im nassen Gras findet er unter einem blühenden Rosenbusch einen roten Ball. Onkel Fritz sagt zu ihm: „Gib deiner kleinen Schwester den Ball!" Karl gibt ihr den Ball—aber nicht gern. Anna, seine Schwester, ist ein liebes, kleines Mädchen—vor allem wenn sie den Ball bekommt.

Etwas später gehen die Eltern ins saubere, zweistöckige Haus. Im Wohnzimmer sehen sie Hans, den Sohn des Onkels. Hans ist ein junger Mann und studiert fleißig an der Universität. Er liegt auf dem bequemen Sofa und denkt an seine blonde Freundin. Sie heißt Hilde und ist achtzehn Jahre alt. Sie hat langes, blondes Haar und studiert auch. Hans telefoniert mit ihr und sagt: "Es ist heute so heiß, gehen wir schwimmen."

Hans und Hilde fahren in Hildes neuem Sportwagen an den Strand. Der Himmel ist blau, der Sand ist heiß, aber das Wasser ist kühl. Hans und Hilde sind gute Schwimmer. Zuerst schwimmen sie, dann liegen sie im Sand. Am Abend sind sie braun von der Sonne.

Alle sind sich einig, der heutige Tag war nicht aufregend, aber angenehm und entspannend.

A.　*Übung*

Without looking at the text, try to complete the statements with the correct words from the list scrambled below.

Beispiel: Der Vater trinkt s̶c̶h̶w̶a̶r̶z̶e̶n̶ ̶K̶a̶f̶f̶e̶e̶.

1.　Karl hat einen . . . .

2.　Er findet den Ball unter einem . . . .

3. Die Erwachsenen essen Brot mit....................
4. Hans ist ein....................
5. Seine Freundin hat....................
6. Das Wasser ist....................
7. Hildes Sportwagen ist....................
8. Hilde und Hans sind....................

guter Marmelade, neu, junger Mann, langes, blondes Haar, roten Ball, kühl, großen Rosenbusch, gute Schwimmer

4.   Demonstrative adjectives (other der words)

German has a group of *der words* or *dieser words* which change their endings exactly like *der, die, das. Dieser (this)* is a good example. The ending to these words depends on the gender, number, and case of the noun it modifies.

	Masculine	Feminine	Neuter	Plural
Nominative	dies*er*	dies*e*	dies*es*	dies*e*
Accusative	dies*en*	dies*e*	dies*es*	dies*e*
Dative	dies*em*	dies*er*	dies*em*	dies*en*
Genitive	dies*es*	dies*er*	dies*es*	dies*er*

der Tisch—dies*er* Tisch   die Tür—dies*e* Tür
das Kind—dies*es* Kind   die Leute—dies*e* Leute

Learn these so-called *der words:*

dies-	*this, that, these; the latter*
jed-	*each, every (only used in the singular)*
jen-	*that, those; the former*
manch-	*many a, several, some*
solch-	*such, such a*
welch-	*which*

A.   *Übung*

Replace the italicized definite article with the appropriate form of the cued *der word*.

1. Ich habe *das* Buch nicht gelesen....................   *jen-*
2. Frau Braun kauft immer *die* Zeitung....................   *dies-*
3. *Die* Kinder besuchen mich....................?   *welch-*
4. Siehst du *den* kleinen Jungen?....................   *jen-*
5. *Die* Platten kaufe ich nie....................   *solch-*

Wiederholung

A.   Write sentences using all the words given. Be sure to use the correct articles. Also watch adjective endings.

Beispiel: im/deutsch/Fernsehen/geben/es/keine/langweilig/Werbungen
Im deutschen Fernsehen gibt es keine langweiligen Werbungen.

1. ich/hören/jeden/Abend/Nachrichten
2. heute/kaufen/wir/ein/neu/Auto
3. d-/Arzt/können/d-/Krank-/nicht/helfen
4. trinken/Sie/gerne/schwarz-/Kaffee?
5. weil/d-/Wetter/heiß/sein/, gehen/wir/heute/schwimmen

B. Review adjectives and adverbs by matching the ones on the left with their opposites on the right.

1.	langweilig	a.	weiß
2.	bekannt	b.	oft
3.	neu	c.	alt
4.	gut	d.	klein
5.	schwarz	e.	subjektiv
6.	selten	f.	immer
7.	nie	g.	dumm
8.	objektiv	h.	unbekannt
9.	warm	i.	schlecht
10.	kalt	j.	kühl
11.	intelligent	k.	heiß
12.	groß	l.	wenig
13.	faul	m.	froh
14.	kurz	n.	lang
15.	gesund	o.	nah
16.	arm	p.	dort
17.	hier	q.	krank
18.	weit	r.	fleißig
19.	viel	s.	reich
20.	traurig	t.	interessant

Wortschatz

Nouns

das brot, -e bread
die Debatte, -n debate
der Dokumentarfilm, -e documentary
die "Deutsche Welle" German radio program (short wave)
der Eistee, -s ice tea
die Eltern parents
der Erwachsene, -n adult, grown-up
der Farbfernseher, - color television set
das Fernsehen television
der Fisch, -e fish
der Garten, ¨ garden
das Gras, ¨er grass
die Kirche, -n church
der Krimi, -s detective story

das Mädchen, - girl
die Marmelade, -n marmelade
der Onkel, - uncle
die Opernübertragung, -en opera broadcast
das Programm, -e program
das Radioprogramm, -e radio program
der Rosenbusch, ¨e rose bush
die Sendung, -en broadcast
die Sportübertragung, -en sports broadcast
der Sportwagen, - sports car
das Stück, -e piece
die Unterhaltungssendung, -en entertainment show
der Verwandte, -n relative

die Werbung, -en advertisement, commercial
das Wohnzimmer, - living room

Verbs

sich an·hören to listen to
sich an·sehen, (sieht an), sah an, ange-sehen to look at
beißen, biß, gebissen to bite
besteigen, bestieg, bestiegen to climb
brennen, brannte, gebrannt to burn
duften to smell pleasantly
fern·sehen, (sieht fern) sah fern, fern-gesehen to watch television
gähnen to yawn
halten von, (hält von), hielt von, gehalten to think of
(sich) informieren to inform
klopfen to knock
stören to disturb, to bother
verpassen to miss
(sich) unterhalten, (unterhält), unter-hielt, unterhalten to enjoy oneself
um·schalten to switch over, to change a channel

Other Words

albern silly
angenehm pleasant
aufregend exciting
ausländisch foreign
bekannt known
bequem comfortable
beschäftigt busy, occupied
bestimmt certain

einseitig one-sided
entspannend relaxing
fast almost
faul lazy
frisch fresh
frischgemäht just mowed
froh glad
gemütlich cozy, comfortable
hübsch pretty
hungrig hungry
katholisch Catholic (adj.)
langweilig boring
leise softly
möglich possible
naß wet
politisch political
rot red
sachlich factual
schwarz-weiß black and white
schwierig difficult
traurig sad
unbekannt unknown
verrückt crazy
vor allem above all
voreingenommen biased
zweimal twice
ziemlich rather
zweistöckig two-story

Idiomatic Expressions

das geht nicht that doesn't work
nichts Besonderes nothing special
es ist noch nicht vorbei it isn't over yet
schade too bad
sich einig sein to be in agreement

Kapitel 8

Sports, Physical Education and Recreation

Culture Notes

German-speaking people are sports- and recreation-minded. The huge number of sports clubs and recreation associations bear witness to that fact. Even small villages often have their own sports club, usually a "Fußballklub" (soccer club) or a "Turnverein" (gymnastics club). If one had to identify a national sport, soccer and skiing would win that poll, the latter especially in Austria, Switzerland, and Southern Germany. But people engage in many other sports too.

Physical education is a required and important part of the school curriculum for all age levels. Intramurals are stressed more than interschool rivalries. Top level competitors use clubs—not schools—as their home base for training and competition. Universities are not engaged in big-time sports competition.

Hiking has always been a favorite past time for young and old in all German-speaking countries. Gentle walks through city parks, short and long hikes through the countryside, and even demanding climbs in the high mountains, all these activities can be considered to be a part of their life style. There is no shortage of hiking paths *anywhere*. Maps for hiking routes are available in every bookstore and often at newspaper stands. In the mountains of Austria and Switzerland, many huts are maintained by different Alpine clubs. They enable hikers and climbers to explore the serenity and beauty of the Alps.

Swimming pools can be found in almost any community, large or small. But don't look for public tennis courts in parks or high schools. There aren't any. For this sport, one has to belong to a club or rent a court by the hour.

DIALOGE

Laufen

Herr K.: Fräulein Rieger, laufen Sie mit?

Frl. R.: Ich glaube nicht, Sie laufen so viel schneller als ich.

Jogging

Miss Rieger, will you jog along?

I don't believe so. You run so much faster than I.

Herr K.: Oh, das stimmt gar nicht. Gestern bin ich mit einem älteren Ehepaar nach Fürberg* gelaufen. Da war ich der Langsamste.

Oh, that's not true. Yesterday I ran to Fürberg with an older couple. At that time I was the slowest.

Frl. R.: Na gut, ich laufe mit. Aber bitte warten Sie nicht auf mich, wenn ich langsamer werde. Das wäre mir peinlich.

O.K. then. I will jog along. But please don't wait for me if I run slower. That would be embarrassing for me.

Herr K.: Einverstanden.

Agreed.

Schilaufen

Skiing

Andrea: Brrr, heute ist es viel kälter als gestern, nicht wahr?

Brr, today it is much colder than yesterday. Isn't it?

Trude: Ja, aber die Luft ist trockener. Und es ist auch nicht so windig wie gestern.

Yes, but it is less humid. (the air is drier) And it isn't as windy as yesterday.

Andrea: Wenn nur bald die Sonne herauskäme.

If only the sun would come out soon.

Trude: Ja, das wünschte ich mir auch. Aber der Schnee ist herrlich. Reiner Pulver! Heute ist keine Abfahrt vereist.

Yes, I wish that too. But the snow is wonderful. Pure powder. Not one downhill run is icy today.

Andrea: Prima, dann können wir ja ein bißchen schussen.

Great, then we can go straight down.

Am Tennisplatz - beim Spiel

At the Tennis Court-at play

Herr A.: Frau Müller, wer schlägt auf?

Mrs. Müller, who serves?

Frau M.: Ich glaube Sie; wir haben gerade aufgeschlagen.

I believe you do. We just served.

Herr S.: Frau Müller, Ihre Vorhand ist die Beste im Klub, und Ihre Rückhand wird auch immer besser.

Mrs. Müller, your forehand is the best in the club, and your backhand is getting better and better.

Frau M.: Herr Schulz, Sie übertreiben. Wenn das stimmte, hätte ich beim letzten Turnier mehr Matches gewonnen.

Mr. Schulz, you are exaggerating. If that were true, I would have won more matches at the last tournament.

Herr S.: Ich wäre gern Ihr Partner beim gemischten Doppel gewesen.

I would have liked to have been your partner in the mixed doubles.

Frau M.: Hätten Sie mich doch gefragt. Wie steht's?

You should have asked me. What's the score?

Herr S.: Einstand?

Deuce?

Frau M.: Nein, ich glaube Vorteil Aufschläger. (schlägt auf)

No, I think it's advantage server. (is serving)

Herr S.: Ach nein, schon wieder ein Aß! Ihr Aufschlag wird auch immer besser und schneller.

Oh, no, another ace! Your serve is getting better and faster too.

Frau M.: Das ist Spiel, stimmt's? Ja, so einen Aufschlag hätte ich im letzten Satz gebraucht.

That's game, correct? Well, I would have needed such a serve in the last set.

*Small village at Lake Wolfgangsee in Austria.

Wandern und Bergsteigen	*Hiking and Mountain Climbing*

Herr A.: Herr Wagner, machen Sie morgen einen Ausflug?

Herr W.: Ja, wenn das Wetter schön bleibt würden wir gern auf den Stoderzinken gehen.

Herr A.: Stoderzinken? Das ist doch der höchste Berg in dieser Gegend. Der ist ja noch höher als die Lammspitze. Dort wollen Sie hinauf?

Herr W.: Stimmt, aber wir lassen uns Zeit. Wir sollten es in fünf Stunden schaffen.

Herr A.: Ja, wenn ich zehn Jahr jünger wäre, würde ich mitkommen.

Herr W.: Ich glaube, Sie würden es noch heute schaffen.

Mr. Wagner, are you going on a hiking trip tomorrow?

Yes, if the weather stays nice, we would like to go to the Stoderzinken.

Stoderzinken? That is the highest mountain in this area, isn't it? It's even higher than the Lammspitze. Do you want to go up there?

That's correct. But we take our time. We should make it in five hours.

Well, if I were ten years younger, I would come along.

I think you would make it even today.

Grammar

1. The comparative of adjectives and adverbs
Life and language are full of comparisons. That's why we need a

positive:	fast	schnell
comparative:	faster	schneller
superlative:	fastest	am schnellsten
	the fastest	der, die, das Schnellste

The Positive

Seine Wohnung ist so groß wie mein Haus.
His apartment is as large as my house.
Hans ist so alt wie Ingrid.
Hans is as old as Ingrid.
Der BMW fährt so schnell wie ein Mercedes.
The BMW drives as fast as a Mercedes.

When things and persons are the same, use *so...wie*

A. Übung

Respond as indicated in this example.

Ich arbeite viel. Und Gerda?
Sie arbeitet so viel wie ich.

1. Ingrid ist 25 Jahre alt. Und Herbert? Er ist...
2. Otto läuft schnell. Und Karin? Sie läuft...
3. Heute ist es heiß. Und gestern? Gestern war...
4. Du hast wenig Zeit. Und die Nachbarn? Sie haben...
5. Mary versteht gut Deutsch. Und John? John versteht Deutsch...
6. Robert bezahlt viel für seine Wohnung. Und Sie? Ich bezahle...

The Comparative

The comparative is formed in German by adding -*er* to the stem of the adjective or adverb.

weit	weiter	*far*	*farther*
billig	billiger	*cheap*	*cheaper*
klein	kleiner	*small*	*smaller*
schön	schöner	*beautiful*	*more beautiful*

One-syllable adjectives and adverbs usually add an umlaut to the stem vowel (except with the diphthong -*au*-)

jung	jünger	*young*	*younger*
groß	größer	*big*	*bigger*
alt	älter	*old*	*older*

B.   *Übung*

Respond using "noch" + comparative.

Beispiel: Meine Wohnung ist ziemlich klein.   *My apartment is rather small.*
         Ist Ihre Wohnung auch so klein?   *Is your apartment that small too?*
         Meine Wohnung ist noch kleiner.   *My apartment is even smaller.*

1.   Ist Texas so groß wie die Bundesrepublik? Ich glaube, Texas ist...
2.   Ist die Fahrt von München nach Salzburg so weit wie die Fahrt von Würzburg nach Nürnburg? Nein, die Fahrt von München nach Salzburg ist...
3.   Dauert der Flug von Frankfurt nach Wien so lange wie der Flug nach Köln? Nein, der Flug nach Wien...
4.   Ist euer Hotelzimmer so billig wie unseres? Unser Zimmer ist...
5.   Ist Mainz so alt wie Hamburg? Nein, Mainz ist...
6.   Sind die Berge in Alaska so hoch* wie in Österreich? Nein, die Berge in Alaska sind...
7.   War dieser Sommer so warm wie der letzte? Ich finde, er war...

Dissimilarities are often expressed by *comparison* + *als*.
Ich bin größer *als* er.

The Superlative

The German superlative is formed by adding -*st*- to the stem of the adjective. One-syllable adjectives often add an umlaut.

schnell	der, die, das *Schnellste*
Der BMW fährt *schnell*.	Dieser Mercedes ist der *schnellste* Wagen, or: Dieser Mercedes fährt *am schnellsten*.
Ist dieses Geschäft *billig?*	Ja, es ist das *billigste* Geschäft in der Stadt.
Kauft man dort *billig?*	Ja, dort kauft man *am billigsten*.

The superlative construction with *am* + *adjective/adverb* + *ending* is just an alternative form of the superlative and is usually used when the superlative modifies a verb. If the stem of the adjective ends in -*d*, -*t*, -*z*, a linking -*e*- is inserted between the stem and the ending to facilitate pronunciation.

*When "hoch" is used before a noun, then it becomes "hoh-," z.B. Der Großglockner ist ein sehr hoher Berg.

Das ist ein leichtes Bier.   Es ist das leichteste Bier.
Wo gibt es ein gesundes Klima?   Wo gibt es das gesündeste Klima?
Diese Stadt ist alt.   Sie ist die älteste Stadt.
Der Februar ist kurz.   Er ist der kürzeste Monat.

C. Übung

Complete with the superlative. Remember to use the correct endings.

> Beispiel: Hans ist mein ältest .... Bruder.
>   Hans ist mein ältester Bruder.

1. Ilse ist seine jüng .... Schwester.
2. Er kauft immer das schnell .... Auto.
3. Das ist die größ .... Firma in dieser Gegend.
4. Gestern hatten wir das schön .... Wetter.
5. Mainz ist die ält .... Stadt.

Irregular Comparison

German has a number of common comparatives and superlatives which are irregular just like English: good, better, best. They must be memorized!

gut	besser	best-	*good*	*better*	*best*
viel	mehr	meist-	*much*	*more*	*most*
gern	lieber	liebst-	*gladly*	*rather*	*best*
hoch	höher	höchst-	*high*	*higher*	*highest*
nahe	näher	nächst-	*near*	*nearer*	*nearest*

The "irregulars"— quite different, but common!

D. Übung

Restate each sentence in the comparative and superlative.

> Beispiel: Ich esse Huhn gern. Fisch esse ich noch lieber.
>   Aber Kuchen esse ich am liebsten.

1. In München regnet es viel. In Wien noch ...., und in Salzburg am ....
2. Dieses Bier schmeckt gut. Pils schmeckt noch .... Aber Löwenbräu schmeckt mir am ....
3. Die Zugspitze ist hoch. Der Dachstein ist noch .... Aber der Großglockner ist am ....
4. Wir wandern gern, aber noch .... fahren wir Schi, und Tennis spielen wir am ....

The comparative and superlative play a prominent role in the world of advertisement. Here are a few samples of the German "Werbung," the language of advertisement.

- Für die Schönheit nur das Beste.   *Only the best for beauty.*
- Das beste Persil, das es je gab.   *The best Persil (detergent) there ever was.*

• Niemand ist schöner als die Venus von Milo.

No one is more beautiful than the Venus of Milo.

• Es gibt nichts Schöneres als reine Seide.

There is nothing more beautiful than pure silk.

• Bei uns ist das Beste gerade noch gut genug.

At our place the best is barely good enough.

• Elba macht Beton in 86 Ländern: für die kleinste Künstlerklause und für die größten Wolkenkratzer.

Elba makes concrete in 86 countries: for the smallest artist's hermitage and for the largest skyscrapers.

DIALOGE

Frau J.:	Stimmt's, daß Sie letzten Winter in Österreich waren?	Is it correct that you were in Austria last winter?
Frau L.:	Leider nicht. Wir wären gern nach St. Christof am Arlberg gefahren, aber wir konnten kein Quartier finden.	Unfortunately not. We would have liked to have gone to St. Christof at the Arlberg, but we couldn't find any lodging.
Frau J.:	Fahren Sie dieses Jahr?	Are you going this year?
Frau L.:	Schön wär' es! Wir würden gern fahren, aber diesen Winter haben wir keinen Urlaub.	It would be nice. We would love to go, but this winter we don't have any vacation.

Beim Wandern
(vor der Wanderung in einem Geschäft)

Going Hiking
(before the hike in a store)

Herr A.:	Könnten Sie uns eine Wanderkarte dieser Gegend zeigen? Wir möchten morgen den... besteigen.	Could you show us a hiking map for this area? We would like to climb....tomorrow.
Verkäufer:	Wie wär's mit dieser? Sie hat Maßstab... und ist billiger als die größere.	How about this one? It has a scale of...and is cheaper than the bigger one.
Herr A.:	Bill, sollten wir noch etwas mitnehmen?	Bill, should we take something else along?
Bill:	Mir fällt nichts mehr ein.	I can't think of anything.

Wandern und Bergsteigen

Hiking and Mountain Climbing

Karl:	Wie weit ist es noch bis zum Gipfel?	How far is it still to the top?
Fritz:	Ich glaube etwa zwei Stunden.	I believe about two hours.
Karl:	Zwei Stunden! Wenn ich das gewußt hätte, wäre ich vielleicht nicht mitgekommen. Wie wär' es mit einer kurzen Rast und einer Flasche Bier?	Two hours! If I had known that, I may not have come along. How about a short rest and a bottle of beer?
Fritz:	Ich würde kein Bier trinken. Alkohol macht müde.	I wouldn't drink beer. Alcohol makes you tired.
Karl:	...und meine Schuhe drücken mich auch.	And my shoes hurt too.

Fritz:	Neue Schuhe? Das kenne ich. Damit hätte ich auch Schwierigkeiten. Neue Schuhe sollte man immer vor einer Tour ein bißchen eingehen.	New shoes? I know how that is. I would have difficulties with those too. One should always break in new shoes a little before a tour.
Karl:	Ja, das hätte ich tun sollen.	Yes, I should have done that.
Fritz:	Gehen wir weiter. Wir schaffen es schon.	Let's continue. We will make it.

Laufen		*Jogging*
Frau S.:	Sie sehen so fit aus. Wie machen Sie das nur?	You look so fit. How do you do it?
Frau B.:	Ich laufe fast jeden Tag und ich bin nicht mehr die Jüngste.	I jog almost every day and I am no longer the youngest.
Frau S.:	Fast jeden Tag?	Almost every day?
Frau B.:	Je mehr ich laufe, desto besser fühle ich mich.	The more I run, the better I feel.
Frau S.:	Sagen Sie, wären Sie gestern auch gelaufen? Es hat doch so geregnet.	Tell me, would you have jogged yesterday too? It rained terribly.
Frau B.:	Ich bin gelaufen.	I did jog.
Frau S.:	Unglaublich. Das dürfte ich nicht. Ich bekäme sofort eine Erkältung. Wie oft laufen Sie in der Woche?	Unbelievable. I couldn't do that. I would catch a cold immediately. How often do you run a week?
Frau B.:	Na, ich würde sagen, etwa drei- oder viermal. Wenn ich mehr Zeit hätte, würde ich noch öfter laufen.	Well, I would say three or four times. If I had more time, I would jog more often.
Frau S.:	Und wie weit laufen Sie?	And how far do you run?
Frau B.:	Das kommt darauf an, wie ich mich fühle. Wenn ich müde vom Büro nach Hause komme, laufe ich 3-4 Kilometer. Und wenn ich mich frisch fühle, laufe ich etwas weiter.	That depends on how I feel. If I come home tired from the office, I run about 3-4 kilometers. And if I feel fresh, then I run a bit farther.
Frau S.:	Toll!	Fantastic.

---

2. The subjunctive mood

Every language finds ways to distinguish between reality and unreality. It is the subjunctive which deals with contrary-to-fact conditions, with wishes, conjectures, and suppositions.

Compare:	**indicative**	*When I have time, I read a lot.*
		Wenn ich Zeit habe, lese ich viel.
	subjunctive	*If I had time, I would read a lot.*
		Wenn ich Zeit hätte, würde ich viel lesen.

There are two ways to express the subjunctive in the present and future time frame.

A. The general subjunctive which derives its form from the past tense:

PAST TENSE INDICATIVE	*PRESENT/FUTURE SUBJUNCTIVE*
Ich lernte gern Deutsch.	Ich lernte gern Deutsch.
I gladly learned German.	*I would like to learn German.*
Er spielte oft Tennis.	Er spielte oft Tennis.
He often played Tennis.	*He would play tennis often.*

Present subjunctive of *regular* (weak) verbs is formed by adding *t* plus these endings: ich = e; du = est; er, sie, es = e; wir = en; ihr = et; Sie, sie = en.

As you can see, with so-called regular (weak) verbs, the distinction between past tense indicative and the present tense subjunctive can only be made in context. However, with irregular (strong) verbs, a vowel change takes place, and if the stem vowel is *a, o,* or *u,* an umlaut is added. To form the present subjunctive of *irregular* (strong) verbs, add the subjunctive personal endings to the stem of the past indicative.

PAST TENSE INDICATIVE	*PRESENT TIME SUBJUNCTIVE*
Er kam heute nach Hause.	Er käme heute nach Hause, wenn…
He came home today.	*He would come home today, if…*
Ich ging ins Kino.	Ich ginge ins Kino, wenn…
I went to the movies.	*I would go to the movies, if…*
Ich war sehr glücklich.	Ich wäre sehr glücklich, wenn…
I was very happy.	*I would be very happy, if…*
Ich hatte nie Zeit.	Ich hätte nie Zeit, wenn…
I never had time.	*I would never have time, if…*

In every day German, the subjunctive forms "**wäre**" and "**hätte**" are used a great deal, but most other subjunctive verb forms are not.

B. The subjunctive mood in the present and future time frame can be expressed through *würde + infinitive of the verb*. It is this *würde* construction which is primarily used in modern German, especially in conversation.

INDICATIVE	*SUBJUNCTIVE*
Ich gehe gern ins Museum.	Ich würde gern ins Museum gehen.
I like to go to the museum.	*I would like to go to the museum.*
Inge besucht ihre Verwandten.	Inge würde ihre Verwandten besuchen.
Inge visits her relatives.	*Inge would visit her relatives.*
Mieten Sie dieses Auto?	Würden Sie dieses Auto mieten?
Are you renting this car?	*Would you rent this car?*

The *würde + indicative* construction of the present subjunctive is simple and uncomplicated. Use it often.

A. Übung

Restate each sentence as an unreal condition. Use the *würde* form in the conclusion clause.

> Beispiel: Wenn das Fahrrad noch gut ist, kaufe ich es.
> Wenn das Fahrrad noch gut wäre, würde ich es kaufen.

1. Wenn Hans nicht krank ist, läuft er täglich vier Kilometer.
2. Was machen Sie, wenn Sie Kopfschmerzen haben?
3. Wenn wir Urlaub haben, reisen wir ins Ausland.
4. Lernen Sie Deutsch?
5. Ich wandere gern, wenn es warm ist.
6. Wir fahren mit Ihnen, wenn es Ihnen recht ist.

3. Modals in the subjunctive

The present tense subjunctive forms of these modals, and some special verbs, are also used frequently. They often express politeness.

können	ich könnte, du könntest, er könnte, usw.
dürfen	ich dürfte, du dürftest, er dürfte, usw.
müssen	ich müßte, du müßtest, er müßte, usw.
wissen	ich wüßte, du wüßtest, er wüßte, usw.
wünschen	ich wünschte, du wünschtest, er wünschte, usw.

Könnten Sie mir sagen, wann der Bus nach Tölz fährt?
Could you tell me when the bus for Tölz is leaving?

Dürfte ich Sie bitten, mir zu helfen?
May I ask you to help me?

Wir sollten das nicht tun.
We are not supposed to do that.

Wenn ich nur wüßte, wann sie kommen.
If I only knew when they are coming.

Ich wünschte, ich hätte mehr Geduld.
I wish I had more patience.

Er müßte nicht kommen.
He wouldn't have to come.

Wünsche für den Alltag—mit **hätte** *und* **wäre**

Ich wünschte...

    das Wetter wäre besser.
    ich hätte länger Urlaub.
    wir hätten mehr Geld.
    die Preise wären nicht so hoch.
    du hättest mehr Zeit für mich.
    ihr wäret schon hier.
    Sie wären toleranter.
    Sie hätten mehr Spaß.
    ich wäre nicht immer so müde.
    er wäre höflicher.
    sie wären nicht so unfreundlich.
    wir wären schon dort.
    ich wäre nicht so oft krank.
    du wärest Nichtraucher.
    der See wäre wärmer.
    es wäre nicht so kalt.
    es wäre nicht so heiß.
    es wäre nicht so laut hier.
    er hätte nette Freunde.

Ich wünschte…	$\left\{\begin{array}{l}\text{sie wäre…}\\ \text{Sie wären…}\\ \text{er wäre…}\end{array}\right.$
	usw.

Things we ought to do, but don't want to

Ich müßte/sollte/
-will es aber nicht-
$\left\{\begin{array}{l}\text{die Wohnung putzen.}\\ \text{die Wäsche waschen.}\\ \text{den Rasen mähen.}\\ \text{einkaufen gehen.}\\ \text{die Abrechnung erledigen.}\\ \text{mit meinem Rechtsanwalt sprechen.}\\ \text{mit meiner Chefin telefonieren.}\\ \text{schon zurückfahren.}\\ \text{ins Büro gehen.}\\ \text{meine Steuerabrechnung machen.}\\ \text{die Garage sauber machen.}\\ \text{die Fenster putzen.}\\ \text{Briefe schreiben.}\end{array}\right.$

What would you do if…

Was würden Sie tun,
wenn…
$\left\{\begin{array}{l}\text{das Wetter besser wäre?}\\ \text{Sie mehr Energie hätten?}\\ \text{Sie viel Geld hätten?}\\ \text{Sie viel Zeit hätten?}\\ \text{Sie in Europa wären?}\\ \text{Sie längere Ferien hätten?}\\ \text{Sie Politiker wären?}\\ \text{Sie eine Erkältung hätten?}\\ \text{Sie eine Einladung ins Weiße Haus hätten?}\end{array}\right.$

4. The past subjunctive

How do you express a contrary-to-fact condition in the past tense? It's quite simple:

Just one for three! The past subjunctive for all past tenses—past, present perfect, past perfect—is formed from the *past* indicative.

hätt-

wär-   + past participle

ich hätte…	ich wäre…
er	er
sie hätte…	sie wäre…
es	es
wir hätten…	wir wären…
Sie hätten…	Sie wären…
sie hätten…	sie wären…
du hättest…	du wärest…
ihr hättet…	ihr wäret…

*Consult Kapitel 5 for the use of *haben* or *sein* as an auxiliary p.78.

I would have given it to him, if he had come.
Ich hätte es ihm gegeben, wenn er gekommen wäre.
We would have gone to the concert, if the program had been interesting.
Wir wären ins Konzert gegangen, wenn das Programm interessant gewesen wäre.

A. Übung

Supply the proper form of *haben* or *sein* in the subjunctive to complete the sentence.

> Beispiel: Ich .....wäre........ nach Hause gefahren, wenn ich
> Zeit gehabt .....hätte;........

1. Wir .... das Tennismatch gewonnen, wenn wir besser gespielt
   ....
2. Wenn er es gewußt ...., ... er es mir gesagt.
3. Hans und Inge .... hier geblieben, wenn das Wetter besser
   gewesen ....
4. Wir .... das Haus verkauft, wenn wir einen guten Preis
   bekommen ....
5. Unser Freund .... am Wochenende gekommen, wenn er Zeit
   gehabt ....

B. Übung

Express these brief sentences   a) in the present subjunctive
                                 b) in the past subjunctive

> Beispiel: If I only had the time!
> Wenn ich nur Zeit hätte!
> Wenn ich nur Zeit gehabt hätte!

1. If I only knew that.

   a)
   b)

2. If it only were warmer.

   a)
   b)

3. If we only would find the dog.

   a)
   b)

4. If we only had more vacation.

   a)
   b)

5. If he only had the money.

   a)
   b)

You have noticed that many hypothesis clauses begin with "wenn."

Wenn ich heute nicht so müde wäre, würde ich mitkommen.
If I weren't so tired today, I would come along.
Wenn meine Mutter nicht arbeitete, würde sie mich besuchen.
If my mother didn't work, she would visit me.

Without "wenn" it's
V-S word order!

But you can also omit the "wenn" without changing the meaning of the sentence. Just begin the sentence with the verb and apply V-S word order.

Wäre ich heute nicht so müde, würde ich mitkommen.
Arbeitete meine Mutter nicht, würde sie mich besuchen.

Wiederholung

A.   Put into the *comparative.*

Beispiel: Ich schlafe am Sonntag lang.
          Und Otto schläft noch .....länger........

1.   Herbert spricht so schnell. Aber Fritz spricht noch ....
2.   Unser Auto ist groß. Müllers Auto ist noch ....
3.   Gestern war es heiß. Aber heute ist es noch ....
4.   Sie haben wenig Geld. Und ich habe noch ....
5.   Bei Schmidts kauft man billig. Aber im Kaufhof kauft man noch ....
6.   Nach Innsbruck ist es weit von hier. Nach Zürich ist es noch.......... ....

B.   Now do the same with the next sentences. But watch out. All adjectives are *irregular.*

1.   Das kostet viel. Und das noch ....
2.   Das schmeckt gut! Doch das schmeckt noch ....
3.   Ich esse Fisch gern. Doch Wiener Schnitzel esse ich noch ....
4.   Mein Fernseher ist gut. Aber Ihrer ist noch ....
5.   Denver liegt sehr hoch. Aber Aspen liegt noch ....

C.   Say the *superlative.*

Beispiele: Dieser Film dauert lang. Aber „Vom Winde verweht"
           (Gone with the Wind) dauert ....am längsten...
           Dieses Bild ist schön.
           Gewiß, aber das hier ist ....das Schönste..

1.   Bei uns ist es kalt. Doch in Sibirien ist es ....
2.   Mein Job ist schwer. Aber Ihrer ist ....
3.   Ich esse Bratwurst gern. Doch Steak esse ich ....
4.   Das Essen ist in diesem Restaurant teuer. Doch das Übernachten ist
     ....
5.   Im Hotel „Adler" ißt man gut. Doch im „Steirerhof" ißt man.......... ....
6.   Nach Italien fahre ich gern. Doch nach Schweden fahre ich ....

D. Put these sentences into a contrary-to-fact condition. Change the sentences from indicative into *subjunctive*. Make it easy on yourself and use *würde +* *infinitive* in the conclusion whenever possible—but only in the present tense.

> Beispiele: Ich bleibe gern länger hier.
> Ich würde gern länger hier bleiben.
> Wir sind nach Amerika geflogen.
> Wir wären nach Amerika geflogen.

1. Im Sommer wandern wir gern in den Bergen.
2. Ich frage sie nicht.
3. Wir glauben ihm nicht.
4. Wer bekommt das Geld?
5. Das wünschen wir uns auch.
6. Ich zahle die Rechnung morgen.
7. Mir hat dieses Kleid besser gefallen.
8. Er ist zu spät gekommen.
9. Wir sind gern nach Österreich gefahren.
10. Sie haben es nicht getan.

E. Translate these contrary-to-fact statements into good English. Try to be precise. Use the correct tense, too.

1. Wenn wir länger Urlaub gehabt hätten, wären wir noch eine Woche länger in der Schweiz geblieben.
2. Ich ginge heute ins Kino, wenn ich nicht meine Steuerabrechnung machen müßte.
3. Wäre ich Politiker, so würde ich das nicht sagen.
4. Wenn das Wetter besser gewesen wäre, hätten wir einen Ausflug gemacht.
5. Ich wünschte, ich könnte etwas gegen meine Kopfschmerzen tun.
6. Es wäre so schön, wenn wir mehr Geld zum Reisen hätten.
7. Gäbe es eine bessere Wanderkarte für diese Gegend, so würde ich sie sofort kaufen.
8. Was hätten Sie gern gesehen, wenn Sie nach Deutschland gefahren wären?

Wortschatz

Nouns

die Abfahrt, -en downhill run

die Abrechnung, -en settlement (of accounts)

das Aß, -sse ace

der Aufschläger, - server

der Aufschlag, ̈e serve (tennis)

der Ausflug, ̈e trip, outing

der Chef, -s boss, male

die Chefin, -nen boss, female

die Bundesrepublik (BRD) The Federal Republic (of Germany)

der Einstand deuce (tennis)

die Erkältung, -en cold, flu

das Fahrrad, ̈er bicycle

das Fernsehen, - television

der Fernseher, - television

die Gegend, -en area

das gemischte Doppel mixed doubles (tennis)

der Gipfel, - peak, summit

das Huhn, ̈er chicken

Italien Italy

der Kaufhof German department store chain

das Kleid, -er dress

Kopfschmerzen pl. headache(s)

die Luft air

der Maßstab, ¨e scale

der Nichtraucher, - non-smoker

das Quartier, -e lodging

der Rasen, - lawn

die Rast, -en rest

der Rechtsanwalt, ¨e lawyer

die Rückhand backhand

der Politiker, - politician

der Satz, ¨e set (tennis)

der Schnee snow

der Schuh, -e shoe

der See, -n lake

der Spaß, ¨e fun

die Steuerabrechnung, -en tax return

das Turnier, -e tournament

das Übernachten overnight stay

der Unfall, ¨e accident

der Vertrag, ¨e contract

die Vorhand forehand (tennis)

die Wanderung, -en hike

die Wanderkarte, -n hiking map

die Wäsche laundry

Verbs

auf·schlagen (schlägt auf), schlug auf, aufgeschlagen to serve (tennis)

aus·sehen (sieht aus), sah aus, ausgesehen to look, appear

besteigen, bestieg, bestiegen to climb

drücken to press, to pinch

ein·laden (lädt ein), lud ein, eingeladen to invite

erledigen to finish, to settle

geschehen (geschieht), geschah, ist geschehen to happen

gewinnen, gewann, gewonnen to win

heraus·kommen, kam heraus, ist herausgekommen to come out

mähen to mow

mit·kommen, kam mit, ist mitgekommen to come along

mit·nehmen, nahm mit, mitgenommen to take along

putzen to clean

schaffen to make (it), to accomplish

schussen to ski straight down hill

stimmen to be correct

übertreiben, übertrieb, übertrieben to exaggerate

waschen, (wäscht), wusch, gewaschen to wash

sich wohl·fühlen to feel well

Other Words

herrlich wonderful, marvelous

hinauf up, upward(s)

höflich polite

langsam slow

peinlich embarrassing

toll fantastic, great

trocken dry

unfreundlich unfriendly

unglaublich unbelievable

vereist icy

windig windy

Idiomatic Expressions

Das spielt kein Rolle. That doesn't make any difference.

das Weiße Haus The White House (USA)

Es fällt mir nichts ein. I can't think of anything.

Es kommt darauf an... It depends upon...

sich Zeit lassen to take one's time

Wie steht's? What's the score?

Kapitel 9

Communication:
The Telephone, Post Office, Newspapers, Train Station, and Airport

Culture Notes

The systems of communication and transportation such as postal service, telephone, railroads, and airlines are not precisely the same in the two Germanies (The Federal Republic of Germany and The German Democratic Republic), in Austria, and in Switzerland. But there are some features they share:

Most of these services are owned or controlled by the governments of the country. Neither the postal service nor the railroads nor the telephone companies make money; on the contrary, they need to be heavily subsidized by the government. But they perform vital services. Here is a brief listing of some of the typical features of these services.

Trains are still the major means of public transportation in all German-speaking countries; trains provide excellent and frequent service to places near and far; are usually on time, clean and comfortable, and cost a reasonable amount. There are just two classes—no need to travel first class to have a comfortable trip—and special price reduction for senior citizens and students. *Liegewagen* with make-shift beds which serve as seats during the day (three people to a compartment) provide an economic alternative to fairly expensive *Schlafwagen* (sleeper) on overnight trips. Foreign travelers should consider the purchase of a Eurail-Pass which allows unlimited travel for a certain period of time—usually 1–3 months, throughout many parts of Europe. Train stations in larger cities often have a *Bahnhofs-Postamt* which is also open on weekends and holidays—sometimes 24 hours a day.

Postal service: Dependable and fast; at a post office one can buy stamps, pay bills (with *Zahlkarten*), use a *Postsparbuch* (post office savings account) for depositing and withdrawing money at any post office within the country, and make local and long-distance calls. The *Hauptpost* (main post office) in a large city is open 24 hours a day throughout the year. The postal service also runs buses to places which cannot be reached by train.

Airlines and airports: Services and procedures follow the pattern of air transportation throughout the Western world. Differences are negligible. Security may be tighter than at airports in the USA. Frisking with metal detectors or by airport personnel is often standard procedure.

Newspapers and press: see *Lesestück* in this chapter, p. 129–130.

DIALOGE

*Auf der Post**	*At the Post Office*
Kunde: Wieviel Porto brauche ich für diesen Brief nach Irland?	How much postage do I need for this letter to Ireland?
Beamter: (zeigt auf den Brief) Ist das der Brief, den Sie schicken wollen?	(pointing to the letter) Is that the letter which you want to send?
Kunde: Ja, und diese Postkarte auch.	Yes, and this post card too.
Beamter: (wiegt den Brief) (DM1, 50) - eine Mark fünfzig. Und für die Postkarte brauchen Sie eine siebzig Pfennig Marke.	(weighs the letter) (DM1, 50) - one mark fifty. And for the post card you need a seventy Pfennig stamp.
Kunde: (gibt dem Postbeamten einen Hundertmarkschein) …Es tut mir leid. Können Sie wechseln?	(gives the postal clerk a hundred mark bill) …I am sorry. Do you have change for this?
Beamter: Hätten Sie es nicht kleiner? Ich habe heute wenig Kleingeld.	Don't you have anything smaller? I have very little change today.
Kunde: Ich seh' nochmal nach. Leider nicht.	I'll check again. Sorry, no.
Beamter: Na, es wird schon gehen. Aber ärgern Sie sich nicht über die 10 Markscheine, die ich Ihnen jetzt geben muß.	Well, it will be o.k. But don't become annoyed about the 10 mark bills which I have to give to you now.
Kunde: Nein, nein, das macht nichts.	No, no, that's o.k.

Am Telefon	*On the Phone*
Herr A.: Guten Tag. Könnte ich mit Herrn Lindner sprechen?	Hello. Could I speak with Mr. Lindner?
Herr T.: Mit wem wollen Sie sprechen?	With whom do you want to speak?
Herr A.: Mit Herrn Lindner.	With Mr. Lindner.
Herr T.: Bei uns gibt's keinen Herrn Lindner.	There is no Mr. Lindner with us.
Herr A.: Spreche ich nicht mit der Firma Wolfram und Blohm?	Isn't this the Wolfram and Blohm Company?
Herr T.: Nein, hier ist das Finanzamt.	No, this is the Internal Revenue Service.
Herr A.: Oh, entschuldigen Sie bitte. Ich muß falsch gewählt haben. (zu sich selbst) Ja, ich habe wirklich die falsche Nummer!	Oh, please excuse me. I must have dialed the wrong number. (to himself) Yes, that's really the wrong number!

---

*The Post Office is also called *das Postamt*.

Am Telefon

J. Tyler:	(wählt eine Nummer)
	...Schon wieder besetzt.
	(nach einer Minute wählt er wieder)
	Guten Tag. Hier spricht John Tyler. Könnte ich bitte mit Frau Leitner sprechen.
Sekret:	Einen Augenblick. Ich verbinde. ...Frau Leitner spricht gerade. Möchten Sie warten, oder wollen Sie später wieder anrufen?
J. Tyler:	Ich rufe in fünfzehn Minuten wieder an.
Sekret:	Gut. Wie war der Name bitte?
J. Tyler:	John Tyler.
Sekret:	Danke. Ich sage Frau Leitner, daß Sie angerufen haben.

On the Telephone

	(dials a number)
	...Busy again.
	(after a minute he dials again).
	Hello, John Tyler speaking. Could I speak with Mrs. Leitner please.
	Just a moment, I'll connect you. ...Mrs. Leitner is on the phone right now. Would you like to wait, or do you want to call back later?
	I'll call back in fifteen minutes.
	Fine. What was your name, please?
	John Tyler.
	Thank you. I will tell Mrs. Leitner that you called.

Am Bahnhof

Kunde:	Bitte einmal Schnellzug, zweite Klasse, nach Düsseldorf.
Beamter:	Einfach oder hin und zurück?
Kunde:	Hin und zurück, bitte. Ich habe zwei Koffer, die ich nicht ins Abteil mitnehmen will.
Beamter:	Geben Sie sie als Reisegepäck auf.
Kunde:	Und wie kann ich das tun?
Beamter:	Gehen Sie zum Ausgang zurück, und dann links. Dort ist der Schalter fürs Reisegepäck.
Kunde:	Vielen Dank.

At the Train Station

	One ticket, second class Express train to Düsseldorf, please.
	One way, or a return ticket?
	A return ticket, please. I have two suitcases which I don't want to take into the compartment.
	Check them through.
	And how can I do that?
	Go back to the exit, and then left. There is the luggage window.
	Many thanks.

Am Flughafen

Kundin:	Entschuldigen Sie bitte, von wo fliegt Lufthansaflug 426 nach Madrid ab?
Beamtin:	Halle B, Gate 5.
Kundin:	Können Sie mir sagen, wie ich dorthin komme?
Beamtin:	Nehmen Sie die Rolltreppe dort drüben und folgen Sie dem Zeichen "B."
Kundin:	Vielen Dank.
Beamtin:	Gern geschehen.

At the Airport

	Excuse me please, from where does Lufthansa Flight 426 to Madrid depart?
	Concourse B, gate 5.
	Could you tell me how to get there?
	Take the escalator over there and follow the sign "B."
	Many thanks.
	My pleasure.

Grammar

1. Relative pronouns

What are relative pronouns and how are they used? Look at these examples and their English equivalents. The most frequent relative pronouns in English are *that, which, who, whom* and *whose*.

Nominative   Der Schaffner, der nach der Fahrkarte fragte, war ein junger Mann.
The conductor, who asked for the ticket, was a young man.

Die Frau, die mit uns sprach, war Kanadierin.
The woman, who talked to us, was a Canadian.

Das Haus, das wir mieten, kostet DM 1,000 pro Monat.
The house, which we are renting, costs 1000 marks per month.

Die Freunde, die wir einluden, kamen alle zu spät.
The friends, whom we invited, were all late.

Accusative   Der Winter, den wir in der Schweiz verbrachten, war sehr kalt.
The winter, which we spent in Switzerlalnd, was very cold.

Die Information, die ich am Bahnhof bekam, war falsch.
The information, which I received at the railroad station, was wrong.

Das Gulasch, das meine Mutter macht, schmeckt am besten.
The goulash, which my mother makes, tastes best.

Die Briefmarken, die ich auf der Post gekauft habe, sind Sondermarken.
The stamps, which I bought at the post office, are commemorative stamps.

Dative   Der Professor, mit dem wir korrespondieren, besucht uns dieses Jahr.
The professor, with whom we are corresponding, is visiting us this year.

Die Friseuse, zu der ich immer gehe, ist leider auf Urlaub.
The hair dresser, to whom I always go, unfortunately is on vacation.

Das Flugzeug, mit dem ich nach Europa flog, war eine Boeing 747.
The plane, with which I flew to Europe, was a Boeing 747.

Die Touristen, denen wir die Stadt zeigten, waren Österreicher.
The tourists, whom we showed the city, were Austrians.

Genitive   Der Deutsche, dessen BMW eine Panne hatte, schimpfte sehr.
The German, whose BMW broke down, complained a lot.

Die Schweizerin, deren Buch ich gelesen habe, ist sehr berühmt.
The Swiss woman, whose book I read, is very famous.

Das Auto, dessen Nummernschild ich nicht lesen konnte, fuhr sehr schnell.
The car, whose license plate I could not read, drove very fast.

Die Wälder, deren Bäume sterben, bekamen zu viel ''sauren Regen.''
The forests, whose trees are dying, received too much acid rain.

The chart below shows you the close relationship between the definite articles **der, die, das,** and the use of their forms as relative pronouns.

	MASCULINE	*FEMININE*	*NEUTER*	*PLURAL*
NOMINATIVE	der	die	das	die
ACCUSATIVE	den	die	das	die
DATIVE	dem	der	dem	*denen*
GENITIVE	*dessen*	*deren*	*dessen*	*deren*

Keep in mind the following principles guiding the use of relative pronouns:

a. They have the same gender and number as the nouns to which they refer.
b. They introduce a dependent clause, and therefore cause V-L (verb last) word order.
c. They have case endings appropriate to their function within the dependent clause.
d. The case is determined by the preposition or the function of the relative pronoun within the dependent clause.
e. The clauses they introduce are always set off by commas.

A. *Übung*

Complete with the appropriate *relative* pronoun.

> Beispiel: Das ist der Berg, ...den........ wir besteigen wollen.

1. Hier ist der Koffer, ... sehr schwer ist.
2. Dort steht die Frau, mit .... Sie sprechen wollen.
3. Das ist die Zeitung, ... ich gern lese.
4. Die Leute, mit .... wir gesprochen haben, waren sehr nett.
5. Der Mann, ... Adresse ich vergessen habe, lehrt an der Universität.
6. Der Koffer, ... ich als Reisegepäck schicken möchte, ist sehr groß.
7. Wo ist das Auto, ... du gekauft hast?
8. Das Flugzeug, mit .... wir fliegen, hat Verspätung.
9. Die Schweizer, ... Dialekt ich nicht verstehe, kommen aus Zürich.
10. Die Straßenbahn, mit .... wir gefahren sind, war Linie 5.

Remember: The case is determined by the preposition. But the gender and the number are determined by the noun to which it refers.

When referring to a place, *wo* is often used instead of a preposition and relative pronoun.

> Dort ist das Gasthaus, *wo* (in dem) wir gegessen haben.
> *There is the inn where we ate.*
> Herr Mayer zeigte uns die Stadt, *wo* (in der) er aufgewachsen ist.
> *Mr. Mayer showed us the city where he grew up.*

Wer and *was* serve as relative pronouns when there is no antecedent person or when the antecedent person, idea, or thing is not specifically identified.

> Wer wandert, soll einen Rucksack mitnehmen.
> *Whoever goes hiking should take along a knapsack.*
> Er weiß nicht, mit wem er gesprochen hat.
> *He doesn't know with whom he has spoken.*
> Das ist alles, was sie uns gesagt haben.
> *That's all they told us.*

A *wo-compound* may also be used to replace a preposition and the indefinite pronoun *was*. The *wo-compound* then serves as a relative pronoun.

> Ich weiß nicht, wofür (für was) er sich interessiert.
> *I don't know in what he is interested.*

B.   *Übung*

Complete with a *wo* or *wo-compound* used as a relative pronoun.

> Beispiele: Dort ist das Büro, ...wo......... ich arbeite.   *where*
> Ich weiß, ...wofür....... ich arbeite.   *for what*

1. Ich zeige Ihnen das Haus, ... ich gewohnt habe.   *where*
2. Wir wissen nicht, ... er kommt.   *from where*
3. Er hat uns nicht gesagt, ... er das bezahlen kann. *with what*
4. Ich frage mich, ... ich so schwer gearbeitet habe. *what for*
5. Sie sagen uns, ... sie fahren wollen.   *where to*

Relative pronouns are not "grammatical baggage." They are used in literature as well as daily life. Let's look at some examples from the world of communication and travel. Find the proper English translation for each of them.

*Relative Pronouns in Action**

AM BAHNHOF

1. Am Bahnsteig 7 steht der Schnellzug, der nach Hannover fährt.
2. Am Schalter 2 wartet die Gruppe, die nach Hamburg reist.
3. Die Wechselstube, die sich in der Abfahrtshalle befindet, ist von 8-18 Uhr geöffnet.
4. Die Amerikaner, denen man den Fahrplan erklärt, fahren nach München.
5. Der Fahrplan, den man mir gezeigt hat, gilt nicht mehr.
6. Das Restaurant, in dem wir gegessen haben, befindet sich im zweiten Stock.
7. Der Reisende, dessen Uhr stehengeblieben ist, kommt zu spät.
8. Das Reisegepäck, das zu schwer ist, schicken wir mit der Bahn.

DIE PRESSE

1. Der Artikel, der mich interessierte, stand gestern in der *Süddeutschen Zeitung.*
2. Der Artikel, den ich gern gelesen hätte, war in der gestrigen Zeitung.

*For translation see answers on pp. 175–176.

3. Der Journalist, dessen Stil mir gut gefällt, heißt Peter Wallner.
4. Die Anzeigen, deren Inhalt ich manchmal nicht verstehe, findet man auf Seite 30.
5. Die Journalisten, mit denen wir diskutierten, glaubten alles zu wissen.

AUF DER POST

1. Hier sind die Marken, mit denen Sie Ihre Briefe frankieren müssen.
2. Sie müssen die Zahlkarte, die Sie mir gegeben haben, ausfüllen.
3. Das ist ein Postsparbuch, mit dem man bei jeder Post Geld abheben kann.
4. Es gibt keine Postämter, wo man nicht telefonieren kann.
5. Für jeden Anruf, den man auf der Post macht, muß man beim Schalter bezahlen. (unless you use a postal phone credit card.)

AM TELEFON

1. Die Dame, deren Namen ich nicht verstehen konnte, sprach zu leise.
2. Der Herr, der vor mir in die Telefonzelle ging, sprach sehr lange.
3. Die Telefonnummer, die man mir gegeben hat, stimmt nicht.
4. Das Telegramm, das mir die Post brachte, war von meinen Eltern.
5. Mein Postsparbuch, dessen Nummer ich vergessen habe, liegt bei mir zu Hause.

Lesestück

Etwas über die Presse in den deutschsprachigen Ländern.

Es gibt keine Demokratie, die ohne Pressefreiheit eine Demokratie bleiben kann. Die ältere Generation in Deutschland, der man in der Nazizeit diese Freiheit nahm, erlebte das.

In der Schweiz, wo es seit Jahrhunderten eine erfolgreiche Demokratie gibt, erschien 1597 in Goldach (Kanton St. Gallen) die erste Zeitung Europas. Das Recht auf unabhängige Information ist für ein Land, in dem man frei leben will, sehr wichtig. Jeder soll schreiben dürfen, was er will; und jeder soll lesen können, was er mag. Es ist kein Zufall, daß man in der kleinen Schweiz (4 Millionen Einwohner) über 400 Zeitungen finden kann.

In der Bundesrepublik Deutschland, in der heute 63 Millionen Menschen leben, gibt es ungefähr 1250 Zeitungen. Sie repräsentieren verschiedene politische Meinungen, so zum Beispiel die *Süddeutsche Zeitung* (liberal), die *Frankfurter Allgemeine Zeitung* (konservativ-liberal) oder die *Welt* (konservativ). Dazu kommen noch politische Wochenblätter wie *Die Zeit* (liberal) oder der *Rheinische Merkur* (konservativ). Eine Sonderstellung hat in der westdeutschen Presse *Der Spiegel*, ein Nachrichtenmagazin, das dem amerikanischen *Time* und *Newsweek* ähnlich ist. *Der Spiegel* sieht seine Rolle als ''politischer Wachhund.'' Politiker, mit denen der *Spiegel* auf Kriegsfuß steht, fürchten die scharfe und oft arrogante Kritik dieser Zeitschrift.

Sieben von zehn Zeitungen, die die Westdeutschen täglich lesen, kommen als Abonnement ins Haus. In der Bundesrepublik gehört die Presse zur Privatwirtschaft; in der Deutschen Demokratischen Republik ist es der Staat, der die Presse kontrolliert.

Auch in Österreich garantiert die Verfassung die Pressefreiheit. Die *Neue Kronenzeitung,* der *Kurier* und *Die Presse* zählen zu jenen Zeitungen Österreichs, die man überall im Lande kaufen kann. Von den regionalen Zeitungen sind besonders die «Salzburger Nachrichten" für ihre unabhängige Berichterstattung bekannt.

Interessant ist auch die Tatsache, daß es im heutigen Deutschland—in der Bundesrepublik wie auch in der Deutschen Demokratischen Republik—weniger Zeitungen als vor dem Zweiten Weltkrieg gibt. So erschienen im Jahre 1932 in Deutschland 2889 Zeitungen, also mehr als doppelt so viele wie heute. Wer sind bei diesem «Zeitungssterben" die Verlierer gewesen? Es waren lokale Zeitungen, die mit den großen Zeitungen nicht mehr konkurrieren konnten, und Parteizeitungen, denen heute das politische «Hinterland" fehlt.

«Die Großen fressen die Kleinen auf." Dieser Trend im deutschen Pressewesen macht vielen Deutschen Sorgen. Es ist ein Trend, der ein Problem für die Pressefreiheit werden könnte. In einer echten Demokratie möchte man, ja muß man viele Stimmen hören....

A. *Übung*

Answer the following questions by marking the correct answer(s). More than one answer may be possible.

I.   Warum ist die Pressefreiheit wichtig?

1.   Viele Leute können Zeitungen lesen.
2.   Man braucht kein Fernsehen.
3.   Die Zeitungen bleiben billig.
4.   Sie ist so wichtig für die Demokratie.

II.   Wann gab es die meisten Zeitungen in Deutschland?

1.   Während des Zweiten Weltkrieges.
2.   Nach dem Zweiten Weltkrieg.
3.   Vor dem Zweiten Weltkrieg.
4.   Heute.

III.   Warum ist es kein Zufall, daß es in der Schweiz über 400 Zeitungen gibt?

1.   Die Schweiz ist groß.
2.   Die Schweiz hat eine alte Demokratie.
3.   Die Schweiz ist neutral.
4.   Der Staat kontrolliert die Presse.

IV.   Was ist *Der Spiegel?*

1.   Ein Nachrichtenmagazin.
2.   Eine berühmte Zeitung in der DDR.
3.   Das Äquivalent zu *Time* und *Newsweek.*
4.   Eine sehr alte Zeitung.

V.   Was bedeutet «Zeitungssterben?"

1.   Es gibt mehr Zeitungen.
2.   Es gibt weniger Zeitungen.
3.   Die Zeitungen kosten zu viel.
4.   Man hört weniger Stimmen, weil es weniger Zeitungen gibt.

2. German word order: A summary

A. Where does the verb go?

The position of verbs in a German sentence or clause is of special importance. While other words can be placed in different positions depending on what the speaker or writer wants to emphasize, the rules about the placement of the verb, auxiliary verb, or modal auxiliary are firm. The chart below may assist you in using correct German word order.

1. *main clause* = verb is second grammatical unit	Wir **lernen** diesen Sommer Deutsch. Diesen Sommer **lernen** wir Deutsch. Deutsch **lernen** wir diesen Sommer.	*We are learning German this summer.*
2. *main clause* with modals = modal second unit	Er **will** morgen seine Freunde **besuchen**. Seine Freunde **will** er morgen **besuchen**. Morgen **will** er seine Freunde **besuchen**.	*He wants to visit his friends tomorrow.*
3. *main clause* separable prefix verb = stem of verb second unit, prefix last (present and past tense)	Fritz **kommt** heute abend **an**. Heute abend **kommt** Fritz **an**. Fritz **kam** gestern abend **an**. Gestern abend **kam** Fritz **an**.	*Fritz is arriving tonight. Fritz arrived last night.*
4. *main clause* compound tenses = auxiliary verb second unit, past participle last.	Ich **habe** gestern zuviel **gegessen**. Gestern **habe** ich zuviel **gegessen**. Zuviel **habe** ich gestern **gegessen**. Wir **sind** oft nach Europa **geflogen**. Oft **sind** wir nach Europa **geflogen**. Nach Europa **sind** wir oft **geflogen**.	*I ate (have eaten) too much yesterday. We often flew to Europe.*
5. In questions without a question word (wo, wie, etc.) = the conjugated VERB always begins the sentence.	**Lernen** wir diesen Sommer Deutsch? **Will** er morgen seine Freunde **besuchen**? **Kommt** Fritz heute abend **an**? **Habe** ich gestern zuviel **gegessen**? **Sind** Sie oft nach Europa **geflogen**?	*Are we learning German this summer? Does he want to visit his friends tomorrow? Is Fritz arriving tonight? Did I eat too much yesterday? Did you fly to Europe often?*
If a question begins with a question word, V-S (verb-subject) word order is used.	Wo **lernen** Sie Deutsch? Wann **will** er seine Freunde **besuchen**? Um wieviel Uhr **kommt** Fritz **an**? Warum **habe** ich soviel **gegessen**? Wie oft **sind** Sie nach Europa **geflogen**?	*Where are you learning German? When does he want to visit his friends? At what time is Fritz arriving? Why did I eat so much? How often did you fly to Europe?*

6. Commands and re-   **Fahren** Sie langsam, bitte!   *Drive slowly, please.*
   quests (imperative) =   **Bleiben** Sie hier!   *Stay here!*
   infinitive first + "Sie"   **Kommen** Sie mit!   *Come along!*

7. Main + dependent   Hans kommt heute nicht, weil   *Hans isn't coming today*
   clause = verb last in   er krank **ist.**   *because he is sick.*
   dependent clause.

8. If dependent clause   Weil er krank **ist, kommt**   *Because he is sick, Hans*
   comes first, verb in   Hans heute nicht.   *isn't coming today.*
   main clause comes
   first.

Wiederholung

A.   You are first at a post office in Germany and then at a train station and you want to do the following things:

1.   Buy a stamp for a letter to the USA -
2.   Send a postcard to Austria -
3.   Buy a round trip ticket to Munich -
4.   Check your heavy suitcases as "Reisegepäck" -
5.   Find a telephone booth -
6.   Fill out a money order -

What would you say or ask to accomplish these tasks?

1.   ....
2.   ....
3.   ....
4.   ....
5.   ....
6.   ....

B.   Rewrite each sentence using the cue as your new antecedent. Make all necessary changes.

   Beispiel: Dort ist der Mann, mit dem ich gesprochen habe.   *die Frau*
             Dort ist ..... die Frau ....., mit ..... der .... ich gesprochen habe.

1.   .... Bitte fragen Sie die Verkäuferin, die dort   *der Mann*
      steht.
2.   .... Hier ist der Artikel, den ich Ihnen zeigen   *die Anzeige*
      wollte.
3.   .... Wo ist die Fahrkarte, die du gekauft hast?   *der Fahrplan*
4.   .... Wie heißt das Kind, dessen Name ich   *die Ärztin*
      vergessen habe?
5.   .... Das ist der Koffer, der so schwer ist.   *die Tasche*
6.   .... Ist das der Schweizer, den wir getroffen   *die Schweizer*
      haben?

C. Übersetzen Sie!

1. This is the article which I read.
2. The number is busy. Please call again in 15 minutes.
3. Is there a telephone booth from which I can call?
4. There is the post office where you can buy stamps.
5. Who was the gentleman with whom I have spoken?
6. That's all (that) I know.
7. This is the mountain which we want to climb.
8. Do you have a knapsack which I can take along?

D. What can you do with these words? See if you can come up with a meaningful sentence or question using the given words. Extend the sentence if you wish and use any structure or tense of your choice. Watch tense.

Beispiel: warten   Wir müssen warten, weil Flug 404
       der Flug 404   Verspätung hat.
       Verspätung

1. kaufen / eine Fahrkarte / Hin- und Rückfahrt / nach Wien / ich
2. der Koffer / schwer / als Reisegepäck / aufgeben / wir
3. Geld / abheben / heute / wir// weil / die Bank / geschlossen / am Wochenende
4. sich ärgern / ich// wenn die Telefonnummer / immer / besetzt
5. suchen / die Abflughalle / nicht finden / Sie / können / aber

Wortschatz

Nouns

die Abfahrtshalle, -n departure hall

das Abonnement, -s subscription

die Anzeige, -n classified ad

der Artikel, - article

der Ausgang, "-e exit

die Bahn, -en here: railroad

der Bahnsteig, -e platform (train station)

der Beamte, -n civil servant

der Baum, "-e tree

die Berichterstattung, -en reporting

die Briefmarke, -n postage stamp

die Bundesrepublik Deutschland (BRD) The Federal Republic of Germany

die Dame, -n lady

die Demokratie, -n democracy

die Deutsche Demokratische Republik (DDR) German Democratic Republic

der Dialekt, -e dialect

die Fahrkarte, -n ticket

der Fahrplan, "-e time table, schedule

der Fahrschein, -e ticket

das Finanzamt, "-er internal revenue service

die Freiheit freedom

die Friseuse, -n hair dresser

die Gruppe, -n group

die Halle, -n hall (departure or arrival)

die Hin- und Rückfahrt, -en return (round) trip

der Hundertmarkschein, -e hundred mark bill

der Inhalt, -e content

das Jahrhundert, -e century

der Kanadier, - Canadian, male

die Kanadierin, -nen Canadian, female

der Kanton   canton (state) in Switzerland

das Kleingeld   change (money)

der Kunde, -n   customer

das Nummernschild, -er   license plate

die Marke, -n   stamp

die Meinung, -en   opinion

das Nachrichtenmagazin, -e   news magazine

die Nazizeit   Nazi period (in Germany 1933–45)

die Panne, -n   breakdown (car)

der Pfennig, -e   penny (100 Pf. = 1 Mark)

das Postamt, ⁻er   post office

der Postbeamte, -n   postal clerk

das Postsparbuch, ⁻er   postal savings book

die Presse   press, newspaper

die Pressefreiheit   freedom of the press

die Privatwirtschaft   private industry

das Recht, -e   right

der saure Regen   acid rain

das Reisegepäck   baggage, luggage

der Reisende, -n   traveler

die Rolltreppe, -n   escalator

der Rucksack, ⁻e   knapsack

der Schaffner, -   conductor, male

die Schaffnerin, -nen   conductor, female

der Schalter, -   ticket window

der Sekretär, -e   secretary, male

die Sekretärin, -nen   secretary, female

die Seite, -n   page

die Sondermarke, -n   commemorative stamp

die Sonderstellung   special place, position

der Stil, -e   style

die Stimme, -n   voice

die Telefonzelle, -n   telephone booth

der Verlierer, -   looser

die Verspätung   delay

der Wachhund, -e   watchdog

die Wechselstube, -n   money exchange office

das Wochenblatt, ⁻er   weekly newspaper

die Zahlkarte, -n   money order

(der Erlagschein, -e -)   in Austria

das Zeichen, -   sign

die Zeitschrift, -en   magazine

das Zeitungssterben   demise of newspapers

der Zufall, ⁻e   coincidence

Verbs

ab·fliegen, flog ab, ist abgeflogen   to fly off, depart

ab·heben, hob ab, abgehoben   to withdraw (money)

auf·wachsen (wächst auf) wuchs auf, ist aufgewachsen   to grow up

sich ärgern   to be annoyed

aus·füllen   to fill out

sich befinden, befand, befunden   to be located, situated

beitragen, trug bei, beigetragen   to contribute

bringen, brachte, gebracht   to bring

erklären   to explain

erleben   to experience

erscheinen, erschien, ist erschienen   to appear, to be published

frankieren   to prepay, stamp (mail)

fürchten   to be afraid, to fear

garantieren   to guarantee

gelten (gilt), galt, gegolten   to be valid

korrespondieren   to correspond

kontrollieren   to control

lehren   to teach, instruct

repräsentieren   to represent

schicken   to send, mail

schimpfen   to complain, scold

stehen·bleiben, blieb stehen, ist stehengeblieben   to stop, halt

sterben (stirbt), starb, ist gestorben   to die

stimmen   to be correct (something is…)

verbinden, verband, verbunden   to connect

zahlen   to pay

Other Words

ähnlich   similar

deutschsprachig   German-speaking

doppelt   double

dorthin   to that place, over there

echt genuine
erfolgreich successful
gerade just, at that moment
gestrig yesterday's
gültig valid
grün green
lokal local
nochmals once more
politisch political
scharf sharp
täglich daily
unabhängig independent
ungefähr approximately
verschieden different
wechseln to change (money)
wichtig important

Idiomatic Expressions

auf Kriegsfuß stehen to be in conflict with…to be on a war path

Das macht mir Sorgen. That worries me.

Das macht nichts. That doesn't matter.

Es steht in der Zeitung. It's written in the newspaper.

Es wird gehen. It will work out, I can manage.

Gern geschehen. Gladly, don't mention it.

Hin und zurück. Back and forth.

Kapitel   10

Selbstbiographisches

In diesem letzten Kapitel möchten wir Ihnen zeigen, wie Sie auf deutsch über sich selbst sprechen können. Wir nennen das Kapitel »Selbstbiographisches,« denn Sie sind der Mittelpunkt.

DIALOGE

Sie sind in *Köln* auf der Polizei, denn man hat Ihnen alle wichtigen Papiere (Paß, Führerschein, Flugkarte, usw.) gestohlen. Der Polizist spricht kein Englisch. Aber das macht nichts, denn Sie können seine einfachen Fragen verstehen und auf deutsch beantworten. Zunächst müssen Sie ein Formular ausfüllen. Daher der Telegrammstil.

Polizist:	Nachname (Familienname)
Sie:	Cook
Polizist:	Vorname
Sie:	Richard
Polizist:	Wohnort
Sie:	zur Zeit Köln
Polizist:	Straße
Sie:	Rheinallee 27, bei Biebers
Polizist:	Telefon
Sie:	63-54-72
Polizist:	Geburstag (Geburtsdatum)
Sie:	20. Juli 1959
Polizist:	Geburtsort
Sie:	Columbus, Ohio
Polizist:	Staatsangehörigkeit
Sie:	Amerikaner
Polizist:	Beruf
Sie:	Drogist
Polizist:	Paßnummer
Sie:	Weiß ich nicht, denn man hat mir meinen Paß gestohlen.
Polizist:	Größe
Sie:	1, 68 m (ein Meter achtundsechzig)
Polizist:	Gewicht
Sie:	75 Kilo
Polizist:	Haarfarbe
Sie:	blond

Polizist:	Augenfarbe
Sie:	blau-grau
Polizist:	Besondere Kennzeichen
Sie:	Narbe über dem rechten Auge.
Polizist:	Wo können wir Sie erreichen?
Sie:	Ich bin bis Montag in Köln.
	Sie haben ja meine Adresse.

Wir sprechen natürlich nicht in Stichwörtern (Telegrammstil), sondern in Sätzen. Wiederholen wir also das Gespräch.

Wie heißen Sie?	Ich heiße Richard Cook.
Wo wohnen Sie?	Zur Zeit wohne ich in Köln auf der Rheinallee bei Biebers.
Was ist Ihre Telefonnummer?	Meine Nummer ist 63-54-72.
Wann und wo sind Sie geboren?	Ich bin am 20. Juli 1959 in Columbus, Ohio geboren.
Welche Staatsangehörigkeit haben Sie?	Ich bin Amerikaner.
Was sind Sie von Beruf?	Ich bin Drogist.
Wissen Sie Ihre Paßnummer?	Nein, denn man hat mir meinen Paß gestohlen.
Wie groß sind Sie?	Ich bin 1,68 m groß.
Wieviel wiegen Sie?	Ich wiege 75 Kilo.
Was ist Ihre Haarfarbe?	Blond.
Und Ihre Augenfarbe ist?	Blau-grau.
Haben Sie besondere Kennzeichen?	Ja, ich habe eine Narbe über dem rechten Auge.

Wir möchten noch viel mehr über Sie wissen. Jetzt sind Sie aber nicht mehr auf der Polizei, sondern auf einer Party, wo Sie mit einem Gast sprechen. Der Gast scheint sehr neugierig zu sein, denn Sie werden so richtig ausgefragt.

Gast:	Also, Herr Cook. Wie lange sind Sie schon in Köln?
Sie:	Seit zwei Wochen.
Gast:	Was bringt Sie denn in unsere Stadt?
Sie:	Ich habe eine Konferenz besucht.
Gast:	Was haben Sie denn in Ihrer Freizeit gemacht?
Sie:	Mir wurden fast alle Sehenswürdigkeiten der Stadt gezeigt.
Gast:	Haben Sie Ihre Frau mitgebracht?
Sie:	Ich bin noch ledig.
	Und Sie?
Gast:	Ich bin schon 20 Jahre verheiratet.
Sie:	Haben Sie auch Kinder?
Gast:	Ja, zwei Töchter und einen Sohn.
	Die Älteste ist Volksschullehrerin, und die zweite ist Verkäuferin in einem Kinderwarengeschäft.
	Mein Sohn....
Sie:	Entschuldigen Sie, ich muß noch schnell mit Frau Kurz sprechen.

Frau Kurz ist leider auch sehr neugierig, und so werden Sie weiter ausgefragt.

Frau K.:	Haben Sie schon unsere Oper besucht?
Sie:	Ja, letzte Woche bin ich von einem Kollegen zum „Freischütz" eingeladen worden.
Frau K.:	Und wie hat Ihnen die Oper gefallen?
Sie:	Ja, gut, aber eigentlich bin ich Wagnerliebhaber.

Frau K.:	Da müssen Sie nach Bayreuth.
Sie:	Das ist mir von anderen auch gesagt worden.
Frau K.:	Es ist aber schwer, Karten zu bekommen.
Sie:	Man hat sie mir auf dem Reisebüro schon besorgt.
Frau K.:	Wie lange bleiben Sie in Köln?
Sie:	Noch drei Tage. Entschuldigen Sie, ich sehe gerade Herrn Dietrich. Er hat einen Brief für mich.
Frau K.:	Natürlich.

Interview Check List

Jetzt müssen Sie keine Fragen mehr beantworten. Wir haben aber eine Interviewliste, die Sie vielleicht ausfüllen möchten. Wenn Sie eine Frage nicht beantworten können, sehen Sie sich die Listen über Berufe und Hobbys an.

Name...
Vorname...
Adresse...
(Wohnort, Straße)
Telefonnummer...
Beruf...
Familienstand...   (ledig, verheiratet, geschieden, Witwer, Witwe)
Hobbys...
Interessen...
Reisen, die Sie gemacht haben...
Klubs/Vereine...
Lieblings
    Autor(in)...
    Komponist(in)...
    Sänger(in)...
    Filmschauspieler(in)...
    Film...
    Buch...
    Stadt...
    Sport...
    Getränk...
    Essen...
    (see Chapter 3 for list)

Und was sind *Sie* von Beruf?

architect	Architekt(in)
artist	Künstler(in)
baker	Bäcker(in)
bookkeeper	Buchhalter(in)
businessman	Geschäftsmann
businesswoman	Geschäftsfrau
chemist	Chemiker(in)
civil servant	Beamter (Beamtin)
clerk	Angestellter (Angestellte)
dentist	Zahnarzt (Zahnärztin)
druggist	Drogist(in)
electrician	Elektriker(in)

engineer	Ingenieur(in)
judge	Richter(in)
lawyer	Rechtsanwalt (Rechtsanwältin)
librarian	Bibliothekar(in)
mechanic	Mechaniker(in)
minister	Pastor(in), Pfarrer
nurse (female)	Krankenschwester
nurse (male)	Krankenpfleger
officer (military)	Offizier(in)
pilot	Pilot(in)
physician	Arzt (Ärztin)
professor	Professor(in) für Musik, Mathematik, Chemie, usw.
plumber	Installateur(in)
psychologist	Psychologe, Psychologin
sales clerk	Verkäufer(in)
secretary	Sekretär(in)
teacher	Lehrer(in)

Was ist Ihr Hobby? oder *Was machen Sie gern in Ihrer Freizeit?*
Ich spiele Tennis, Golf, Karten, Basketball, Fußball, usw.
Ich spiele Klavier, Gitarre, Cello, Trompete, Flöte, Geige*, usw.   *violin
Ich schwimme, lese, schreibe, koche, wandere, bastle*, sammle* Briefmarken/   *do crafts *to collect
   Münzen, arbeite im Garten, stricke*, surfe, laufe Schi, sehe fern, höre Radio,   *to knit
   usw.

Wofür interessieren Sie sich?
Ich interessiere mich für Sport, Musik, Kunst, Politik, Literatur, Film, Tanz,
   Technik, Theater, Astrologie, usw.

A.   Übung

Find a suitable verb for these sentences. Choose from the list. More than one
choice may be correct.

   Beispiel: Mein Freund ....geht......... gern ins Kino.

1.   Mein Vater .... gern Klavier.
2.   Mein Bruder .... gern Autos.
3.   Meine Schwester .... gern über Politik.
4.   Mein Nachbar .... gern im Garten.
5.   Meine Nachbarin .... gern Romane.
6.   Mein Chef .... gern Briefmarken.
7.   Mein Sohn .... gern Platten.
8.   Meine Tante .... gern.
9.   Meine Tochter .... gern lange am Telefon.
10.   Mein Mann .... gern in guten Restaurants.

sammeln, reparieren, spielen, lesen, arbeiten, sprechen, essen, diskutieren, hören,
basteln

B.   Übung

Answer these "personal" questions in complete German sentences.

> Beispiel: Wie oft waren Sie schon in Europa?
> Ich war schon dreimal dort.

1. Was machen Sie meistens am Wochenende?
2. Welches Land möchten Sie besuchen?
3. Wie oft gehen Sie ins Kino?
4. Wieviele Kinder haben Sie?
5. Wo sind Sie geboren?
6. Woher kommen Sie?
7. Was machen Sie in Ihren Ferien? (im Urlaub)
8. Warum sind Sie mit Ihrem Beruf zufrieden (unzufrieden)?
9. Beschreiben Sie Ihren Chef/Ihre Chefin.
    Er (sie) ist...
10. Meine Freunde sagen, daß ich .... bin.
    (klug, charmant, nett, intelligent, reich, arm, freundlich, interessant, alt, jung, sportlich, impulsiv, attraktiv, natürlich, populär, pünktlich, eingebildet, liberal, konservativ, vorsichtig, mutig, kräftig, schlank)

C.   Übung

Was sind diese Menschen von Beruf? Fill in the blanks with the appropriate occupation.

> Beispiel: Herr Frisch lehrt in der Schule. Er ist ....Lehrer.........

1. Hans verkauft Schuhe in einem Schuhgeschäft. Er ist ....
2. Herr Klein reparierte gestern mein Auto. Er ist ....
3. Mein Bruder predigt jeden Sonntag in der Kirche. Er ist ....
4. Meine Schwester arbeitet im Krankenhaus, wo sie Patienten pflegt. Sie ist
    ....
5. Ich verkaufe Aspirin, Hustensaft, usw. in einer Drogerie. Ich bin...........
6. Herr Schmidt hat meinen elektrischen Ofen repariert. Er ist ....
7. Fräulein Jung hilft uns, die richtigen Bücher zu finden. Sie arbeitet in einer
    Bibliothek und ist ....
8. Karl arbeitet für TWA. Er gibt Auskunft über die Flüge, verkauft Flugkarten
    und hilft den Fluggästen. Er ist ....
9. Karin hat Medizin studiert. Sie arbeitet jetzt im Johanniterkrankenhaus als
    ....
10. Meine Tochter arbeitet im Büro. Sie tippt Briefe, telefoniert, öffnet die Briefe
    für den Chef, usw. Sie ist dort ....

Grammar

1.   The future tense

The future tense in German, as in English, is formed with an auxiliary plus an infinitive. In German the auxiliary is *werden*. The infinitive goes to the end of a main clause.

Ich werde nach Hause fahren.
I shall go home.
Wann werden Sie Ihr Buch schreiben?
When are you going to write your book?
Du wirst morgen krank sein.
You will be sick tomorrow.

Conjugation of werden

ich	werde		wir	werden
er			Sie	
sie	wird		sie	werden
es			ihr	werdet
du	wirst			

A. *Übung*

Übersetzen Sie.

1. I will receive mail soon.
2. Will you write to me this week?
3. When is she going to work?
4. He is going to buy good tickets.
5. The bus will come in 15 minutes.

2. The passive voice

The passive voice is usually used to describe a condition in which the *subject* is acted upon. In other words, the subject is not doing the action, but someone or something is doing something to the subject. A form of the verb *werden* is needed to express the passive.

Because you have to know the verb forms of *werden* in order to express or to recognize the passive, we should review them quickly.

If used as main verb, *werden* means *to become*. (Do not confuse it with *bekommen* = *to receive*.) *Werden* plus *infinitive* denotes *future* tense.

Das Kind wird krank.	*The child is getting sick.*
Das Kind wurde krank.	*The child became sick.*
Das Kind ist krank geworden.	*The child has become sick.*
Das Kind wird krank werden.	*The child will become sick.**

A. *Übung*

Complete with the correct form of *werden*. Watch tense.

1. Hans .... gestern krank.   *simple past*
2. Erika .... Sekretärin.   *present*

*We are only giving the present, simple past, present perfect and future tenses because the past perfect and future perfect are seldom used. However, you will find these forms in the appendix.

3.   Wir . . . . nach Hause fliegen   *future*
4.   Wieviel . . . . du verdienen?   *future*
5.   Er . . . . berühmt . . . .   *present perfect*

B.   Übung

Decide whether you should use *werden* or *bekommen*. Watch tense.

Beispiele: Frau Braun . . . bekommt . . . . . . jeden Tag die Zeitung.
Fritz . . . . wird . . . . Elektriker.

1.   Mein Opa . . . . im Mai neunzig   *present perfect*
Jahre . . . .
2.   . . . . du auch einen Brief   *present perfect*
von Erika . . . . ?
3.   Der bekannte Schauspieler . . . . schnell   *past*
erkannt.
4.   Gestern . . . . ich endlich meinen Paß.   *past*
5.   Wir . . . . erst im Juli Urlaub.   *present*

Now let's see how *werden* is used in the PASSIVE.

THE PASSIVE

Das Buch wird geschrieben.	*The book is being written.*
Das Buch wurde geschrieben.	*The book was being written.*
Das Buch ist geschrieben worden.*	*The book has been written.*
Das Buch wird geschrieben werden.	*The book will be written.*

*Note: In the perfect tense of the passive the special form of *worden* (not *geworden*) is used.

Unser Auto wird heute repariert.	*Our car is being repaired today. (present)*
Das Haus wurde von uns gereinigt.	*The house was being cleaned by us. (past)*
Das Buch ist von allen Studenten gelesen worden.	*The book has been read by all students. (present perfect)*
Die Rechnung wird von den Gästen bezahlt werden.	*The bill will be paid by the guests. (future)*

Essentially you need to know three things to form the passive from the active. Please compare:

Er hat den Brief geschrieben.	*He has written the letter.*
Der Brief ist von ihm geschrieben worden.	*The letter has been written by him.*

1.   The accusative object of the active sentence becomes the nominative subject of the passive sentence:
Der Brief...

2. The active verb form is replaced by a form of *werden:*

    ist .... geschrieben worden.

3. The subject of the active sentence is replaced by *von* + *dative* (of subject in active sentence):

    von ihm...

Therefore, the new passive sentence reads:

Der Brief ist von ihm geschrieben worden.

C. Übung

Supply the correct form of *werden.*

Beispiel: Die Geschichte ...ist... erzählt ...worden   *present perfect*

1. Der Student .... von dem Professor gefragt.   *present*
2. Die Schauspielerin .... interviewt.   *present*
3. Die Briefe .... geschickt ....   *present perfect*
4. Die Kinder .... zur Party eingeladen.   *future*
5. Du .... von mir angerufen ....   *present perfect*
6. Ich .... von Dr. Lange untersucht.   *past*
7. Die Zeitung .... von uns allen gelesen ....   *present perfect*
8. Dieses Lied .... oft gesungen.   *present*

D. Übung

Change the active sentences into the *passive.* Watch tense.

Beispiel: Frau Kurz hat mich zum Essen eingeladen.
Ich bin (von Frau Kurz) zum Essen eingeladen worden.

1. Um sieben Uhr servieren wir das Essen.
2. Thomas Mann hat viele Romane geschrieben.
3. Dr. Müscher behandelt meine Mutter.
4. Meine Sekretärin hat die Briefe abgeschickt.
5. Ein Mechaniker reparierte gestern mein Auto.
6. Die reiche Dame hat viele Kleider gekauft.
7. Dr. Erismann wird mich operieren.   *(future)*

E. Übung

Translate these sentences into English. Note that not all sentences have an agent.

Beispiel: Das Haus wird verkauft   *The house is being sold.*

1. Sein Buch wurde in zwei Sprachen übersetzt.
2. Das Paket ist gestern abgeschickt worden.
3. Der Gast wurde ausgefragt.
4. Frau Kleins Paß ist gestohlen worden.
5. Während des Krieges ist Hamburg durch Bomben zerstört worden.*
6. Amerika wurde 1492 von Columbus entdeckt.

*When the agent is an impersonal force such as the natural elements or a concept, *durch* is used with an accusative object.

7. Der Film wird hoffentlich gemacht werden.
8. Der Mann ist ermordet worden.
9. Die Wohnung wird einmal die Woche gereinigt.
10. Wo wird der Volkswagen hergestellt?

3. *Man* as a substitute for the passive

Man—one, a person, you, they—is often used to avoid the passive, especially in spoken German. The *man* construction expresses essentially the same idea as the passive construction.

Beispiele: Ich werde angerufen.	*I am being called.*
Man ruft mich an.	*They are calling me.*
Fritz ist ausgefragt worden.	*Fritz was being (has been) questioned.*
Man hat Fritz ausgefragt.	*They questioned Fritz.*

A.   *Übung*

Restate in the active voice, using the *man* construction.

1. Es wurde viel getanzt.
2. Wir sind besucht worden.
3. Ich bin gefragt worden.
4. Die Frau wird interviewt.
5. Dort wurde viel gegessen und getrunken.
6. In dem Zimmer ist nicht geraucht worden.
7. Dem Lehrer wurde nicht geantwortet.

Wie schreibt man eine Karte oder einen Brief?
Note: All *personal pronouns* are capitalized.

---

eine Geburtagskarte an eine Freundin	*a birthday card to a friend*
...den 13. Oktober	*October 13th*

Liebe Karin!	*Dear Karin,*
Zu Deinem 35. Geburtstag gratuliere ich Dir recht herzlich. Ich wünsche Dir fürs nächste Jahr vor allem gute Gesundheit und weiteren Erfolg in Deiner neuen Stellung.	*For your 35th birthday I am sending you my heartiest congratulations. For the next year I wish you above all good health and continued success in your new job.*
Herzlichst	*Yours,*
Deine Erika	*Erika*

---

eine Einladung an einen Kollegen zu einer Party	*an invitation to a colleague for a party*
...den 15. Juli	*July 15th*

Lieber Herr Schmidt!	*Dear Mr. Smith,*
Am 22. Juli wollen wir den Geburtstag von Herrn Kluge bei uns zu Hause	*On July 22nd we want to celebrate Mr. Kluge's birthday at our house. We*

feiern. Wir möchten Sie und Ihre Frau recht herzlich zu einer Party einladen. Wir erwarten Sie zwischen 20:00 und 20:30 Uhr.
Mit freundlichen Grüßen
Ihre Gabriele Jost

would like to cordially invite you and your wife to a party. We will be expecting you between 8:00 and 8:30.

Best regards,
your Gabriele Jost

---

ein Dankschreiben
Sie möchten sich für ein Geschenk von guten Freunden bedanken.
Liebe Ingrid und lieber David,
Herzlichen Dank für die schöne Platte, die Ihr mir zum Geburtstag geschenkt habt. Sie hat mir schon viel Freude gemacht. Es war besonders nett von Euch, daß Ihr Euch an meinen Lieblingskomponisten Mozart erinnert habt.
Viele liebe Grüße
Eure Elke

a thank-you note
You would like to thank good friends for a present.
Dear Ingrid and dear David,
Thank you so much for the beautiful record which you sent for my birthday. I have enjoyed it a lot already. It was especially nice that you remembered my favorite composer, Mozart.

With love,
your Elke

Beschwerdeschreiben
Manchmal muß man leider auch einen Beschwerdebrief schreiben.
An das
Versandhaus Wenz
Bahnhofstraße 15
5000 Frankfurt/M 3

letter of complaint
Unfortunately, sometimes one has to write a letter of complaint.
The Wenz Company
Bahnhof Street 15
5000 Frankfurt/M 3

Sehr geehrt Damen und Herren!
Am 11. August bestellte ich bei Ihnen vier blaue Badehandtücher mit passenden Waschlappen. Das Paket, das Sie mir am 20. August schickten, enthielt aber vier gelbe Badehandtücher und vier blaue Waschlappen. Leider bezahlte ich die Nachnahme, bevor ich das Paket öffnete. Ich bitte Sie daher, mir die *blauen* Badehandtücher zu schicken. Sobald ich die neue Ware erhalten habe, werde ich die *gelben* Handtücher zurücksenden.

Hochachtungsvoll
Karin Maier

Ladies and Gentlemen,
On August 11th I ordered from you (your company) four blue bath towels with matching wash cloths. However, the package which you mailed to me on August 20th contained four yellow bath towels and four blue wash cloths. Unfortunately, I paid the C.O.D. charge before I opened the package. Therefore, please send the blue bath towls. After I have received the new merchandise, I will return the yellow towels immediately.
Sincerely,
Karin Maier

die Antwort der Firma Wenz
Frau
Karin Maier
Provinzial Straße 23
5411 Urbar bei Koblenz

the answer of the Wenz Company

Mrs. Karin Maier
Provinzial St. 23
5411 Urbar near Koblenz

Sehr geehrte Frau Maier!
Wir bedauern außerordentlich, daß Ihr
Auftrag vom 11. August nicht richtig
ausgeführt wurde. Mit gleicher Post
wurden Ihnen die blauen Badehandtücher zugeschickt. Sobald Sie die
falsche Ware zurückgeschickt haben,
werden wir natürlich für Ihre Unkosten
aufkommen. Es liegt uns viel daran,
daß unsere Kunden zufrieden sind.
Hochachtungsvoll
gez. Franz Kraft

Dear Mrs. Maier,
We are very sorry that your order of
August 11th was filled incorrectly. With
the same mail we have sent you the
blue bath towels. As soon as you have
returned the wrong merchandise, we will,
of course, cover your costs. We are very
interested in keeping our customers
satisfied.

Sincerely,
(signed Franz Kraft)

Hints on letter writing

1. die Anrede	*1. addressing a person*
Lieber Vater,	Dear Father,
Lieber Karl,	Dear Karl,
Mein lieber Freund,	My dear friend,
Mein lieber Johann,	My dear Johann,
Lieber Herr Müller!	Dear Mr. Müller,
Sehr geehrter Herr Klein!	Dear Mr. Klein,
Liebe Mutter!	Dear Mother,
Liebe Heidi!	Dear Heidi,
Meine liebe Freundin,	My dear friend,
Meine liebe Gertrud,	My dear Gertrud,
Liebe Frau Carsten,	Dear Mrs. Carsten,
Sehr geehrte Frau Braun,	Dear Mrs. Braun,
Liebe Mutter und lieber Vater,	Dear Mother and Father,
Liebe Ellen und lieber Franz,	Dear Ellen and Franz,
Sehr geehrte Herren,	Gentlemen:
Sehr geehrte Frau Dr. Kurz,	Dear Dr. Kurz:
Sehr geehrter Herr Professor Lange,	Dear Professor Lange:
Sehr geehrte Damen und Herren!	Dear Ladies and Gentlemen:

Note: When addressing a letter, consider whether you are addressing a family
member, a good friend, someone whom you address by a last name,
business letters, or those written to people who because of their status in
life require a special form of address.

2. *Briefschluß*	2. *How to end a letter*
Privatbriefe:	Personal Letters:
Herzliche Grüße	Cordially, or With love,
Dein Freund Karl	Your friend Karl
Viele Grüße an Euch alle	Greetings to all of you,
Herzlichst, Deine...	With all my best,
Es grüßt Sie herzlich	Cordially, your
Ihr (Ihre)	
Geschäftsbriefe:	Business Letters:
Hochachtungsvoll (most often used)	Respectfully, or
	Sincerely,
Mit vorzüglicher Hochachtung	With great respect...
Mit freundlichen Grüßen	Sincerely,

One final note, when addressing the envelope, Europeans usually write the return address on the back and the address in the center of the front.

Absender: *(return address)*	Dr. Karl Jost
	Bonner Weg 23
	4600 Dortmund
Adresse: *(address)*	Herrn Dr. Fritz Klein
	Bahnhofstraße 5
	6000 Frankfurt/M 52

A.   *Übung*

1. Sie möchten Ihre gute Freundin Klara zum Abendessen einladen. Schreiben Sie eine kurze Einladung.
2. Ihr Chef hat Sie zum Wochenende eingeladen. Sie können leider nicht kommen. Schreiben Sie einen kurzen Entschuldigungsbrief.
3. Sie bedanken sich bei Ihren Eltern (Kindern) für ein Weihnachtsgeschenk.

Wiederholung

A.   *Übung*

Match the occupations on the left with the activities on the right.

1.	Zahnarzt	a.	reparierte meinen Toaster
2.	Bäcker	b.	verkauft Schuhe
3.	Elektriker	c.	arbeitet in einem Krankenhaus
4.	Professor	d.	arbeitet auf der Post
5.	Verkäuferin	e.	macht meine Zähne sauber
6.	Krankenschwester	f.	backt jeden Tag Brot
7.	Drogist	g.	schreibt ein Buch
8.	Postbeamter	h.	verkauft Aspirin, Hustensaft, usw.

B. Übung

Fill in the blanks of the letter with appropriate words from the list below.

.... Hans,

  Jetzt bin ich schon drei .... in Bonn. Es gefällt mir wirklich gut. Jeden Tag gehe ich am Rhein spazieren. Leider ist das .... nicht so schön. Es hat jeden Tag .... Letzten Sonntag war ich bei Familie Schmidt .... Sie gaben eine große Party für mich. Die meisten Gäste wollten wissen, wo ich ...., ob ich verheiratet bin, und was ich in Bonn mache. Ich war auch schon in der Oper in Köln. Wie Du weißt, ist Köln nicht .... von Bonn. Natürlich vermisse ich meine lieben .... in Amerika. Aber bald sehe ich Dich und die anderen wieder. Für heute also .... Grüße

  .... Bob

eingeladen, lieber, Dein, herzliche, Wochen, geregnet, wohne, Wetter, weit, Freunde, liebe, Dein, mache

Wortschatz

Nouns

der Architekt, -en architect, male
die Architektin, -nen architect, female
der Auftrag, ̈e order
das Auge, -n eye
die Augenfarbe color of eyes
die Auskunft, ̈e information
das Badehandtuch, ̈er bath towel
Bayreuth city in Bavaria, location of Wagner festivals
der Beamte, -n civil servant, male
die Beamtin, -nen civil servant, female
der Beruf, -e occupation
der Beschwerdebrief, -e letter of complaint
der Bibliothekar, -e librarian, male
die Bibliothekarin, -nen librarian, female
die Bombe, -n bomb
der Chemiker, - chemist, male
die Chemikerin, -nen chemist, female
das Dankschreiben, - thank-you note
der Drogist, -en druggist, male
die Drogistin, -nen druggist, female
der Entschuldigungsbrief, -e letter of apology
der Erfolg, -e success
der Familienname, -n last (family) name
der Familienstand marital status

die Ferien vacation
der Filmschauspieler, - movie actor, male
die Filmschauspielerin, -nen movie actor, female
die Flöte, -n flute
der Fluggast, ̈e airline passenger
die Flugkarte, -n airplane ticket
der „Freischütz" opera by Karl Maria von Weber
die Freizeit leisure time, free time
der Führerschein, -e driver's license
die Gartenarbeit, -en gardening
die Geburtstagskarte, -n birthday card
die Geige, -n violin
das Geschenk, -e present, gift
die Gesundheit health
das Gewicht, -e weight
die Gitarre, -n guitar
die Größe, -n height
die Haarfarbe, -n color of hair
der Hustensaft, ̈e cough syrup
der Ingenieur, -e engineer, male
die Ingenieurin, -nen engineer, female
der Installateur, -e plumber, male
die Installateurin, -nen plumber, female
der Kaufmann, die Kaufleute businessman

das Kennzeichen, - identification
der Klub, -s club
der Komponist, -en composer, male
die Komponistin, -nen composer, female
die Konferenz, -en conference
das Krankenhaus, ¨er hospital
der Krankenpfleger, - nurse, male
die Krankenschwester, -n nurse, female
die Kunst, ¨e art
die Liste, -n list
die Manieren (pl.) manners
der Mittelpunkt, -e center (of attention)
die Münze, -n coin
die Nachnahme, -n cash on delivery (C.O.D.)
der Nachname, -n last name
die Narbe, -n scar
der Ofen, ¨n stove
das Paket, -e parcel, package
die Papiere (pl.) documents
die Paßnummer, -n passport number
der Pastor, -en minister, pastor, male
die Pastorin, -nen minister, pastor, female
der Physiker, - physicist, male
die Physikerin, -nen physicist, female
der Pilot, -en pilot, male
die Pilotin, -nen pilot, female
die Polizei police
der Polizist, -en police officer, male
die Polizistin, -nen police officer, female
die Prüfung, -en test, exam
der Psychologe, -n psychologist, male
die Psychologin, -nen psychologist, female
das Reisebüro, -s travel agency
der Richter, - judge
der Roman, -e novel
der Sänger, - singer, male
die Sängerin, -nen singer, female
der Satz, ¨e sentence
die Sehenswürdigkeit, -en site of interest
das Selbstbiographische autobiographical matters
die Staatsangehörigkeit citizenship
die Stellung, -en position

das Stichwort, ¨er key word, cue
die Technik technology
der Telegrammstil telegram style (very brief)
der Tierarzt, ¨e veterinarian, male
die Tierärztin, -nen veterinarian, female
der Toaster, - toaster
die Trompete, -n trumpet
die Unkosten (pl.) expenses
der Verkäufer, - salesman
die Verkäuferin, -nen saleswoman
der Verein, -e club, association
das Versandhaus, ¨er mail order house
der Volksschullehrer, - elementary school teacher, male
die Volksschullehrerin, -en elementary school teacher, female
der Vorname, -n first name
der Wagnerliebhaber, - lover of Wagnerian music
die Witwe, -n widow
der Witwer, - widower
der Wohnort, -e place of residence
der Zahn, ¨e tooth
der Zahnarzt, ¨e dentist, male
die Zahnärztin, -nen dentist, female

Verbs

ab·schicken to send off
auf·kommen (für), kam auf, ist aufgekommen to assume the cost
aus·fragen to question, quiz
aus·führen to carry out, implement
basteln to do crafts, to tinker
beantworten to answer
sich bedanken (für) to thank, say thanks
bedauern to regret
behandeln to treat
diskutieren to discuss
entdecken to discover
erreichen to reach, contact
erwarten to expect
feiern to celebrate
her·stellen to manufacture
mit·bringen, brachte mit, mitgebracht to bring along
nähen to sew

operieren   to operate
pflegen   to take care of, to nurse
predigen   to preach
reinigen   to clean
reparieren   to repair
sammeln   to collect, gather
Schi·fahren (fährt Schi), fuhr Schi, ist Schi gefahren   to ski
stehlen (stiehlt) stahl, gestohlen   to steal
stricken   to knit
surfen   to surf
tippen   to type
übersetzen   to translate
verdienen   to earn
vermissen   to miss
zerstören   to destroy
zurück·senden   to send back

Other Words

arm   poor
attraktiv   attractive, good looking
berühmt   famous
besonders   special
charmant   charming
dasselbe   the same
eigentlich   actual(ly)
einfach   simple

eingebildet   arrogant
falsch   false
freundlich   friendly
geschieden   divorced
hochachtungsvoll   respectful
impulsiv   impulsive
klug   smart
kräftig   strong
ledig   single
meistens   mostly, most of the time
natürlich   naturally, of course
neugierig   curious
passend   suitable, matching
reich   rich
sauber   clean
schlank   slender
sondern   but, on the contrary
sportlich   athletic
verheiratet   married
vorsichtig   careful
weit   far
zufrieden   satisfied, pleased

Idiomatic Expressions

Es liegt uns viel daran...   We are very much concerned, it matters to us
Freude machen   to give joy, to bring joy

Answers for Exercises

This section of the book provides answers for all exercises in the 10 chapters. We suggest that you check each answer *after* you have done the exercise.

Kapitel 1

A.   Übung p. 4

Sample responses:

1.   Wo wohnen Sie? Wo arbeiten/leben/spielen/bleiben…Sie?
2.   Wie heißen Sie? Wie heißt er/sie? Wie ist das Wetter? Wie geht's?
3.   Wer ist sie/er? Wer kommt heute? Wer spielt Tennis?
4.   Was machen Sie? Was trinken Sie? Was fragt sie/er?
5.   Wieviel kostet das? Wieviele Kinder haben Sie? Wieviele Kinder hat er/sie?
6.   Wie lange fahren wir? Wie lange bleibt er/sie? Wie lange arbeiten Sie heute?
7.   Wohin gehen wir? Wohin fahren Sie? Wohin reist er/sie? Wohin wandern wir heute?
8.   Woher kommen Sie? Woher kommt er/sie? Woher kommen sie?
9.   Wann kommen Sie? Wann gehen Sie ins Kino?

B.   Übung p. 4

Matching answers and additional sample responses:

1.   .c….Ich wohne in Chicago. Ich wohne zu Hause. Ich wohne hier.
2.   .d….Ich heiße Karl Schmidt.
3.   .b,f..Danke, gut. Und Ihnen?
4.   .i….Aus Bonn. Ich komme aus Amerika/New York/Kalifornien.
5.   .j,e…Ich gehe ins Konzert. Ich fahre nach Wien. Ich spiele Tennis. Ich bleibe zu Hause.
6.   .a….Fünfzig Mark. Es kostet 15 Franken. 30 Schilling.
7.   .g,k..Am fünfzehnten Mai. Am Wochenende. Ich bleibe hier.
8.   .h….Zwei Monate. Wir bleiben zwei Tage. Ich bleibe vier Wochen.
9.   .l….Nach Frankfurt. Ich fahre nach Berlin. Wir fahren nach Hause.
10. .m…Drei. Wir haben zwei Kinder. Wir haben keine Kinder.

C. Übung pp. 4–5

1. Wie geht es Ihnen? (or: Wie geht's?)
2. Wieviel kostet das?
3. Wie heißen Sie?
4. Was machen Sie heute abend?
5. Wo wohnen Sie?
6. Woher kommen Sie?
7. Darf ich vorstellen…?
8. Wohin gehen Sie?
9. Ich heiße…
10. Ich komme aus…
11. Ich wohne (lebe) in…
12. Vielen Dank!
13. Bitte schön! (or: Gern geschehen!)
14. Ich fahre nach München.

A. Übung p. 6

1. Eltern	6. Schwester
2. Geld	7. das Telefon
3. das Auto/der Bus	8. die Milch
4. der Polizist	9. die Gabel/das Messer
5. Bruder	10. der Fernseher

A. Übung p. 7

1. er	6. Sie
2. wir	7. es
3. Sie	8. ich
4. sie	9. sie
5. ich	10. sie (note: if these pronouns start a new sentence, all of them have to be capitalized)

A. Übung p. 8

1. er	6. es
2. es	7. er
3. sie	8. sie
4. er	9. sie
5. es	10. sie

A. Übung p. 9

1. heißen	5. studiert
2. wohnt	6. arbeitet
3. kommt	7. frage
4. kaufe	8. antworten

B. Übung pp. 9–10

1. Hans tanzt gern.
2. Wir lernen gern Deutsch.

3. Ich trinke gern Kaffee.
4. Sie arbeiten gern.
5. Karin schwimmt gern.
6. Ich spiele gern Tennis.
7. Sie reisen gern.
8. Sie singen gern.
9. Er wandert gern.
10. Wir leben gern in Florida.

A.   Übung p. 11

1.	ist	6.	ist
2.	ist	7.	sind
3.	bin	8.	sind
4.	ist	9.	Sind
5.	sind	10.	ist.

B.   Übung p. 11

1.	haben	5.	hat
2.	hat	6.	Hast
3.	habe	7.	Hat
4.	hat	8.	Haben

C.   Übung—Translation for Übung A—p. 11

1. Mr. Braun is an American.
2. Beer is cheap in Germany.
3. I am sick today.
4. Franz is intelligent.
5. We are tired.
6. The suitcase is small.
7. The people are diligent.
8. We are from Switzerland.
9. Are you an American, Mr. Brown?
10. Karin is healthy again.

Translation for Übung B

1. We have a lot of time.
2. Hans has an expensive car.
3. I have a new house.
4. Karin has a (boy)friend.
5. The child has a ball.
6. Do you have a radio?
7. Does he have time?
8. Do Mr. and Mrs. Schmidt have children?

Wiederholung (Review) pp. 12–13

A.

1. Guten Tag! (or: Grüß Gott!)
2. Guten Morgen!

3. Guten Abend!
4. Guten Tag!
5. Guten Tag! (or: Guten Morgen!)

B.

1. Wann arbeitet Herr Schmidt?
2. Was kauft er?
3. Wie ist das Wetter?
4. Wieviel kostet es?
5. Wo wohnt Frau Müller?

C.

1. Ich reise gern.
2. Wie heißen Sie?
3. Wieviel kostet das Radio?
4. Wir spielen gern Tennis.
5. Sie haben keine Zeit.
6. Sie wohnt in München.
7. Entschuldigen Sie bitte.
8. Wohin gehen Sie jetzt?

D.

1. Ja, ich bin Amerikaner.
2. Ich fahre nach...
3. Ich wohne in...
4. Ja, ich reise gern.
5. Ich bleibe...

Kapitel 2

B. Übung p. 18

1. Meine Telefonnummer ist...
2. Meine Zimmernummer ist...
3. Meine Hausnummer ist...
4. Ich weiß nicht (I don't know) or: 4542 Kilometer. (2,823 miles)

C. Übung p. 18

1. dreiunddreißig plus vierzehn ist siebenundvierzig
2. siebenundachtzig minus dreizehn ist vierundsiebzig
3. siebenmal drei ist einundzwanzig
4. vierzig durch acht ist fünf
5. siebzehn plus sechs ist dreiundzwanzig
6. fünfmal sieben ist fünfunddreißig
7. zweiundvierzig minus acht ist vierunddreißig
8. fünfzig durch zehn ist fünf
9. zwölf plus neun ist einundzwanzig
10. fünfundzwanzig minus sechs ist neunzehn

D. Übung p. 19

1. Mt. McKinley ist 6194 Meter (or: 20,320 feet)
2. Ich bin...Meter...
3. Man bekommt heute...Mark
4. Ich habe...Bruder (Brüder) und...Schwester (Schwestern).
5. Ich bin...

A. Übung p. 20

1. Haben wir eine Wohnung?
2. Hat Hans ein Haus?
3. Ist es weit von Berlin nach Wien?
4. Bleiben wir zwei Wochen in Europa?
5. Hat Inge drei Brüder?
6. Hat Herr Braun viel Geld?

B. Übung p. 20

1. Wo
2. Wann
3. Wohin
4. Wo
5. Wie
6. Warum
7. Wieviel
8. Woher
9. Was
10. Wie lange

C. Übung p. 21

1. Wieviel kostet es?
2. Haben sie Kinder?
3. Bleibt sie drei Tage oder vier Tage?
4. Kostet es 38 Schilling oder 83 Schilling?
5. Wie weit ist es von hier?
6. Braucht sie Geld?

D. Übung p. 21

1. Es kostet 15 Mark.
2. Ich habe zwei Brüder und drei Schwestern.
3. Er kauft das Radio.
4. Es ist heute 12 Grad.
5. Sie bekommen morgen das Geld.
6. Ich habe nicht genug Zeit.

A. Übung pp. 22–23

1. Weihnachten ist am fünfundzwanzigsten Dezember. or: am fünfund-zwanzigsten
2. Der Nationalfeiertag der USA ist am vierten Juli.
3. Silvester ist am einunddreißigsten Dezember.
4. Neujahr ist am ersten Januar.
5. Ich fliege am... (nach Europa)
6. Ich fahre am... (nach Deutschland)
7. Ich habe am... Geburtstag.
8. Ich fahre am... nach Hause.

A. Übung (about fractions) p. 23

1. Hälfte	4. siebenzehntel
2. viertel	5. Dreiviertel
3. Achtel	

A. Übung p. 24

1. Fliegt sie am zwanzigsten nach Berlin?
2. Heiratet Hans am siebzehnten Juni?
3. Welcher Tag ist heute? or: Der wievielte (Tag) ist heute?
4. Kommen Sie am vierzehnten?
5. Ist der dreiundzwanzigste ein Montag?

B. Übung p. 24

1. Sie ist am einundzwanzigsten hier.
2. Der fünfte ist ein Samstag.
3. Er kommt am dreißigsten.
4. Wir fliegen am achtzehnten nach Deutschland.
5. Ich kaufe am zehnten Mai ein Haus.

A. Übung pp. 25–26

1. Ich nehme einen Zug.
2. Wir kennen ein Restaurant.
3. Hans sucht ein Buch.
4. Brauchen Sie eine Wohnung?
5. Kennt sie eine Journalistin?
6. Maria kauft einen Pullover.

B. Übung (negation) p. 26

1. kein Auto	5. keinen Bus
2. kein Geld	6. keine Pillen
3. keine Lederhose	7. keine Kinder
4. kein Bier	

C. Übung p. 26

1. kein Restaurant	4. kein Journalist
2. keinen Bahnhof	5. keine Straßenbahn
3. keine Journalistin	6. keinen Paß

A. Übung p. 28

1. mich	5. dich
2. sie	6. Sie
3. uns	7. sie
4. ihn	8. mich

A. Übung p. 28

1. Es/es	3. Er/ihn
2. Sie/sie	4. Es/es

5. Es/es
6. Er/ihn

7. Sie/sie
8. Er/ihn

A. Übung p. 29

1. einen Regenschirm
2. den Park
3. die Stadt
4. das Haus

5. den Zoo
6. den Tisch
7. das metrische System
8. die Frauen

A. Übung p. 30

1. nicht im Hotel
2. es nicht
3. nicht oft
4. morgen nicht
5. nicht schnell
6. heute abend nicht

B. Übung p. 30

1. Kommt er heute nicht?
2. Warum gehen Sie nicht nach Hause?
3. Arbeitet er heute abend nicht?
4. Brauchen Sie das nicht?
5. Warum bleibt sie nicht hier?

C. Übung p. 30

1. Sie geht nicht schnell.
2. Sie sprechen nicht zu schnell.
3. Er arbeitet nicht am Abend.
4. Sie zahlt die Rechnung nicht.
5. Wir essen nicht viel.

A. Übung p. 31

1. Inge geht nie allein in die Stadt.
2. Ich fahre am fünften Mai allein nach Hause.
3. Erich kommt immer pünktlich in die Schule.
4. Er ist morgen leider nicht zu Hause.
5. Ein Bus fährt alle 30 Minuten in die Stadt.

B. Übung p. 31

1. Sind Sie heute abend allein?
2. Sind wir heute pünktlich?
3. Ist er wieder krank?
4. Fährt der Bus alle 15 Minuten?

C. Übung p. 32

1. Herr Schulz kommt pünktlich ins Hotel.
2. Sie ist heute nicht zu Hause.
3. Sie bleiben bis morgen hier.
4. Hans fliegt morgen nach Hause.
5. Wir reisen am siebten nach Österreich.

Wiederholung pp. 32–33

A.

1. Ich trinke Milch.
2. Mein Freund ist krank.
3. Ich sehe dort eine Freundin.
4. Ich brauche 100 Mark.
5. Fritz kommt am 17. März.
6. Ich fahre heute nach Hamburg.
7. Ich komme aus Texas.
8. Ich bleibe bis zum 8. Mai.

B.

1.	kein	5.	keine
2.	nicht	6.	nicht
3.	keinen	7.	nicht
4.	keinen	8.	nichts

C.

1.	klein	5.	immer
2.	faul	6.	morgen
3.	dort	7.	alt
4.	billig	8.	schlecht

D.

1. Achtundsechzig Grad Fahrenheit ist zwanzig Grad Celsius.
2. Dreimal vier ist zwölf.
3. Hält der Bus hier?
4. Ich habe Durst.
5. Hat sie Hunger?
6. Hans und Inge heiraten im Frühling.
7. Welcher Tag ist heute? or: Der wievielte ist heute?
8. Ich frage ihn nicht.
9. Wir kaufen einen Computer.
10. Sie sind nicht gegen sie.

E.

1. Wohin fahren Sie am sechsundzwanzigsten?
2. Wieviel kostet das?
3. Was suchen Sie?
4. Trinken Sie Bier?
5. Gibt es hier ein Restaurant?
6. Brauchen Sie ein Zimmer?
7. Heiratet Otto im Herbst?
8. Sind Sie heute krank?

Kapitel 3

A. Übung pp. 37–38

1. wann der Bus kommt?
2. wohin diese Straßenbahn fährt?

3. wo hier der Ober ist?
4. wie teuer das ist?
5. wen ich frage?
6. warum die Suppe kalt ist?
7. wie der Herr heißt?
8. wann Herr Schmidt nach Hause fährt?

B. Übung p. 38

1. Suchen Sie eine Milchbar?
2. Fährt er mit dem Bus?
3. Nimmt Inge ein Taxi?
4. Kommst du ins Hotel?
5. Seht ihr das Taxi?
6. Finde ich das Restaurant?
7. Wartet sie auf die Straßenbahn?
8. Bestellt er das Menü?
9. Geht Hans zum Schnellimbiß?
10. Steht das Auto vor dem Hotel?

A. Übung pp. 38–39

1. weiß		5. Wissen	
2. wissen		6. weiß	
3. weiß		7. weiß	
4. wissen		8. Weißt	

B. Übung p. 39

1. Wo gibt es ein Restaurant? or: Wo ist ein Restaurant?
2. Weiß Hans, wo der Bus hält?
3. Wieviel kostet die Zeitung?
4. Wissen Sie, warum sie nach Hause fährt?
5. Ich weiß nicht, wann die Straßenbahn kommt.
6. Wir wissen, wie billig das Gasthaus ist.
7. Weißt du, wo ich wohne?
8. Wen frage ich?

DIALOG: WAS SUCHT MR. SMITH? P. 3–5 TRANSLATION

Mr. Smith: Excuse me, please. Where is there a hotel or a restaurant?
passer-by A: A hotel? A restaurant? I am sorry. I don't know. I am not from here.
Mr. Smith: Please (excuse me), is there a hotel or a restaurant?
passer-by B: What are you looking for? A Hotel? No, there isn't a hotel here.
passer-by C: But a restaurant. Good and reasonably priced. Not far from here.
Mr. Smith: How far from here?
passer-by C: Do you see the traffic light over there?
Mr. Smith: Yes, I see it.
passer-by C: Go to the traffic light, and then to the right at the corner.
passer-by B: And from there go straight to the square. There is the restaurant "Zum Adler" (at the eagle).
Mr. Smith: And where do I find a hotel?
passer-by D: Take the bus to the Bahnhofstraße. There is the "Parkhotel".
passer-by C: Or take a Taxi.
Mr. Smith: How much does that cost?
passer-by C: I believe seven marks.
Mr. Smith: Thank you very much.

A. Übung p. 40

1. Bringen Sie ein Glas Wein!
2. Versuchen Sie diese Nachspeise!
3. Kochen Sie ohne Salz!
4. Warten Sie auf den nächsten Bus!
5. Kommen Sie heute abend!
6. Gehen Sie zur Ecke!
7. Wählen Sie das Beefsteak!
8. Fragen Sie den Ober!
9. Nehmen Sie wenig Pfeffer!
10. Fahren Sie mit einem Taxi!

A. Übung p. 42

1. können	6. muß
2. will	7. darf
3. Wollen	8. können
4. kann	9. dürfen
5. sollen	10. willst

A. Übung p. 43

1. möchte eine Tasse Kaffee.
2. möchte eine Tasse Tee trinken.
3. möchte jetzt essen.
4. möchten Sie wohnen?
5. möchte etwas Leichtes essen.
6. möchten zahlen, bitte.
7. möchtest du trinken?
8. möchte einen Tisch bestellen.
9. möchte ein Gasthaus finden.
10. möchten Sie fahren?

C. Übung p. 45

1. bringen Sie	6. Haben Sie
2. möchte	7. Wie teuer ist
3. Möchten Sie	8. möchte
4. Können…empfehlen	9. trinken
5. Wie	10. wieviel

A. Übung p. 46

1. die Restaurants zu teuer sind
2. er mit einem Taxi fährt
3. das Essen billig ist
4. es ein preiswertes Hotel gibt
5. ich wenig Geld habe
6. das Wetter kalt ist

B. Übung pp. 46–47

1. Ich bin glücklich, weil ich jetzt in Deutschland bin.
2. Wir zahlen jetzt, damit wir nach Hause gehen können.
3. Der Kellner empfiehlt das Menü, obwohl es nicht gut ist.

4. Meine Frau bleibt in Europa, während ich hier arbeite.
5. Ich weiß nicht, ob die Obstsuppe kalt ist.
6. Der Kellner gibt uns einen Tisch am Fenster, weil er uns kennt.
7. Herr König fährt oft mit dem Auto, obwohl das Benzin teuer ist.
8. Wissen Sie, wie oft der Bus fährt?

C. Übung p. 47

1. Ich möchte Pilze, wenn sie nicht zu teuer sind.
2. Wir wohnen im Hotel Dresden, bis wir ein Haus kaufen.
3. Er soll nach Hause kommen, weil er kein Geld hat.
4. Ich möchte Sie sehen, obwohl ich krank bin. or: Ich möchte dich sehen…
5. Mein Freund sucht die Kellnerin, damit er zahlen kann.
6. Sie gehen nicht nach Hause, bis Sie kommen.
7. Fritz bestellt eine Vorspeise, wenn er in einem Restaurant ißt.
8. Sie können reisen, wenn Sie Zeit haben.

D. Übung p. 48

1. Ich nehme Gulasch mit Knödel.
2. Essen Sie Austern?
3. Ich empfehle heute Spargelspitzen oder Wiener Schnitzel mit Reis.
4. Ich möchte das Fleisch gut durchgebraten.
5. Bitte bringen Sie mir Schweinebraten mit Kartoffelbrei.
6. Er möchte Tomatensuppe.
7. Möchten Sie das Rippensteak gegrillt?
8. Wieviel kostet der Schinken?

E. Übung pp. 49–50

1. möchte
2. möchten
3. Möchtest

4. möchten
5. Möchtet
6. möchten

F. Übung p. 50 (sample answers)

1. gedämpft/gekocht
2. gebacken/gegrillt/gebraten
3. vom Rost/gegrillt/gebraten
4. gebacken/gegrillt/gebraten
5. gekocht/gefüllt/gebraten
6. geschmort/gegrillt/gebraten
7. vom Rost/gegrillt/gebraten

G. Übung p. 50

1. Frikadellen
2. Äpfel
3. Spargel

4. Zwiebel
5. Pommes frites
6. Trauben

H. Übung p. 50

1. Haben Sie gefüllte Tomaten?
2. Ich möchte mein Steak durchgebraten.
3. Bitte dämpfen Sie die Karotten.
4. Ich habe Früchte/Obst nicht gern.

5. Karin bestellt immer Salat.
6. Möchten Sie im Restaurant oder zu Hause essen?
7. Ich möchte das Menü empfehlen.
8. Bitte bringen Sie mir Faschiertes (Hackbraten) und Kartoffelbrei.

A. Übung p. 51

1. c
2. b.

B. Übung p. 52

1. Wohin fährt der Bus?
2. Kommt der Bus bald?
3. Wieviel kostet es?

C. Übung p. 52

1. Gibt es noch etwas Warmes zu essen?
2. Ich möchte etwas Leichtes.
3. Ich möchte auch ein Zimmer.
4. Wieviel kostet das Zimmer?

D. Übung p. 52

1. Ich bin Amerikaner (Amerikanerin) or: Ich bin Engländer (Engländerin)
2. Ja, ich wohne hier im Hotel.
3. Ich fahre nach…

E. Übung p. 52
Ich wähle c, e, h

F. Übung p. 53 (matching)

1.	b	8.	g
2.	c	9.	h
3.	f	10.	a
4.	j	11.	m
5.	e	12.	l
6.	d	13.	k
7.	i		

Situationen p. 53 (sample answers)

1. Ich möchte etwas Leichtes essen / Ich möchte nur Salat / Ich möchte nur ein Sandwich.
2. Bitte, wo ist eine Milchbar / ein Schnellimbiß?
3. Ist es weit von hier?
4. Soll ich eine Straßenbahn oder einen Bus nehmen?

A. Übung p. 54

1.	der Leberkäse	5.	das Gasthaus
2.	das Naturschnitzel	6.	die Spargelspitzen
3.	der Käsekuchen	7.	das Fruchteis
4.	die Obsttorte		

B. Übung p. 54

1. die Straßenbahn
2. das Gasthaus
3. die Bushaltestelle
4. der Käsekuchen
5. der Stadtplan
6. die Hausfrau
7. der Hotelportier

Wiederholung pp. 54–55

A.

1. Gehen Sie/Fahren Sie geradeaus/nach links/nach rechts
2. Gehen Sie bis zur Ecke/bis zum Schild/über die Brücke
3. Nehmen Sie den Bus/die Straßenbahn/ein Taxi
4. Bringen Sie die Speisekarte/die Zeitung/das Telefonbuch

B.

1. Bringen Sie mir ein Coca Cola/ein Glas Milch/die Speisekarte
2. Ich möchte das Fleisch nicht durchgebraten/durchgebraten
3. Ich möchte das Gemüse gedämpft/gedünstet
4. Ich möchte den Nachtisch mit Schlag/ohne Schlag

C.

1. Wir warten schon lange./Ich warte schon lange.
2. Die Suppe ist kalt.
3. Das Bier ist warm.
4. Das ist versalzen.
5. Das Tischtuch ist nicht sauber.
6. Das Fleisch ist zäh.

D.

1. Wo ist hier ein Telefon? or: Gibt es hier ein Telefon?
2. Bitte noch ein Glas Wein/eine Tasse Kaffee/ein Eis
3. Bitte, ist der Platz besetzt/ist der Platz noch frei
4. Bitte, gibt es noch etwas Warmes (zu essen)?/Mittagessen/Abendessen

E.

1. Die Rechnung bitte. or: Bitte, zahlen/es war gut/wir kommen wieder.
2. Wir waren zufrieden.
3. Entschuldigen Sie bitte. or: Verzeihung.
4. Auf Wiedersehen.

F.

1. f	9. f
2. d	10. c
3. f	11. f
4. d	12. c
5. e	13. d
6. d	14. c
7. e	15. d
8. c	16. b

Kapitel 4

A.   Übung p. 61

1. den Freunden	4. dem Professor
2. dem Arzt	5. dem Mädchen
3. dem Kind	6. der Managerin

A.   Übung pp. 61–62

1. dem Herrn	5. den Freunden
2. den Kindern	6. dem Touristen
3. den Studenten	7. den Touristen
4. dem Freund	

B.   Übung p. 62

1. Geben Sie es den Touristen.
2. Wir zeigen es der Mutter.
3. Ich sage es dem Lehrer.
4. Karl schreibt dem Geschäftsmann.
5. Ich sage es den Leuten.

A.   Übung p. 62

1. dem Bus	4. einem Monat
2. dem Geschäft	5. dem Konzert
3. den Freunden	

A.   Übung p. 63

1. ihm	4. mir
2. uns	5. ihnen
3. ihr	6. dir

A.   Übung pp. 63–64

1. ihr	5. ihm
2. ihm	6. ihr
3. ihnen	7. ihm
4. ihnen	8. ihr

B.   Übung p. 64

1. Bitte helfen Sie der Frau.
2. Glaubt er dem Amerikaner nicht?
3. Das paßt den Österreichern nicht.
4. Wir danken den Deutschen.
5. Diese Wohnung gefällt der Studentin.
6. Das Haus gehört der Firma.
7. Schmeckt es den Gästen?
8. ...daß Sie dem Kind nicht helfen können.

A.   Übung p. 65

1. Wann zieht Maria in die neue Wohnung ein?
2. Bitte nehmen Sie das Buch mit.
3. Herr Braun ruft Sie morgen an.

4. Bitte machen Sie das Fenster zu.
5. Wann fliegen Sie nach Amerika zurück?
6. Der Zug fährt um 16 Uhr 40 ab.
7. Herr Richter kommt am Freitag an.
8. Wann fängt das Konzert an?

B. Übung p. 65

1. …Maria am Mittwoch zurückfliegt.
2. …Ernst im Sommer umzieht.
3. …das Spiel um 19 Uhr anfängt.
4. …Ingrid nach Österreich mitkommt.
5. …er am Sonntag abfährt.
6. …dort immer aussteigt.

A. Übung pp. 66–67

1. a. ihr den Koffer
   b. ihn Elke
   c. ihn ihr
2. a. ihnen ein Haus
   b. es den Amerikanern
   c. es ihnen
3. a. ihnen die Stadt
   b. sie den Freunden
   c. sie ihnen

B. Übung p. 67 (sample answers)

1. Wir zeigen den Deutschen ein Auto.
2. Ich bringe ihnen einen Koffer.
3. Er kauft es ihr.

Kurzer Geschäftsbrief p. 67 (Translation)

Dear Mr. Müller,

My colleague, John Tyler, and I will arrive in Düsseldorf on June 23rd at 3:30 p.m. with Lufthansa flight 79 from Hamburg. Are you picking us up or should we go directly to the hotel? We would be happy if you could pick us up, but it is not necessary.

Please let us know before we depart from here.

Cordially,

your….

A. Übung p. 68

1. die Stadt
2. dem Hotel
3. das Haus
4. einem Mann
5. dem Tisch
6. einen Berg
7. einem Gasthof
8. dem Gasthaus
9. dem Sofa
10. die Ecke

B. Übung pp. 68–69

1. übers Wetter
2. ans Fenster
3. vorm Geschäft
4. ins Büro
5. im Koffer
6. unterm Tisch

C. Übung p. 69

1. Wir wohnen im Hotel.
2. Bringen Sie den Brief ins Büro?
3. Ich arbeite jetzt im Geschäft.
4. Frau Müller reist in die Schweiz.
5. Karin geht in das Gasthaus.

Wiederholung pp. 69–70

A.

1. Gibt es noch ein Zimmer?
2. Ist es ein Einzelzimmer oder ein Doppelzimmer?
3. Wieviel kostet es?
4. Kann ich die Wohnung sehen?
5. Wann kann ich einziehen?
6. Gibt es einen Mietvertrag?
7. Wie lange kann man die Ferienwohnung mieten?
8. Darf man Hunde in der Wohnung haben? or: Sind Hunde in der Wohnung erlaubt?
9. Wieviele Zimmer hat die Wohnung?
10. Wann soll ich anrufen?

B.

1. Ich ziehe diesen Sommer nach Zürich um.
2. Oskar mietet eine Ferienwohnung in Österreich.
3. Die Wohnung hat zwei Zimmer, einen Balkon und eine Küche.
4. Sie bleiben gern in New York.
5. Dieser Koffer gehört mir nicht.
6. Ich möchte sie gern kennenlernen.

C.

1. ihnen	4. einem Studenten
2. ihr	5. den Studenten
3. ihm	6. uns

D.

1. Wir holen Franz am Wochenende ab. We pick up Franz on the weekend.
2. Ich rufe am Sonntag an. I'll call on Sunday.
3. Ich lerne ihn auf der Party kennen. I am meeting him at the party.
4. Er nimmt den Koffer nicht mit. He is not taking along the suitcase.
5. Wo steigen wir aus? Where are we getting off?
6. Wann ziehe ich dort ein? When am I moving in there?
7. Erika kommt am Freitag an. Erika is arriving on Friday.
8. Das Konzert fängt um 19 Uhr an. The concert begins at 7 p.m.

E.

1. ihm das Buch	4. ihn ihr
2. ihn ihr	5. ihm die Schlüssel
3. es dem Gast	6. ihm das Auto

F.

1. Die Wohnung gehört ihr.
2. Wann kommen Sie in Frankfurt an?
3. Das Haus gefällt uns nicht.
4. Sie kommt am Mittwoch zurück.
5. Bitte zeigen Sie mir die Zweizimmerwohnung.
6. Ich möchte sie kennenlernen.
7. Steigen Sie am Markt aus.
8. Die Gäste möchten ein Zimmer mit Dusche.
9. Ich muß um sieben Uhr aufstehen.
10. Bitte helfen Sie dem Mädchen.

Kapitel 5

A.   Übung pp. 75–76

1. viertel nach sechs
2. halbe Stunde
3. neun Uhr fünfunddreißig
4. viertel vor acht
5. ein Uhr
6. viertel nach fünf
7. halb elf

B.   Übung p. 76

1. um sechzehn Uhr fünfundvierzig
2. viertel nach elf, or: elf Uhr fünfzehn
3. um zwanzig Uhr
4. bis viertel vor sechs
5. zweiundvierzig Stunden
6. um halb fünf, or: um vier Uhr dreißig

C.   Übung p. 76

1. Wir essen jeden Tag um viertel vor sechs.
2. Ich komme um halb drei zurück.
3. Bitte rufen Sie mich um halb elf (zehn Uhr dreißig) an.
4. Um wieviel Uhr fährt sie ab?
5. Er ruft mich jede halbe Stunde an.
6. Können Sie uns morgen besuchen?
7. Ich muß um neunzehn Uhr vierzig am Bahnhof sein.
8. Wir sind in drei Stunden zu Hause.

A.   Übung p. 79

1. gewohnt	5. abgeflogen
2. gewesen	6. reserviert
3. geschrieben	7. studiert
4. angerufen	8. vergessen

B.   Übung p. 79

1. Ich habe gern in diesem Büro gearbeitet.
2. Wir sind zwei Tage in Hamburg geblieben.

3. Haben Sie Frau Hödl angerufen?
4. Otto ist nicht zu Hause gewesen.
5. Bist du in den Zoo gegangen?
6. Die Amerikaner haben das Restaurant nicht gefunden.
7. Wohin sind die Kinder gelaufen?
8. Ich habe nie einen Parkplatz gefunden.

D. Übung p. 80 (sample answers)

1. gefahren/gegangen/gereist
2. gelesen/gekauft
3. abgefahren/angekommen
4. gesehen/gehört/gekauft
5. gereist/gefahren
6. gefallen
7. getroffen/gesehen/gefunden
8. gewesen/geblieben
9. gefahren/gegangen
10. getroffen/gefunden/gesehen

A. Übung p. 82

1. Wo ist Karins Vater?
2. Ist das Karls Zimmer?
3. Wissen (Kennen) Sie den Namen des Professors?
4. Ich habe die Adresse des Restaurants nicht.
5. Die Eltern der Kinder sind abgefahren.
6. Möchten Sie Heidis Fotos sehen?
7. Wir können Johns Auto nicht kaufen.

Wiederholung pp. 82–83

A. (sample answers)

7:00 ich stehe auf/ich frühstücke
7:45 ich fahre zur Arbeit/ich komme im Büro an
8:15 ich komme im Büro an/ich gehe zur Arbeit
9:30 ich spreche mit Kunden/ich lese die Post
10:30 ich trinke einen Kaffee/ich spreche mit Kunden
12:30 ich gehe Mittagessen/ich gehe in den Park
13:45 ich gehe ins Büro zurück/ich lese die Zeitung
15:00 ich spreche mit dem Chef/ich telefoniere
16:30 ich arbeite im Büro/ich bespreche mich mit Kollegen
17:15 ich gehe nach Hause/ich fahre nach Hause/ich rufe meine Frau/meinen
      Mann an
17:45 ich kaufe etwas ein
18:00 ich komme zu Hause an/ich lese die Zeitung
19:00 ich esse zu Abend/ich höre mir die Nachrichten an
20:00 ich besuche einen Nachbarn/ich spiele mit den Kindern
21:00 ich sehe fern/ich lese ein Buch/ich spiele Klavier
22:30 ich gehe ins Bett/ich lese im Bett

B.

Am 8. Mai bin ich um 18:15 in Berlin angekommen. Vom Flughafen habe ich ein Taxi genommen und bin sofort zum Hotel gefahren. Ich habe den Portier gefragt, ob er ein Zimmer für mich reserviert hat. Ja, ich habe Glück gehabt. Ich habe ein Zimmer für drei Tage bekommen. Ich bin drei Tage in Berlin gewesen. Ich habe einige deutsche Firmen besucht und ich bin auch öfters bei deutschen Kollegen gewesen. Herr Müller von der Firma Siemens hat mir auch eine neue Fabrik gezeigt. Am Wochenende haben wir einen Ausflug in den Grunewald gemacht. An einem Abend bin ich ins Konzert gegangen. Es hat mir gut gefallen. Die Berliner Philharmoniker haben Beethoven und Mozart gespielt.

Kapitel 6

A. Übung p. 88

1. Der Patient glaubte das nicht.
2. Großvater hörte nicht gut.
3. Was fehlte Ihnen?
4. Der Ausländer sagte nichts.
5. Ich fühlte mich nicht gut.
6. Wir lernten Deutsch.
7. Wo arbeiteten Sie?
8. Der Tourist fragte sehr viel.

B. Übung pp. 89–90

1. Karin nahm die Tabletten. Karin took the tablets.
2. Der Arzt verschrieb Penicillin. The doctor prescribed penicillin.
3. Wer bekam oft Post? Who received mail often?
4. In Deutschland trank man viel Bier. In Germany one (they) drank a lot of beer.
5. Die Amerikaner aßen viele Hamburger. The Americans ate a lot of hamburgers.
6. Die Touristen besuchten viele Museen. The tourists visited many museums.
7. Wir schrieben oft nach Hause. We often wrote home.
8. Ich arbeitete jeden Tag. I worked every day.
9. Frau Müller las ein interessantes Buch. Mrs. Müller read an interesting book.
10. Der Gast verstand die Leute nicht. The guest didn't understand the people.

C. Übung p. 90

1. ...stand ich auf.
2. ...frühstückte ich.
3. ...las ich ein Buch.
4. ...ging ich einkaufen.
5. ...besuchte ich einen Freund.
6. ...aßen wir wieder.
7. ...ging ich nach Hause.
8. ...arbeitete ich im Garten.

9.   ...sah ich einen Film.
10.   ...rief ich meine Mutter an.
11.   ...ging ich ins Bett.

D.   Übung p. 90 (sample answers)

Dialog 1

1.   Er hatte Halsschmerzen.
2.   Er wollte noch ein bißchen warten.
3.   Er hieß Dr. Müscher.
4.   Klaus fuhr ihn zum Arzt.

Dialog 2

1.   Ihr Blinddarm mußte raus.
2.   Er empfahl ihr das Universitätskrankenhaus.
3.   Frau K.s (Kleins) Mutter war auch im Universitätskrankenhaus.

Dialog 3

1.   Ihr war schwindelig.
2.   Karin besuchte sie.
3.   Sie nahm vor einer Stunde zwei Aspirin.
4.   Sie trank zwei Liter.
5.   Hoffentlich fühlst du dich bald besser.

Dialog 4

1.   Er hatte schreckliche Ohrenschmerzen.
2.   Nein, er hatte auch Halsschmerzen.
3.   Er verschrieb Tabletten.

A.   Übung p. 92 (sample answers)

1.	a, b	5.	b, d
2.	c	6.	d
3.	b, d	7.	c, d
4.	b, d		

B.   Übung p. 92 (sample answers)

1.   Ich legte mich ins Bett. / Ich nahm Tabletten.
2.   Ich hatte Halsschmerzen.
3.   Wenn der Blinddarm raus muß. / Wenn man einen Herzanfall hat.
4.   Wenn man Fieber hat. / Wenn man *sehr* krank ist.
5.   Ich nahm Aspirin. / Ich trank viel.
6.   Ja, wir haben einen Hausarzt. / Nein, wir haben keinen Hausarzt.
7.   Sie rauchen zu viel.
8.   Einmal / zweimal im Jahr.
9.   Nein, ich bekomme nicht genug Schlaf.
10.   Wenn man richtig ißt. / Wenn man fit bleibt.

A.   Übung p. 94

1.	sich	3.	sich
2.	sich	4.	sich

5. mir   8. mich
6. uns   9. mir
7. sich   10. sich

B.   Übung pp. 94–95

1. Wir müssen uns beeilen.
2. Herr Johnson rasierte sich nicht (hat sich nicht rasiert).
3. Elke fühlt sich nicht wohl.
4. Ich kaufe mir eine Uhr.
5. Wir treffen uns um 10 Uhr mit Dr. Blume.
6. Ich kann mich an den Namen nicht erinnern.
7. Ich putze mir die Zähne.
8. Karl zieht sich an.
9. Linda, hast du dir die Haare gekämmt?
10. Ich glaube, Sie irren sich.

A.   Übung p. 95

1. ihren   6. Mein
2. seinen   7. unser
3. ihre   8. Ihre
4. ihren   9. dein
5. seinen   10. ihren

B.   Übung p. 96

1. unsere Autoschlüssel   6. Ihr Buch
2. meinen Regenschirm   7. seinen Anzug
3. seinen Koffer   8. mein Wörterbuch
4. ihr Auto   9. unsere Kinder
5. ihre Theaterkarte   10. ihre Schwester

A.   Übung pp. 96–97

1. Als   6. wenn
2. wann   7. Als
3. wann   8. Wann
4. Wenn   9. wann
5. Wenn   10. als

Wiederholung p. 97

A.

1. gehen, ging, ist gegangen
2. schreiben, schrieb, geschrieben
3. essen, aß, gegessen
4. trinken, trank, getrunken
5. fahren, fuhr, ist gefahren
6. ankommen, kam an, ist angekommen
7. sein, war, ist gewesen
8. haben, hatte, gehabt
9. nehmen, nahm, genommen
10. geben, gab, gegeben

B.

1. Kauftest du dir einen Koffer? or: Hast du dir einen Koffer gekauft?
2. Er rasiert sich morgens und abends.
3. Sahst du meinen Bruder? or: Hast du meinen Bruder gesehen?
4. Ich nahm ein Aspirin. or: Ich habe ein Aspirin genommen.
5. Vielleicht hat sie die Grippe.
6. Wir müssen jetzt gehen.

C.

1. Wann war er im Kino?
2. Was hat sich Hans gekauft?
3. Was sind wir gestern gewesen?
4. Wer bekommt nicht genug Schlaf?
5. Wohin fuhr Herr Schwarz gestern?

Kapitel 7

A. Übung p. 101

1. krank	6. schlecht
2. fleißig	7. kalt
3. spät	8. kurz
4. alt	9. laut
5. jung	10. leicht

A. Übung pp. 102–103

1. kurzer	6. roten/weißen
2. nächste	7. frischen
3. billige/saubere	8. lange
4. dummen	9. hohen
5. deutsche	10. kranke

B. Übung p. 103

1. Sie haben hübsches schwarzes Haar.
2. Ich kenne einen guten Arzt.
3. Wir sehen uns einen interessanten Film an.
4. Mir gefällt diese kleine Stadt.
5. Deutsch ist eine leichte Sprache.
6. Franz ist ein schwieriges Kind.
7. Sie sollten oft grünes Gemüse essen.
8. Haben Sie ein billiges Zimmer?
9. Sie gehen immer in teure Restaurants.
10. Wir kaufen ein neues Haus.

A. Übung pp. 103–104

1. Mein Ältester bekommt ein neues Auto.
2. Der Große ist mein Sohn.
3. Ich kenne die Kleine nicht.
4. Meine Jüngste ist Ärztin.
5. Helfen Sie doch der Kranken.
6. In Amerika gibt es viele Arme.
7. Pele ist der Beste.

A. Übung pp. 105–106

1. roten Ball
2. großen Rosenbusch
3. guter Marmelade
4. junger Mann

5. blondes Haar
6. kühl
7. neu
8. gute Schwimmer

A. Übung p. 106

1. jenes
2. diese
3. welche

4. jenen
5. solche

Wiederholung pp. 106–107

A.

1. Ich höre jeden Abend die Nachrichten.
2. Wir kaufen heute ein neues Auto.
3. Der Arzt kann dem Kranken nicht helfen.
4. Trinken Sie gern schwarzen Kaffee?
5. Weil das Wetter heiß ist, gehen wir heute schwimmen. or: Wir gehen heute schwimmen, weil das Wetter heiß ist.

B.

1. t	6. b	11. g	16. s
2. h	7. f	12. d	17. p
3. c	8. e	13. r	18. o
4. i	9. j	14. n	19. l
5. a	10. k	15. q	20. m

Kapitel 8

A. Übung p. 111

1. so alt wie Ingrid
2. so schnell wie Otto
3. es so heiß wie heute

4. so wenig Zeit wie du
5. so gut wie Mary
6. so viel wie Robert

B. Übung p. 112

1. noch größer
2. noch weiter
3. dauert noch länger
4. noch billiger

5. noch älter
6. noch höher
7. noch wärmer

C. Übung p. 113

1. jüngste
2. schnellste
3. größte

4. schönste
5. älteste

D. Übung p. 113

1. mehr/meisten
2. besser/besten

3. höher/höchsten
4. lieber/liebsten

A.   Übung pp. 116–117

1.   Wenn Hans nicht krank wäre, würde er täglich vier Kilometer laufen.
2.   Was würden Sie machen, wenn Sie Kopfschmerzen hätten?
3.   Wenn wir Urlaub hätten, würden wir ins Ausland reisen.
4.   Würden Sie Deutsch lernen?
5.   Ich würde gern wandern, wenn es warm wäre.
6.   Wir würden mit Ihnen fahren, wenn es Ihnen recht wäre.

A.   Übung p. 119

1.   hätten/hätten
2.   hätte/hätte
3.   wären/wäre

4.   hätten/hätten
5.   wäre/hätte

B.   Übung p. 119

1.   a.   Wenn ich das nur wüßte.
     b.   Wenn ich das nur gewußt hätte.
2.   a.   Wenn es nur wärmer wäre.
     b.   Wenn es nur wärmer gewesen wäre.
3.   a.   Wenn wir nur den Hund fänden.
     b.   Wenn wir nur den Hund gefunden hätten.
4.   a.   Wenn wir nur mehr Ferien (Urlaub) hätten.
     b.   Wenn wir nur mehr Ferien (Urlaub) gehabt hätten.
5.   a.   Wenn er nur das Geld hätte.
     b.   Wenn er nur das Geld gehabt hätte.

Wiederholung pp. 120–121

A.

1.   schneller
2.   größer
3.   heißer

4.   weniger
5.   billiger
6.   weiter

B.

1.   mehr
2.   besser
3.   lieber

4.   besser
5.   höher

C.

1.   am kältesten
2.   der Schwerste (am schwersten)
3.   am liebsten

4.   das Teuerste (am teuersten)
5.   am besten
6.   am liebsten

D.

1.   Im Sommer würden wir gern in den Bergen wandern.
2.   Ich würde sie nicht fragen.
3.   Wir würden ihm nicht glauben.
4.   Wer würde das Geld bekommen?
5.   Das würden wir uns auch wünschen.
6.   Ich würde die Rechnung morgen zahlen.

7. Mir hätte dieses Kleid besser gefallen.
8. Er wäre zu spät gekommen.
9. Wir wären gern nach Österreich gefahren.
10. Sie hätten es nicht getan.

E.

1. If we would have had a (longer) vacation, we would have stayed one more week in Switzerland.
2. I would go to the movie today if I did not have to do my taxes.
3. If I were a politician, I would not say that.
4. If the weather had been better, we would have gone on an outing.
5. I wish I could do something for my headaches.
6. It would be so nice if we had more money for traveling.
7. If there were a better map for hiking in this area, I would buy it immediately.
8. What would you have liked to see if you would have traveled to Germany.

Kapitel 9

A. Übung p. 127

1. der	6. den
2. der	7. das
3. die	8. dem
4. denen	9. deren
5. dessen	10. der

B. Übung p. 128

1. wo	4. wofür
2. woher	5. wohin
3. womit	

Am Bahnhof p. 128 (translation)

1. On track 7 is (stands) the express train which goes to Hannover.
2. The group, which travels to Hamburg, is waiting at window 2.
3. The exchange office, which is located in the departure hall, is open from 8 a.m. to 6 p.m.
4. The Americans, to whom they explained the train schedule, are going to Munich.
5. The train schedule, which they showed me, is no longer valid.
6. The restaurant, where we ate, is located on the second (third) floor.
7. The traveler, whose watch has stopped, is (being) late.
8. We are sending the luggage, which is too heavy, by train.

Die Presse pp. 128–129 (translation)

1. The article, which interested me, was in the "Süddeutsche Zeitung" yesterday.
2. The article, which I had wanted to read, was in yesterday's paper.
3. The journalist whose style I like is Peter Wallner.
4. The classified ads, whose content I sometimes don't understand, one finds on page 30.
5. The journalists with whom we had a discussion believed to know everything.

Auf der Post p. 129 (translation)

1. Here are the stamps which you have to put on your letters.
2. You must fill out the money order which you have given me.
3. This is a post office savings book with which you can withdraw money at any post office.
4. There are no post offices from which one can't make a phone call.
5. For every call one makes from the post office one has to pay at the window.

Am Telefon p. 129 (translation)

1. The lady, whose name I couldn't understand, spoke too softly.
2. The gentleman, who went into the telephone booth ahead of me, talked very long.
3. The telephone number, which was given to me, was not correct.
4. The telegram which the post office delivered to me, was from my parents.
5. My postal savings book, whose number I have forgotten, is at my home.

Lesestück pp. 129–130 (translation)
Etwas über die Presse in den deutschsprachigen Ländern (Something about the press in the German-speaking countries)

There is no democracy which can remain a democracy without freedom of the press. The older generation in Germany, from whom this freedom had been taken during the Nazi period, experienced that.

In Switzerland, where there has been a successful democracy for centuries, the first newspaper of Europe was published in 1597 in Goldach (canton St. Gallen). The right to independent information is very important for a country, in which one wants to live in freedom. Everybody should be able to write what he wants to write; and everybody should be able to read what he wants to read. It is no coincidence that one can find over 400 newspapers in little Switzerland (population 4 million).

In the Federal Republic of Germany, in which 63 million people are living today, there are about 1250 newspapers. They represent different political opinions, for instance the *Süddeutsche Zeitung* (liberal), the *Frankfurter Allgemeine Zeitung* (conservative-liberal) or the *Welt* (conservative). Add to that (literally: to that come) political weeklies like *Die Zeit* (liberal) or the *Rheinische Merkur* (conservative).

Der Spiegel, a weekly news magazine which is similar to the American *Time* and *Newsweek,* has a special position in the West German press. The *Spiegel* sees its role as a political watchdog. Politicians who are on the warpath with the *Spiegel* are afraid of biting (sharp) and often arrogant criticism from this magazine.

Seven of ten newspapers which the West Germans are reading every day come into the house as a subscription paper. In the Federal Republic the press belongs to the private sector; in the German Democratic Republic it is the state that controls the press.

In Austria, too, the constitution guarantees the freedom of the press. "Die Neue Kronenzeitung," the "Kurier" and "Die Presse" belong (count) to those newspapers of Austria that one can buy everywhere in the country. Of the regional papers, the *Salzburger Nachrichten* is especially well-known for the independent reporting of the news.

It is an interesting fact that in today's Germany—in the Federal Republic, as well as in the German Democratic Republic—there are fewer newspapers than there were before World War II. In 1932, 2889 newspapers were published (literally appeared) in Germany, more than double the number of today. Who were the losers in this demise of newspapers? They were local newspapers who could no longer compete with the big newspapers, and party newspapers that lack the political "hinterland" today.

"The big ones are devouring the little ones;" this trend in the German press worries many Germans. It is a trend which could become a problem for the freedom of the press. In a genuine democracy one would like to hear, yes, one must hear, many voices.

A.   Übung p. 130

I.	4	IV.	1 and 3
II.	3	V.	2 and 4
III.	2		

Wiederholung pp. 132–133

A. (sample answers and questions)

1. Ich möchte eine Briefmarke für einen Brief nach USA (kaufen).
2. Ich möchte eine Postkarte nach Österreich senden (schicken).
3. Einmal hin und zurück nach München, bitte.
4. Ich möchte meine schweren Koffer als Reisegepäck schicken (aufgeben).
5. Wo ist eine Telefonzelle? / Wo kann ich eine Telefonzelle finden?
6. Wie fülle ich die Zahlkarte aus? / Ich möchte eine Zahlkarte ausfüllen.

B.

1. Bitte fragen Sie den Mann, der dort steht.
2. Hier ist die Anzeige, die ich Ihnen zeigen wollte.
3. Wo ist der Fahrplan, den du gekauft hast?
4. Wie heißt die Ärztin, deren Namen ich vergessen habe?
5. Das ist die Tasche, die so schwer ist.
6. Sind das die Schweizer, die wir getroffen haben?

C.

1. Das ist der Artikel, den ich las (gelesen habe).
2. Die Nummer ist besetzt. Bitte rufen Sie wieder (nochmals) in 15 Minuten an.
3. Gibt es hier eine Telefonzelle, von der ich anrufen kann?
4. Dort ist die Post (das Postamt), wo Sie Briefmarken kaufen können.
5. Wer war der Herr, mit dem ich gesprochen habe?
6. Das ist alles, was ich weiß.
7. Das ist der Berg, den wir besteigen wollen.
8. Haben Sie (hast du) einen Rucksack, den ich mitnehmen kann?

D. (sample answers)

1. Ich kaufe eine Fahrkarte für die Hin- und Rückfahrt nach Wien.
2. Wir haben den schweren Koffer als Reisegepäck aufgegeben.
3. Wir heben heute Geld ab, weil die Bank am Wochenende geschlossen ist.
4. Ich ärgere mich, wenn die Telefonnummer immer besetzt ist.
5. Sie suchen die Abflughalle, aber sie können sie nicht finden.

Kapitel 10

DIALOGUE pp. 136–138 (translation)

You are at the police station in Cologne, for someone stole all your important documents (passport, driver's license, airplane ticket, etc.). The policeman doesn't speak any English. But that doesn't matter because you can understand his simple questions and you can answer in German. First you have to fill out a form. Therefore the "telegram style" (no sentences, just single words).

Of course, we don't talk just in cues (telegram style), but in sentences. Let's therefore repeat the conversation.

What's your name?	My name is Richard Cook.
Where do you live?	Presently I live in Cologne in the Rheinallee with Biebers.
What's your telephone number?	My number is 63-54-72.
When and where were you born?	I was born on July 20, 1959 in Columbus, Ohio.
What is your citizenship?	I am an American.
What's your profession?	I am a druggist.
Do you know your passport number?	No, because they stole my passport.
What's your height?	I am 1 meter and 68 centimeter. (5'7)
How much do you weigh?	I weigh 75 kilo (165 pounds)
What's the color of your hair?	Blond.
And what is the color of your eyes.	Blue-grey.
Do you have any distinguishing marks?	Yes, I have a scar over my left eye.

We want to know much more about you. But now you are no longer at the police station, but rather at a party where you are talking with a guest. The guest seems to be very curious, for he is really quizzing you.

Now then, Mr. Cook, how long have you already been in Cologne?—For two weeks.—And what's bringing you to our city?—I attended a conference.—What have you done with your free time?—They showed me most of the special sights of the city.—Did you bring your wife along?—I am still single. And you?—Oh, I have been married for 20 years.—Do you have any children?—Yes, two daughters and a son. The oldest is an elementary school teacher, and the second one is a saleswoman in a children's store. My son...—Excuse me, I have to talk briefly with Mrs. Kurz.

Unfortunately, Mrs. Kurz is also very curious, and so you are being quizzed some more.

Have you already attended our opera?—Yes, last week I was invited by a colleague to (a performance of) the "Freischütz."—Did you like the opera?—Yes, but actually I am a fan of Wagnerian music. Then you have to go to Bayreuth.—Others have told me that too.—But it is difficult to get tickets.—They already got those for me at the travel agency.
How long are you going to stay in Cologne?—Three more days. Excuse me, please. I just see Mr. Dietrich. He has a letter for me.—Of course.

Interview check-list pp. 138–139 (translation)

Now you don't have to answer any more questions. But we have an interview list which you may want to fill out. If you can't answer a question, check the lists on pp. 138–139 about professions and hobbies.

name/first name/address/(place of residence and street)/telephone number/
profession/marital status (single/married/divorced/widow/widower)
hobbies/interests/trips undertaken/clubs/associations/
favorite: author/composer/singer/moviestar/film/book/city/sport/beverage/meal
And what is your profession? Check list on this pp. 138–139.
What is your hobby? or: What do you like to do in your free time?
I play tennis/golf/cards/basketball/soccer, etc.
I play the piano/the guitar/cello/trumpet/flute/violin, etc.
I swim/read/write/cook/hike/do crafts/collect stamps, coins/work in the yard/
knit/surf/ski/watch TV/listen to the radio, etc.

A. Übung p. 139

1.	spielt	6.	sammelt
2.	repariert	7.	hört
3.	diskutiert/spricht	8.	strickt/näht
4.	arbeitet	9.	spricht
5.	liest	10.	ißt

B. Übung p. 140 (sample responses)

1. Ich arbeite im Garten/repariere mein Auto/spiele Tennis
2. Ich möchte Italien/Österreich/die Schweiz besuchen
3. Ich gehe einmal im Monat/dreimal im Jahr/nie ins Kino
4. Ich habe zwei Kinder/ein Kind/keine Kinder
5. Ich bin in Ohio/New York/in der Schweiz/Springfield geboren
6. Ich komme aus Amerika/Kanada/Kalifornien/Miami
7. Ich fahre nach Österreich/bleibe zu Hause/wandere in den Bergen/schreibe
   ein Buch/besuche Freunde
8. Ich liebe meinen Beruf/verdiene gut/interessiere mich für meinen Beruf/ich
   finde ihn langweilig/ich verdiene nicht genug/habe zu wenig Zeit für meine
   Familie
9. Er/sie ist intelligent/charmant/konservativ
10. ich bin vorsichtig/populär/sportlich

C. Übung p. 140

1.	Verkäufer	6.	Elektriker
2.	Mechaniker	7.	Bibliothekarin
3.	Pfarrer/Pastor	8.	Angestellter
4.	Krankenschwester	9.	Ärztin
5.	Drogist/Drogistin	10.	Sekretärin

A. Übung p. 141

1. Bald bekomme ich Post. or: Bald werde ich Post bekommen.
2. Schreibst du mir dieses Wochenende? or: Wirst du mir dieses Wochenende
   schreiben?
3. Wann wird sie arbeiten?
4. Er wird gute Karten kaufen.
5. Der Bus kommt in 15 Minuten. or: Der Bus wird in 15 Minuten kommen.

A. Übung pp. 141–142

1. wurde
2. wird
3. werden

4. wirst
5. ist berühmt geworden

B. Übung p. 142

1. ist…geworden
2. Hast…bekommen
3. wurde

4. bekam
5. bekommen

C. Übung p. 143

1. wird
2. wird
3. sind/worden
4. werden/werden

5. bist/worden
6. wurde
7. ist/worden
8. wird

D. Übung p. 143

1. Um sieben Uhr wird das Essen von uns serviert.
2. Viele Romane sind von Thomas Mann geschrieben worden.
3. Meine Mutter wird von Dr. Müscher behandelt.
4. Die Briefe sind von meiner Sekretärin abgeschickt worden.
5. Mein Auto wurde gestern von einem Mechaniker repariert.
6. Viele Kleider sind von der reichen Dame gekauft worden.
7. Ich werde von Dr. Erismann operiert werden.

E. Übung pp. 143–144

1. His book was translated into two languages.
2. The package has been (was) mailed yesterday.
3. The guest was being quizzed.
4. Mrs. Klein's passport has been (was) stolen.
5. Hamburg has been (was) destroyed by bombs during the war.
6. America was discovered by Columbus in 1492.
7. I hope (one hopes) that the film will be made.
8. The man has been murdered.
9. The apartment is being cleaned once a week.
10. Where is the Volkswagen being manufactured?

A. Übung p. 144

1. Man tanzte viel.
2. Man hat uns besucht.
3. Man hat mich gefragt.
4. Man interviewt die Frau.
5. Dort aß und trank man viel.
6. Man hat in dem Zimmer nicht geraucht.
7. Man antwortete dem Lehrer nicht.

A. Übung p. 147 (sample letters)

1. Liebe Klara,

   Wir möchten Dich gern für nächsten Freitag (17.3.) um halb sieben zum Abendessen einladen. Hoffentlich kannst du kommen. Bitte rufe mich vor Mittwoch an.

   Auf ein baldiges Wiedersehen

   Deine Brigitte

2. Sehr geehrter Herr Dr. Möller,

   Besten Dank für Ihre freundliche Einladung. Ich würde sehr gern das Wochenende mit Ihrer Familie verbringen, aber wir erwarten am selben Wochenende Besuch von unseren Verwandten aus Österreich.

   Ich hoffe, daß ich Ihre Familie ein anderes Mal besuchen darf.

   Mit freundlichen Grüßen

   Ihr

3. Liebe Mutti, lieber Vati! or Liebe Kinder!

   Das war eine nette Überraschung, als gestern Euer großes Paket ankam. Vielen Dank für Euer Weihnachtsgeschenk, das wir gut gebrauchen können. Die zwei großen Tischdecken mit den 12 Servietten passen gut zu unseren Möbeln im Speisezimmer. Und der Toaster, den Ihr geschickt habt, kam auch zur richtigen Zeit, denn unser alter ist seit zwei Wochen kaputt. Wie habt Ihr das gewußt?

   Vielen Dank und alles Liebe.

   Fröhliche Weihnachten!

Wiederholung pp. 147–148

A.

1.	e	5.	b
2.	f	6.	c
3.	a	7.	h
4.	g	8.	d

B.

Lieber / Wochen / Wetter / geregnet / eingeladen / wohne / weit / Freunde / herzliche / Dein

Reference Grammar

Declension of personal pronoun

	SINGULAR	PLURAL	
ich	*I*	**wir**	*we*
du	*you* (familiar)	**ihr**	*you* (familiar)
er, sie, es	*he, she, it*	**sie**	*they*
Sie	*you* (formal)	**Sie**	*you* (formal)

	SINGULAR					PLURAL			
NOMINATIVE	ich	du	er	sie	es	wir	ihr	sie	Sie
ACCUSATIVE	mich	dich	ihn	sie	es	uns	euch	sie	Sie
DATIVE	mir	dir	ihm	ihr	ihm	uns	euch	ihnen	Ihnen

Conjugation of **sein** *and* **haben**

sein

SINGULAR		PLURAL	
ich **bin**	*I am*	wir **sind**	*we are*
du **bist**	*you are*	ihr **seid**	*you are*
er,sie,es **ist**	*he, she, it is*	Sie, sie **sind**	*you, they are*

haben

SINGULAR		PLURAL	
ich **habe**	*I have*	wir **haben**	*we have*
du **hast**	*you have*	ihr **habt**	*you have*
er,sie,es **hat**	*he, she, it has*	Sie, sie **haben**	*you, they have*

Verb endings in present tense

kaufen *to buy*

SINGULAR	PLURAL
ich kauf**e**	wir kauf**en**
du kauf**st**	ihr kauf**t**
er, sie, es kauf**t**	Sie, sie kauf**en**

Declension of definite and indefinite articles

	MASCULINE	FEMININE	NEUTER	PLURAL
NOMINATIVE	der ein	die eine	das ein	die keine
ACCUSATIVE	den einen	die eine	das ein	die keine
DATIVE	dem einem	der einer	dem einem	den keinen
GENITIVE	des eines	der einer	des eines	der keiner

Conjugation of modal auxiliaries

	dürfen	**können**	**müssen**	**sollen**	**wollen**	**mögen**	
ich	darf	kann	muß	soll	will	mag	möchte
du	darfst	kannst	mußt	sollst	willst	magst	möchtest
er,sie,es	darf	kann	muß	soll	will	mag	möchte
wir	dürfen	können	müssen	sollen	wollen	mögen	möchten
ihr	dürft	könnt	müßt	sollt	wollt	mögt	möchtet
sie, Sie	dürfen	können	müssen	sollen	wollen	mögen	möchten

*"**Studenten**-type" nouns*

	SINGULAR	PLURAL
NOMINATIVE	der Student	die Student**en**
ACCUSATIVE	den Student**en**	die Student**en**
DATIVE	dem Student**en**	den Student**en**
GENITIVE	des Student**en**	der Student**en**

Declension of possessive adjective

	SINGULAR		PLURAL	
	Masculine	Neuter	Feminine	All genders
NOMINATIVE	ein mein unser	ein mein unser	eine meine uns(e)re	keine meine uns(e)re
ACCUSATIVE	einen meinen uns(e)ren	ein mein unser	eine meine uns(e)re	keine meine uns(e)re
DATIVE	einem meinem uns(e)rem	einem meinem uns(e)rem	einer meiner uns(e)rer	keinen meinen uns(e)ren
GENITIVE	eines meines uns(e)res	eines meines uns(e)res	einer meiner uns(e)rer	keiner meiner uns(e)rer

Reflexive pronouns

	PERSONAL PRONOUN			REFLEXIVE PRONOUN	
NOMINATIVE	ACCUSATIVE	DATIVE		ACCUSATIVE	DATIVE
ich	mich	mir		mich	mir
du	dich	dir		dich	dir
er	ihn	ihm			
sie	sie	ihr			sich
es	es	ihm			
wir	uns			uns	
ihr	euch			euch	
sie	sie	ihnen			sich
Sie	Sie	Ihnen			

Endings of definite article

	MASCULINE	NEUTER	FEMININE	PLURAL
NOMINATIVE	-er	-es	-e	
ACCUSATIVE	-en			
DATIVE	-em		-en	
			-er	
GENITIVE	-es			

*Adjective endings after **der**-words or **ein**-words*

	MASCULINE	FEMININE	NEUTER	PLURAL
NOMINATIVE	(der)-**e** (ein)-**er**	-e	(das)-**e** (ein)-**es**	-en
ACCUSATIVE	-en	-e	(das)-**e** (ein)-**es**	-en
DATIVE	-en	-en	-en	-en
GENITIVE	-en	-en	-en	-en

Principal Parts of Strong and Irregular Verbs

INFINITIVE	PRESENT*	PAST	PAST PARTICIPLE	BASIC MEANING
abfahren	fährt ab	fuhr ab	ist abgefahren	*to leave*
abnehmen	nimmt ab	nahm ab	abgenommen	*to decrease*
anfangen	fängt an	fing an	angefangen	*to begin*
anhalten	hält an	hielt an	angehalten	*to stop*
ankommen		kam an	ist angekommen	*to arrive*
(sich) anziehen		zog an	angezogen	*to attract; to dress*
aufgeben	gibt auf	gab auf	aufgegeben	*to assign, mail*
aufstehen		stand auf	ist aufgestanden	*to get up*
aussteigen		stieg aus	ist ausgestiegen	*to get off*
befehlen	befiehlt	befahl	befohlen	*to command*
beginnen		begann	begonnen	*to begin*
behalten	behält	behielt	behalten	*to keep*
bekommen		bekam	bekommen	*to receive*
bitten		bat	gebeten	*to request*
bleiben		blieb	ist geblieben	*to stay*
bringen		brachte	gebracht	*to bring*
denken		dachte	gedacht	*to think*
dürfen	darf	durfte	gedurft	*to allow*
einladen	lädt ein	lud ein	eingeladen	*to invite*
empfehlen	empfiehlt	empfahl	empfohlen	*to recommend*
(sich) entscheiden		entschied	entschieden	*to decide*
erhalten	erhält	erhielt	erhalten	*to receive*
ersteigen		erstieg	erstiegen	*to climb*
essen	ißt	aß	gegessen	*to eat*
fallen	fällt	fiel	ist gefallen	*to fall*
finden		fand	gefunden	*to find*
fliegen		flog	ist geflogen	*to fly*
frieren		fror	gefroren	*to be cold*
geben	gibt	gab	gegeben	*to give*
gefallen	gefällt	gefiel	gefallen	*to please*
gehen		ging	ist gegangen	*to go*
gelingen		gelang	ist gelungen	*to succeed*
genießen		genoß	genossen	*to enjoy*
geschehen	geschieht	geschah	ist geschehen	*to happen*
gewinnen		gewann	gewonnen	*to win*
haben	hat	hatte	gehabt	*to have*
halten	hält	hielt	gehalten	*to hold*
heißen		hieß	geheißen	*to be called*
helfen	hilft	half	geholfen	*to help*
kennen		kannte	gekannt	*to know*
klingen		klang	geklungen	*to sound*
kommen		kam	ist gekommen	*to come*
können	kann	konnte	gekonnt	*to be able to*
lassen	läßt	ließ	gelassen	*to let, leave*
laufen	läuft	lief	ist gelaufen	*to go, run*
leiden		litt	gelitten	*to suffer*
leihen		lieh	geliehen	*to borrow*
lesen	liest	las	gelesen	*to read*
liegen		lag	gelegen	*to lie, be located*

*Only verbs with a vowel change in the third-person singular are listed.

Principal Parts of Strong and Irregular Verbs (continued)

INFINITIVE	PRESENT*	PAST	PAST PARTICIPLE	BASIC MEANING
lügen		log	gelogen	*to tell a lie*
messen	mißt	maß	gemessen	*to measure*
mögen	mag	mochte	gemocht	*to like to*
müssen	muß	mußte	gemußt	*to have to*
nehmen	nimmt	nahm	genommen	*to take*
nennen		nannte	genannt	*to call, name*
raten	rät	riet	geraten	*to advise*
rennen		rannte	ist gerannt	*to run*
rufen		rief	gerufen	*to call*
scheinen		schien	hat *or* ist geschienen	*to appear, shine*
schlafen	schläft	schlief	geschlafen	*to sleep*
schreiben		schrieb	geschrieben	*to write*
schwimmen		schwamm	geschwommen	*to swim*
sehen	sieht	sah	gesehen	*to see*
sein	ist	war	ist gewesen	*to be*
singen		sang	gesungen	*to sing*
sitzen		saß	gesessen	*to sit*
sollen		sollte	gesollt	*to be supposed to*
spazierengehen		ging spazieren	ist spazierengegangen	*to go for a walk*
sprechen	spricht	sprach	gesprochen	*to talk*
stehen		stand	ist *or* hat gestanden	*to stand*
stehlen	stiehlt	stahl	gestohlen	*to steal*
steigen		stieg	ist gestiegen	*to climb*
sterben	stirbt	starb	ist gestorben	*to die*
tragen	trägt	trug	getragen	*to carry, wear*
treffen	trifft	traf	getroffen	*to meet*
trinken		trank	getrunken	*to drink*
tun		tat	getan	*to do*
umziehen		zog um	ist umgezogen	*to move*
(sich) unterhalten	unterhält	unterhielt	unterhalten	*to converse*
unterscheiden		unterschied	unterschieden	*to distinguish*
verbieten		verbot	verboten	*to forbid*
verbringen		verbrachte	verbracht	*to spend time*
verstehen		verstand	verstanden	*to understand*
vorlesen	liest vor	las vor	vorgelesen	*to read aloud*
vorschlagen	schlägt vor	schlug vor	vorgeschlagen	*to suggest*
(sich) waschen	wäscht	wusch	gewaschen	*to wash*
wehtun		tat weh	wehgetan	*to hurt*
werden	wird	wurde	ist geworden	*to become*
werfen	wirft	warf	geworfen	*to throw*
wissen	weiß	wußte	gewußt	*to know*
wollen	will	wollte	gewollt	*to want to*
ziehen		zog	gezogen	*to pull*

*Only verbs with a vowel change in the third-person singular are listed.

Wortschatz:*
Deutsch/Englisch

This vocabulary lists all words used in the text. Nouns are listed in the nominative singular and nominative plural. Strong verbs are entered according to the following model:

geben (i), a, e = geben (gibt), gab, gegeben.

An asterisk (*) indicates that a verb is conjugated with *sein* as the auxiliary verb in the perfect tenses. The forms of irregular verbs are written out. Verbs with a separable prefix are listed with a dot between the prefix and the stem: *ab·fahren.*

The following abbreviations are used:

acc.	accusative
adj.	adjective
adv.	adverb
dat.	dative
fam.	familiar
f.	feminine
m.	masculine
pl.	plural
sing.	singular

A

der Abend, -e evening
  am Abend in the evening
  heute abend tonight
  abends in the evening(s)
ab·fahren*(ä), u, a to depart, leave
die Abfahrt, -en departure; downhill run (skiing)
die Abfahrtshalle, -n departure hall
ab·fliegen*, o, o to fly off, depart

der Abflug, ¨e flight departure
ab·heben, o, o to withdraw (money)
ab·holen to pick up, to fetch
ab·laufen*(ä), ie, au to expire, run out
die Abrechnung, -en settlement
ab·schicken to send off, to mail
der Abschied, -e farewell
acht eight
das Achtel eighth (part)
Achtung! Attention! Careful!
achtunddreißigst- thirty-eighth

der Adler, - eagle
albern silly
der Alkohol alcohol
alle all; every; everyone
allein alone
alles everything
  alles in Ordnung? everything o.k.?
als as; when
alt old
älter older
der Amerikaner, - American, *m.*

*Wortschatz = vocabulary, lit. "treasure of words"

187

die Amerikanerin, -nen
American, *f.*
amerikanisch American
die Ampel, -n traffic light
an at; on; to; by
die Ananas pineapple
ander- other
andere others
an·fangen(ä), i, a to begin
(sich) an·hören to listen to
an·kommen, kam an, ange-
kommen* to arrive
der Anruf, -e telephone call
an·rufen, ie, u to phone, call
an·schauen to look at
an·sehen(ie), a, e to look at, to
view
   (sich) etwas ansehen to take
a look at
(sich) an·stecken to infect; to
catch a disease
antworten dat. to answer
die Anzeige, -n classified ad
*sich an·ziehen, zog an, ange-
zogen* to dress, get dressed
der Anzug, ¨e suit
der Apfel, ¨ apple
der Apfelsaft, ¨e apple cider
der April April
arbeiten to work
der Architekt, -en architect, *m.*
die Architektin, -nen architect,
f.
sich ärgern to be annoyed
arm poor
der Artikel, - article
der Arzt, ¨e physician, *m.*
die Ärztin, -nen physician, *f.*
das Aspirin aspirin
das Aß, -sse ace
attraktiv attractive, good looking
auch also, too
auf on, upon
   auf Kriegsfuß stehen to
be in conflict with
   Auf Wiedersehen! Good-bye
auf·kommen, (für) kam auf,
aufgekommen* to pay for, to
compensate
auf·machen to open
der Aufschlag, ¨e serve (tennis)
auf·schlagen(ä), u, a to serve
(tennis)
der Aufschläger, - server
auf·stehen, stand auf, aufge-
standen* to get up
der Auftrag, ¨e order
auf·wachen to wake up
auf·wachsen*(ä), u, a to grow
up

das Auge, -n eye
die Augenfarbe color of the eyes
der August August
aus from; out of; by
der Ausflug, ¨e outing, trip
aus·fragen to quiz, to question
aus·führen to carry out, to implement
aus·füllen to fill out
der Ausgang, ¨e exit
ausgezeichnet excellent
die Auskunft, ¨e information
das Ausland abroad, foreign
country
der Ausländer, - foreigner, *m.*
die Ausländerin, -nen foreigner, *f.*
ausländisch foreign
aus·sehen(ie), a, e to look like
aus·steigen*, ie, ie to get off,
disembark
die Ausstellung, -en exhibition
aus·suchen to choose, select
die Auster, -n oyster
ausverkauft sold out
aus·ziehen, zog aus, ausge-
zogen* to move out
   sich aus·ziehen to undress
das Auto, -s car
der Autoschlüssel, - car key

B

das Bad, ¨er bath
das Badehandtuch, ¨er bath
towel
die Bahn, -en railroad
der Bahnhof, ¨e railroad station
der Bahnsteig, -e track (train)
bald soon
der Balkon, -e balcony
der Ball, ¨e ball
die Banane, -n banana
die Bank, -en bank
basteln to tinker, to do crafts
der Baum, ¨e tree
Bayreuth city in Bavaria; location
of Wagner Festivals
der Beamte, -n civil servant, *m.*
die Beamtin, -nen civil servant,
f.
beantworten to answer
sich bedanken (für) to thank,
to say thanks
bedauern to regret
sich beeilen to hurry
sich befinden, a, u to be located
die Beförderung, -en promotion
die Begrüßung, -en greeting
behandeln to treat

bei with; at
die Beilage, -n side dish, gar-
nishing
bekannt known
das Benzin gasoline
bequem comfortable
der Berg, -e mountain
Berlin city in Germany
der Beruf, -e profession
berühmt famous
beschäftigt busy, occupied
der Beschwerdebrief, -e letter
of complaint
sich beschweren to complain
besetzt occupied, full
besonder special
besteigen, ie, ie to climb
bestellen to order
bestimmt certain(ly)
besuchen to visit
das Bett, -en bed
bevor before
die Bibliothek, -en library
der Bibliothekar, -e librarian,
m.
die Bibliothekarin, -nen librarian, *f.*
der Bienenstich honey-almond
cake; bee sting
das Bier, -e beer
billig cheap, inexpensive
die Billion, -en trillion
die Biologie biology
bis as far as; up to
   bis bald till then
   bis später until later
   von...bis from...to
bißchen a little bit
bitte please
   bitte schön you are welcome
blaß pale
bleiben*, ie, ie to stay, remain
der Blinddarm, -e appendix
die Blutprobe, -n blood test
die Bohne, -n bean
die Bombe, -n bomb
das Boot, -e boat
brauchen to need
braun brown
brechen, a, o to break
der Brief, -e letter
die Briefmarke, -n postage
stamp
bringen, brachte, gebracht to
bring
das Brot, -e bread
die Brücke, -n bridge
der Bruder, ¨ brother
das Buch, ¨er book
die Bundesrepublik The Federal Republic (of Germany)

das Büro, -s office
der Bus, -se bus
die Bushaltestelle, -n bus stop
die Butter butter

C

charmant charming
der Chef, -s boss, *m.*
die Chefin, -nen boss, *f.*
das Cola coke
der Chemiker, - chemist, *m.*
die Chemikerin, -nen chemist, *f.*
der Computer, - computer
die Cremeschnitte, -n creme tart

D

da there
damit so that
dämpfen to steam (cooking)
der Dank thanks
Danke (schön)! Thanks! Thank you!
Vielen Dank! Thanks a lot!
danken dat. to thank
Danke, gut. Fine, thank you.
nichts zu danken don't mention it
das Dankschreiben, - thank-you note
dann then
das the, that, this
daß that
dasselbe the same
die Debatte, -n debate
die Demokratie, -n democracy
deshalb that's why, therefore, for that reason
deutsch German (language)
der Deutsche, -n German, *m.*
die Deutsche, -n German, *f.*
die Deutsche Demokratische Republik (DDR) German Democratic Republic
die „Deutsche Welle" German radio program (on short wave)
das Deutschland Germany
der Dezember December
der Dialekt, -e dialect
dir to you, *fam., dat.*
diskutieren to discuss
diesmal this time
der Dokumentarfilm, -e documentary film
der Donnerstag, -e Thursday
das Doppelzimmer, - double room

dort there, over there
dort drüben over there
dorthin to that place
drei three
dreimal three times
dreißig thirty
dreiundfünfzigst- fifty-third
dreiundsechzig sixty three
dreizehnt- thirteenth
dritt- third
das Drittel one third
der Drogist, -en druggist, *m.*
die Drogistin, -nen druggist, *f.*
drücken to punch, to push
durch through; divided by
durchgebraten well done
dürfen (darf) may, to be allowed (to)
der Durst thirst
Haben Sie Durst? Are you thirsty?
die Dusche, -n shower
sich duschen to take a shower
Düsseldorf city in Germany

E

die Ecke, -n corner
eigentlich actually
ein(e) a; one
das Einbettzimmer, - single room
einfach simple
eingebildet arrogant
ein halb one half
einig in agreement
sich einig sein to be in agreement
der Einkauf, ¨e shopping, purchase
ein·laden(ä), u, a to invite
die Einladung, -en invitation
einmal once, one time
ein·setzen to implant
eins one
einseitig one-sided
(der) Einstand deuce (tennis)
ein·steigen, ie, ie* to board, to get on
einunddreißig thirty one
einundzwanzig twenty one
einverstanden! agreed!
das Einzelzimmer, - single room
ein·ziehen, zog ein, eingezogen* to move in
das Eis, - ice cream; ice
das Eisbein pig's knuckles
elf eleven

die Eltern parents
empfehlen(ie), a, o to recommend
der Engländer, - inhabitant of England, *m.*
die Engländerin, -nen inhabitant of England, *f.*
der Enkel, - grandson
die Enkelin, -nen granddaughter
entdecken to discover
entschuldigen to excuse
Entschuldigen Sie, bitte! Excuse me, please!
der Entschuldigungsbrief, -e letter of apology
die Entzündung, -en inflammation
die Erbse, -n pea
der Erfolg, -e success
erfolgreich successful
sich erinnern to remember
sich erkälten to catch a cold, get the flu
die Erkältung, -en cold, flu
erklären to explain
erlauben to allow
erleben to experience
erledigen to finish, to complete
erreichen to reach, to contact
erscheinen, ie, ie* to appear; to be published
erst- first
erst um not until
der Erwachsene, -n adult
erwarten to expect
das Essen, - meal
essen(ißt), aß, gegessen to eat
etwa approximately
euch you, *fam. pl.*
das Europa Europe

F

fahren(ä), u, a* to go; to drive
die Fahrkarte, -n ticket
der Fahrplan, ¨e timetable, schedule
das Fahrrad, ¨er bicycle
der Fahrschein, -e ticket
die Fahrt, -en trip, journey
fallen(ä), fiel, gefallen* to fall
falsch false
die Familie, -n family
der Familienname, -n last name
der Familienstand marital status
die Farbe, -n color

der Farbfernseher, -   color television set

das Faschierte   minced meat (hamburger)

fast   almost

faul   lazy

der Februar   February

fehlen   to miss

   was fehlt Ihnen?   what's wrong with you?

feiern   to celebrate

das Fenster, -   window

die Ferien   vacation

die Ferienwohnung, -en   vacation apartment

fern·sehen(ie), a, e   to watch television

das Fernsehen   television

der Fernseher, -   television set

fett   fat

das Fieber, -   fever

der Fiebermesser, -   clinical thermometer

der Filmschauspieler, -   movie actor, *m.*

die Filmschauspielerin, -nen   movie actor, *f.*

das Finanzamt, ¨er   internal revenue office

finden, a, u   to find

die Firma, die Firmen   company, firm

der Fisch, -e   fish

die Flasche, -n   bottle

das Fleisch   meat

fleißig   diligent

fliegen, o, o*   to fly

die Flöte, -n   flute

der Flug, ¨e   flight

der Fluggast, ¨e   airline passenger

der Flughafen, ¨   airport

die Flugkarte, -n   airplane ticket

folgen   to follow

das Foto, -s   photo, picture

die Frage, -n   question

   eine Frage stellen   to ask a question

fragen   to ask

der Franken, -   Swiss franc

frankieren   to prepay, to stamp

die Frau, -en   woman; wife

das Fräulein, -   Miss; young woman

frei   free; vacant

die Freiheit   freedom

der „Freischütz"   opera by K.M. von Weber

der Freitag, -e   Friday

die Freizeit   leisure time, free time

die Freude, -n   joy

   Freude machen   to bring (give) joy to somebody (with dat.)

sich freuen   to enjoy, to be glad

sich freuen auf   to look forward to

   es freut mich   my pleasure

der Freund, -e   friend, *m.*

die Freundin, -nen   friend, *f.*

die Frikadellen   croquettes

frisch   fresh

der Friseur, -e   hair dresser, *m.*

die Friseuse, -n   hair dresser, *f.*

die Frittatensuppe   broth with pancake stripes

froh   glad

die Frucht, ¨e   fruit

das Fruchteis   fruit ice cream, sherbet

früh   early

der Frühling   spring

das Frühstück, -e   breakfast

frühstücken   to have breakfast

der Frühstückssaal, -säle   breakfast room

(sich) fühlen   to feel

der Führerschein, -e   driver's license

fünft-   fifth

fünfzehn   fifteen

für   for

(sich) fürchten   to fear, to be afraid

furchtbar   terrible

das Fußball   soccer

das Fußballspiel, -e   soccer match

der Fußball, ¨e   soccer ball

G

die Gabel, -n   fork

ganz   quite, completely

gar nicht   not at all

der Garten, ¨   garden

die Gartenarbeit   gardening

der Gast, ¨e   guest

der Gastgarten, ¨   outdoor sitting area of a restaurant

die Gastgeberin, -nen   hostess

das Gasthaus, ¨er   inn

der Gasthof, ¨e   inn, hotel

die Gaststätte, -n   inn, restaurant

gebacken   baked

geben(i), a, e   to give

   es gibt   there is, there are

geboren   born

gebraten   roasted

der Geburtstag, -e   birthday

die Geburtstagskarte, -n   birthday card

gedämpft   steamed (cooking)

gefallen(ä), gefiel, gefallen dat.*   to like, to please

gefüllt   filled, stuffed

gegen   against

die Gegend, -en   area, region

gegrilled   grilled

gehen, ging, gegangen*   to go; to drive

   das geht nicht   that won't do

   es geht los   it starts, it begins

   es wird gehen   it will work out, I can manage

   Wie geht es Ihnen? (Wie geht's)   How are you?

gehören dat.   to belong

die Geige, -n   violin

gekocht   cooked

das Geld, -er   money

gelten(i), a, o   to be valid

das gemischte Doppel   mixed doubles (tennis)

das Gemüse, -   vegetable

genug   enough

geöffnet   open

das Gepäck   luggage

gerade   just; straight

geradeaus   straight ahead

geräuchert   smoked

gern + verb   to like

   gern geschehen   You are welcome; don't mention it

das Geschäft, -e   store, business

der Geschäftsbrief, -e   business letter

die Geschäftsfrau, -en   businesswoman

der Geschäftsmann, ¨er   businessman

die Geschäftsleute   business people

geschehen(ie), a, e*   to happen

das Geschenk, -e   gift

geschieden   divorced

geschlossen   closed

geschmort   braised

das Gespräch, -e   talk, discussion

gestern   yesterday

gestrig   yesterday's

gesund   healthy

die Gesundheit   health

das Getränk, -e   beverage

das Gewicht, -er   weight

gewinnen, a, o   to win

der Gipfel, -   peak

die Gitarre, -n   guitar

das Glas, ¨er   glass

glauben dat.   to believe

gleich   same, equal; right away
glücklich   happy
das Golf   golf
der Grad, -e   degree
das Gras, ¨er   grass
Grindlwald   town in Switzerland
die Grippe, -n   influenza
groß   large, big; great; tall, high
die Größe, -n   size, height
grün   green
die Gruppe, -n   group
der Gruß, ¨e   greeting
Grüß Gott!   Good day! (Southern
German and Austrian)
das Gulasch   goulash
gültig   valid
die Gurke, -n   cucumber
gut   good
   Guten Abend!   Good evening!
   Guten Morgen!   Good morning!
   Guten Tag!   Hello! Good day!
   Gute Nacht!   Good night!

H

das Haar, -e   hair
die Haarfarbe   hair color
der Hackbraten   meat loaf
halb   half
   halb durchgebraten   medium
well
die Hälfte   half
die Halle, -n   hall, departure hall
der Hals, ¨e   throat
die Halsschmerzen *pl.*   sore
throat
halten (ä), ie, a   to stop; to hold
halten von   to think of
Hamburg   city in Germany
der Hamburger   inhabitant of
Hamburg, *m.*
die Hamburgerin   inhabitant of
Hamburg, *f.*
das Hauptgericht, -e   main
course
der Hauptplatz   main square
das Haus, ¨er   house
   zu Hause   at home
   nach Hause   home
der Hausarzt, ¨e   family doctor,
m.
die Hausärztin, -nen   family
doctor, *f.*
die Hausfrau, -en   housewife,
homemaker
die Hausnummer, -n   house
number
heiraten   to marry

heiß   hot
heißen, ie, ei   to be called
   Wie heißen Sie?   What's your
name?
helfen (i), a, o *dat.*   to help
heraus·kommen, kam
heraus, herausgekommen*
to come out
der Herbst   autumn
der Herr, -en   gentleman; Mr.
herrlich   great, splendid
her·stellen   to manufacture
herzlich   cordial
der Herzschrittmacher, -   pacemaker
heute   today
   heute abend   tonight
   heute morgen   this morning
   heute nachmittag   this afternoon
hier   here
hier·bleiben*, ie, ie   to remain,
to stay
hin   (to) there
hinauf   up
der Hinflug, ¨e   flight to
hin·kommen, kam hin, hin-
gekommen*   to get there
hinter   behind
die Hin- und Rückfahrt   round
trip
hin und zurück   back and forth
hoch   high
hochachtungsvoll   respectful
hoffentlich   it is to be hoped, I
hope
höflich   polite
hören   to hear
das Hotel, -s   hotel
der Hotelportier, -s   hotel clerk,
m.
die Hotelportierin, -nen   hotel
clerk, *f.*
hübsch   pretty
das Huhn, ¨er   chicken
der Humor   sense of humor
der Hund, -e   dog
hundertmal   hundred times
der Hundertmarkschein, -e
hundred mark bill
das Hundertstel   hundreth
der Hunger   hunger
   Haben Sie Hunger?   Are
you hungry?
der Hustensaft, ¨e   cough syrup

I

ich   I
ihm   (to) him *dat.*

ihn   him, it *acc.*
ihnen   them *dat.*
Ihnen   you form. *sing./pl.*
im, in dem   in the
immer   always
impfen   to vaccinate
impulsiv   impulsive
in   in, into, to
die Information, -en   information
informieren   to inform
der Ingenieur, -e   engineer, *m.*
die Ingenieurin, -nen   engineer,
f.
innen   inside
ins, in das   in the
der Inhalt, -e   content
der Installateur, -e   plumber,
m.
die Installateurin, -nen   plumber, *f.*
das Italien   Italy
intelligent   intelligent
interessant   interesting

J

ja   yes; indeed
das Jahre, -e   year
das Jahrhundert, -e   century
der Januar   January
die Jausenstation, -en   snack
bar (Austrian)
jeder (jede, jedes)   every, each
jetzt   now
der Job, -s   job
der Journalist, -en   journalist,
m.
die Journalistin, -nen   journalist, *f.*
der Juli   July
jung   young
der Junge, -n   boy
der Juni   June

K

der Kaffee   coffee
das Kaffeehaus, ¨er   coffee
house
der Kaiserschmarren   shredded
pancake filled with marmelade,
covered with sugar
der Kalender, -   calendar
kalt   cold
(sich) kämmen   to comb
der Kanadier, -   Canadian, *m.*
die Kanadierin, -nen   Canadian,
f.
der Kanton, -e   canton (state in
Switzerland)

die Karte, -n card, postcard
der Käse, - cheese
der Käsekuchen, - cheesecake
der Katholik, -en Catholic, *m.*
die Katholikin, -nen Catholic, *f.*
katholisch Catholic adj.
die Katze, -n cat
kaufen to buy
der Kaufhof German department store chain
die Kaufleute business people
der Kaufmann businessman
kein no, not a
der Kellner, - waiter
die Kellnerin, -nen waitress
kennen, kannte, gekannt to become acquainted with, to know
das Kennzeichen, - mark, emblem
das Kilo, - kilogram
der Kilometer, - kilometer
das Kind, -er child
das Kino, -s movie theater
die Kirche, -n church
die Kirsche, -n cherry
das Klavier, -e piano
das Kleid, -er dress
klein small, little
das Kleingeld change (money)
klingeln to ring (bell)
klopfen to knock
der Klub, -s club
klug smart
der Knödel, - dumpling
kochen to cook
der Koffer, - suitcase
der Kollege, -n colleague, *m.*
die Kollegin, -nen colleague, *f.*
Köln Cologne (city in FRG)
kommen*, kam, gekommen to come
der Komponist, -en composer, *m.*
die Komponistin, -nen composer, *f.*
die Konferenz, -en conference
können (kann), konnte, gekonnt can, to be able to
konservativ conservative
das Konzert, -e concert
die Kopfschmerzen pl. headache
korrespondieren to correspond
kosten to cost
die Krabbe, -n shrimp; crab
kräftig strong
krank ill, sick
das Krankenhaus, ̈er hospital
der Krankenpfleger, - nurse, *m.*

die Krankenschwester, -n nurse, *f.*
der Krimi, -s detective story
die Küche, -n kitchen
der Kuchen, - cake
kühl cool
der Kunde, -n customer
die Kunst, ̈e art
der Künstler, - artist, *m.*
die Künstlerin, -nen artist, *f.*
küssen to kiss
kurz short

L

lachen to laugh
die Lampe, -n lamp
landen to land
die Landezeit, -en landing time
lang long
langsam slow
langweilig boring
(sich) lassen (läßt), ließ, gelassen to let; to leave; to make, to have done
laufen*(äu), ie, au to run, to jog
laut loud
leben to live, reside
der Leberkäse meatloaf
die Leberknödelsuppe liver-dumpling soup
die Lederhose, -n leather pants
ledig single
lehren to teach
der Lehrer, - teacher, *m.*
die Lehrerin, -nen teacher, *f.*
leicht light; easy
leider unfortunately
leid·tun, tat leid, leid getan dat. to be sorry
es tut mir leid I am sorry
leise soft(ly), quietly
lernen to learn
lesen(ie), a, e to read
letzt- last
die Leute pl. people
lieb dear
lieber rather
liegen, a, e to lie, to be located
es liegt uns viel daran we are very much concerned
der Liegewagen, - train compartment with makeshift beds
links left
die Linsensuppe lentil soup
die Liste, -n list
das Liter, - liter
der Löffel, - spoon
die Luft air

der Lufthansaflug flight of Lufthansa airline
die Lungenentzündung pneumonia

M

machen to do
das macht nichts that doesn't matter
das Mädchen, - girl
mähen to mow
der Mai May
man one, you, they, people
der Manager, - manager, *m.*
die Managerin, -nen manager, *f.*
manchmal sometimes
die Mandeln tonsils
die Manieren pl. good manners
der Mann, ̈er man; husband
der Mantel, ̈ overcoat
die Mark, - mark (German)
die Marke, -n stamp
der Marktplatz, ̈e market square
die Marmelade, -n marmalade, jam
der März March
der Maßstab, ̈e scale
das Medikament, -e medicine, drug
die Medizin medicine
mehr more
mein my
die Meinung, -en opinion
meistens mostly
der Mensch, -en person; *pl.* people
das Messer, - knife
mich me
mieten to rent
die Milch milk
die Milchbar, -s dairy bar
der Mietvertrag, ̈e lease
die Milliarde, -n billion
die Million, -en million
das Mineralwasser, - mineral water
minus minus, less
die Minute, -n minute
mir to me
mit with
mit·bringen, brachte mit, mitgebracht to bring along
mit·fahren*(ä), u, a to drive along, come along
mit·kommen*, kam mit, mitgekommen to come along

mit·nehmen (nimmt mit), nahm mit, mitgenommen to take along

mit·spielen to play (with), to participate

das Mittagessen, - lunch

mittags at noon, midday

der Mittelpunkt center (of attention)

die Mitternacht midnight

der Mittwoch Wednesday

möchten would like to

mögen (mag), mochte, gemocht to like to

möglich possible

der Monat, -e month

der Montag, -e Monday

morgen tomorrow
  Guten Morgen! Good morning!

morgens in the morning

der Motor, -e motor

müde tired

der Mund, ¨er mouth

die Münze, -n coin

das Museum, die Museen museum

die Musik music

müssen (muß), mußte, gemußt must, to have to

die Mutter, ¨ mother

N

na well (interjection)

nach to

der Nachbar, -n neighbor

der Nachmittag, -e afternoon
  am Nachmittag in the afternoon

die Nachnahme C.O.D., cash on delivery

der Nachname, -n last name

die Nachricht, -en news

das Nachrichtenmagazin, -e news magazine

nach·sehen (ie), a, e to look (up), to inquire, to check out

die Nachspeise, -n dessert

nächst- next

die Nacht, ¨e night
  Gute Nacht! Good night!

nahe near

nähen to sew

der Name, -n name

die Narbe, -n scar

naß wet

der Nationalfeiertag, -e national holiday

die Natur nature

natürlich naturally, of course

das Naturschnitzel, - cutlet

die Nazizeit period of the Nazi regime in Germany (1933–1945)

nebelig foggy

neben next

nehmen (nimmt), nahm, genommen to take

nett nice

neu new

neugierig curious

(das) Neujahr New Year's Day

nicht not
  nicht wahr? isn't it? right?

der Nichtraucher, - nonsmoker, *m.*

die Nichtraucherin, -nen nonsmoker, *f.*

nichts nothing

nie never

noch still, yet

nochmals once more
  noch einmal, bitte! again, please
  noch mehr even more

nötig necessary

der November November

null zero

das Nummernschild, -er license plate

nur only

O

ob whether

oben top; above

der Ober, - head waiter, *m.*

das Obst fruit

die Obsttorte, -n fruitcake, fruit tart

obwohl although

oder or

der Ofen, ¨ stove

offen open

öffnen to open

oft often

ohne without

die Ohrenschmerzen pl. earache

der Oktober October

das Öl, -e oil

der Onkel, - uncle

die Oper, -n opera

die Opernübertragung, -en opera broadcast

operieren to operate

die Orange, -n orange

der Orangensaft, ¨e orange juice

der Ort, -e place

der Osten East

Österreich Austria

der Österreicher, - Austrian, *m.*

die Österreicherin, -nen Austrian, *f.*

P

(ein) paar a few

das Paket, -e package, parcel

die Panne, -n breakdown (car)

die Papiere pl. documents, papers

der Park, -s park

der Parkplatz, ¨e parking lot, place

der Partner, - partner

die Party, -s party

der Paß, ¨sse passport

passen dat. to suit, fit

passend suitable, matching, fitting

die Paßnummer, -n passport number

der Pastor, -en pastor, minister, *m.*

die Pastorin, -nen pastor, minister, *f.*

der Patient, -en patient

peinlich embarrassing

der Pfeffer pepper

der Pfennig, -e penny (100 Pf. = 1 Mark)

pflegen to take care of, to nurse

das Pfund, -e pound

der Physiker, - physicist, *m.*

die Physikerin, -nen physicist, *f.*

die Pille, -n pill

der Pilot, -en pilot, *m.*

die Pilotin, -nen pilot, *f.*

der Pilz, -e mushroom

die Platte, -n record

plus plus

der Politiker, - politician, *m.*

die Politikerin, -nen politician, *f.*

politisch political

die Polizei police

der Polizist, -en police officer, *m.*

die Polizistin, -nen police officer, *f.*

der Portier, -s desk clerk (hotel), *m.*

die Portierin, -nen desk clerk (hotel), *f.*

das Porto postage

die Post post office; mail

das Postamt, ¨er post office

der Postbeamte, -n postal worker, *m.*

die Postbeamtin, -nen postal worker, *f.*

die Postkarte, -n postcard

das Postsparbuch, ¨er post office savings book

predigen to preach

der Preis, -e price

preiswert low-priced

die Presse press, newspaper(s)

die Pressefreiheit freedom of the press

die Privatwirtschaft private enterprise

pro pro; in favor of

der Professor, -en professor, *m.*

die Professorin, -nen professor, *f.*

das Programm, -e program

protestantisch Protestant *adj.*

die Prüfung, -en exam, test

der Psychologe, -n psychologist, *m.*

die Psychologin, -nen psychologist, *f.*

der Pullover, - sweater, pullover

pünktlich punctual

(sich) putzen to brush, clean

Q

die Qualität, -en quality

das Quartier, -e quarter; room

R

das Radfahren bicycling

das Radio, -s radio

das Radioprogramm, -e radio program

der Rasen, - lawn

(sich) rasieren to shave

die Rast, -en rest; break

die Raststätte, -n restaurant (at Autobahn)

rauchen to smoke

raus·müssen, mußte raus, rausgemußt to get out, have to leave

rechnen to calculate, figure

die Rechnung, -en bill

das Recht, -e right

recht adv. really, quite

 recht gut quite well

rechts right (direction)

der Rechtsanwalt, ¨e lawyer

der Regen, - rain

 der saure Regen acid rain

der Regenschirm, -e umbrella

regnen to rain

reich rich

rein pure

reinigen to clean

der Reis rice

die Reise, -n trip, journey

das Reisebüro, -s travel agency

das Reisegepäck baggage, luggage

reisen to travel

der Reisende, -n traveler, *m.*

die Reisende, -n traveler, *f.*

die Reklame, -n advertisement

die Renovierung, -en renovation

reparieren to repair

repräsentieren to represent

reservieren to reserve

das Restaurant, -s restaurant

das Rezept, -e prescription

der Richter, - judge, *m.*

die Richterin, -nen judge, *f.*

das Rippensteak rib steak

roh raw

die Rolltreppe, -n escalator

der Roman, -e novel

der Rosenbusch, ¨e rosebush

rot red

die Roulade, -n rolled and braised meat

die Rückhand backhand (tennis)

der Rucksack, ¨e knapsack

rufen, ie, u to call

der Ruhetag, -e day of rest, off day

S

die Sache, -n matter, thing

die Sachertorte Viennese layer-cake

sachlich objective

sagen to say, tell

der Salat, -e salad

das Salz salt

Salzburg Salzburg (city in Austria)

sammeln to collect, gather

der Samstag, -e Saturday

der Sänger, - singer, *m.*

die Sängerin, -nen singer, *f.*

der Satz, ¨e set (tennis); sentence

sauber clean

schade too bad

schaffen to make, to accomplish

der Schaffner, - conductor, *m.*

die Schaffnerin, -nen conductor, *f.*

der Schalter, - ticket window

scharf sharp, pungent

schattig shady

die Scheckkarte, -n credit card

scheinen, ie, ie to seem; to shine

schicken to send, to mail

schi·fahren*(ä), u, a to ski

das Schild, -er sign

der Schilling, -e shilling (currency of Austria)

schimpfen to complain; to scold

der Schinken, - ham

der Schirm, -e umbrella

schlafen(ä), ie, a to sleep

der Schlag whipped cream; hit

schlank slender

schlecht bad, poor

schließen, schloß, geschlossen to close; to lock

schlimm bad

der Schlüssel, - key

schmecken dat. to taste

der Schmerz, -en pain

schmutzig dirty

der Schnee snow

schnell fast, quick

der Schnellimbiß snack bar

der Schnellzug, ¨e express train

das Schnitzel, - cutlet

schon already

schön beautiful

 wie schön! how nice!

schreiben, ie, ie to write

der Schuh, -e shoe

die Schule, -n school

schussen to ski straight down

schwarz-weiß black and white

das Schweden Sweden

der Schweinebraten pork roast

die Schweiz Switzerland

der Schweizer, - Swiss, *m.*

die Schweizerin, -nen Swiss, *f.*

schwellen*, o, o to swell

schwer heavy; difficult

die Schwester, -n sister

schwierig difficult

schwimmen, a, o to swim

schwindelig dizzy

sechs six

sechsundzwanzig twenty-six

der See, -n lake

sehen(ie), a, e to see

die Sehenswürdigkeit, -en sight(s) of interest

sehr very much

sein*, (ist), war, gewesen to be

sein pron. his; its

seit since

die Seite, -n page; side

selbst (selber) self

das Selbstbiographische autobiographical matters
selten seldom
das Seminar, -e seminar
senden to send
die Sendung, -en broadcast
der September September
sicher for sure, sure; safe; certainly
sie she; they
Sie you form. *sing./plur.*
sieben seven
siebzehn seventeen
Silvester New Year's Eve (also:
Sylvester)
sitzen, saß, gesessen to sit
sobald as soon as
das Sofa, -s couch, sofa
sofort at once, immediately
der Sohn, ¨e son
solange as long as
sollen ought (to), to be supposed
(to)
der Sommer, - summer
die Sondermarke, -n commemorative stamp
sondern but, on the contrary
die Sonderstellung, -en special
position, place
der Sonntag, -e Sunday
sparen to save
die Spargelspitzen asparagus
tips
der Spaß, ¨sse fun
spät late
später later
spazieren·gehen, ging spa-
zieren, spazierengegangen*
to take a walk
die Speise, -n food
das Spiel, -e game; match
spielen to play
das spielt keine Rolle that
doesn't make any difference
der Spinat spinach
der Sport sport
der Sportler, - sportsman
die Sportlerin, -nen sports-
woman
sportlich athletic
die Sportübertragung, -en
sports broadcast
der Sportwagen, - sports car
die Sprache, -n language
sprechen(i), a, o to speak
die Sprechstunde, -n office
hour
die Staatsangehörigkeit citizenship
die Stadt, ¨e city
der Stadtplan, ¨e city map

stehen*, stand, gestanden to
stand
es steht in der Zeitung it's
written in the newspaper
wie steht's? what's the score?
stehen·bleiben*, ie, ie to stop
stehlen(ie), a, o to steal
die Stellung, -en position
sterben*(i), a, o to die
die Steuer, -n tax
die Steuerabrechnung, -en
income tax declaration
das Stichwort, ¨er catchword,
cue
der Stil, -e style
stimmen to be correct
das stimmt that's correct
der Stock, die Stockwerke
floor, story
im 1. Stock on the second floor
(1.Stock = 2nd floor)
stören to disturb, to bother
die Straße, -n street, road
die Straßenbahn, -en streetcar
*die Straßenbahnhaltestelle, -
n* streetcar stop
stricken to knit
das Stück, -e piece; play
der Student, -en student, *m.*
die Studentin, -nen student, *f.*
das Studentenheim, -e student
dormitory
studieren to study
die Stunde, -n hour; lesson
vor einer Stunde an hour ago
stündlich hourly
suchen to look for, to search
die Suppe, -n soup
surfen to surf
das System, -e system
das metrische System the
metric system

T

die Tablette, -n pill, tablet
der Tag, -e day
Guten Tag! Good day!
das Tagesmenü, -s special of
the day
täglich daily
tanzen to dance
die Tasche, -n bag; pocket
die Tasse, -n cup
die Technik technology; tech-
nique
der Tee, -s tea
das Telefon, -e telephone
die Telefonzelle, -n telephone
booth

der Telegrammstil telegram
style (in writing)
(das) Tennis tennis
die Tennisstunde, -n tennis
lesson
teuer expensive
das Theater, - playhouse, theater
die Theaterkarte, -n theater
ticket
das Tier, -e animal
der Tierarzt, ¨e veterinarian, *m.*
die Tierärztin, -nen veterinarian, *f.*
tippen to type
der Tisch, -e table
das Tischtuch, ¨er table cloth
die Tochter, ¨ daughter
toll! It's great!
die Tomate, -n tomato
die Tomatensuppe tomato soup
der Tourist, -en tourist, *m.*
die Touristin, -nen tourist, *f.*
tragen(ä), u, a to wear; to carry
treffen(i), traf, getroffen to
meet
sich treffen to meet each other,
to get together
trinken, a, u to drink
das Trinkgeld, -er tip
trocken dry
die Trompete, -n trumpet
tschüß! bye now!
tun(tut), tat, getan to do
die Tür, -en door
das Tournier, -e tournament

U

üben to exercise
über over; about
überall everywhere
das Übernachten overnight
stay
übersetzen to translate
die Übung, -en exercise
übertreiben, ie, ie to exaggerate
die Uhr, -en clock; watch
um 11 Uhr at 11 o'clock
um around; about; in order to; at
um·schalten to switch over; shift
um·ziehen, zog um, umge-
zogen* to move
sich um·ziehen to change clothes
unabhängig independent
unbekannt unknown
der Unfall, ¨e accident
unfreundlich unfriendly
ungefähr approximate(ly)
ungerade uneven
unglaublich unbelievable

die Universität, -en university

das Universitätskrankenhaus, ̈-er university hospital, clinic

die Unkosten pl. expenses

uns us

unser our

unten below; under; among

unter below; at the bottom

sich unterhalten to enjoy oneself, to converse

die Unterhaltungssendung, -en entertainment show

untersuchen to examine

sich untersuchen lassen to have oneself examined

der Urlaub, -e leave, vacation

V

der Vater, ̈ father

die Verabredung, -en appointment

verbinden, a, u to connect

verbringen, verbrachte, verbracht to spend (time)

verdienen to earn

der Verein, -e club, association

vereist icy

vergessen(i), vergaß, vergessen to forget

vergleichen, i, i to compare

verheiratet married

verkaufen to sell

der Verkäufer, - salesman

die Verkäuferin, -nen saleswoman

der Verkehr traffic

verlieren, o, o to lose

vermieten to rent

verpassen to miss

verrückt crazy

versalzen to salt too much, to oversalt

das Versandhaus, ̈-er mail-order house

verschieden different

verschreiben, ie, ie to prescribe (medicine)

versetzen to transfer

sich verspäten to be late, delayed

die Verspätung, -en delay

verstehen, verstand, verstanden to understand

versuchen to try

der Verwandte, -n relative

verwenden to use

Verzeihung! Excuse me, please!

viel, viele much, many

vier four

das Viertel fourth

viertel quarter

vierundzwanzig twenty-four

vierzig forty

der Volksschullehrer, - elementary schoolteacher, *m.*

die Volksschullehrerin, -nen elementary schoolteacher, *f.*

voll full

von from; of

von…bis from…to

vor in front of; before

vor allem above all

voraussichtlich presumably; probably

vorbei along, by; over, past

nicht vorbei not over yet

voreingenommen biased

vorbei·kommen*, kam vorbei, vorbeigekommen to stop by

die Vorhand forehand (tennis)

der Vormittag, -e morning

am Vormittag in the morning

der Vorname, -n first name

vor·schreiben, ie, ie to order, to specify

vorsichtig careful

die Vorspeise, -n appetizer

der Vertrag, ̈-e contract

W

der Wachhund, -e watchdog

der Wagnerliebhaber, - a fan of Wagnerian music

wählen to choose; to dial

wahr true

das ist nicht wahr that isn't true

während during; while; whereas

wandern to hike

die Wanderung, -en hike

die Wanderkarte, -n hiking map

wann when

ab wann from what time on

warm warm

warten to wait

warum why

was what

die Wäsche laundry

waschen(ä), u, a to wash

der Waschlappen, - wash cloth

das Wasser water

die Wechselstube, -n exchange office (money)

der Wecker, - alarm clock

der Weg, -e way, path

wegen because, on account of

weh·tun (tut weh), tat weh, wehgetan to hurt

Weihnachten Christmas

weil because

der Wein, -e wine

die Weinstube, -n wine tavern

das Weiße Haus The White House (USA)

weit far

weiter further

welch which

wen whom

wenig few

wenigstens at least

wem to whom

wenn if; when, whenever

wer who

die Werbung, -en advertisement

werden*(i), u, o to become, to get

wessen whose

der Westbahnhof railroad station (west)

das Wetter weather

wichtig important

wie how; as; like

Wie bitte? What was that?

Wie geht es Ihnen? How are you?

Wie heißen Sie? What's your name?

wieder again

das Wiedersehen reunion

Auf Wiedersehen! Good-bye!

wie lange how long

Wien Vienna

das Wiener Schnitzel, - breaded veal cutlet

wieviel how much

wieviele how many

der wievielte Tag ist heute? What day is today?

der Windbeutel, - cream puffs

windig windy

der Winter, - winter

wir we

wirklich really

die Wirtschaft economy

der Wirtschaftsprüfer, - certified public accountant, *m.*

die Wirtschaftsprüferin, -nen certified public accountant, *f.*

wissen(weiß), wußte, gewußt to know

die Witwe, -n widow

der Witwer, - widower

wo where

die Woche, -n   week
das Wochenblatt, ⸚er   weekly newspaper
das Wochenende, -   weekend
wofür   why, for what
woher   from where
wohin   where to
sich wohl·fühlen   to feel well
wohnen   to live, reside
der Wohnort, -e   place of residence
die Wohnung, -en   apartment
das Wohnzimmer, -   living room
wollen(will), wollte, gewollt   to want, wish
das Wörterbuch, ⸚er   dictionary
wunderbar   wonderful
wünschen   to wish
würden   would

Z

zäh   tough
die Zahl, -en   number

zahlen   to pay
zählen   to count
die Zahlkarte, -n   money order (in Austria: der Erlagschein, -e)
der Zahn, ⸚e   tooth
der Zahnarzt, ⸚e   dentist, *m.*
die Zahnärztin, -nen   dentist, *f.*
zehn   ten
das Zehntel, -   tenth
das Zeichen, -   sign
zeigen   to show
die Zeit, -en   time
  sich Zeit lassen   to take one's time
die Zeitschrift, -en   magazine
die Zeitung, -en   newspaper
zerstören   to destroy
ziehen, zog, gezogen   to move; to pull
ziemlich   fairly, rather
das Zimmer, -   room
die Zimmernummer, -n   room number

der Zoo, -s   zoo
zu   to; at; too
der Zufall, ⸚e   coincidence
zufrieden   satisfied
der Zug, ⸚e   train
zu·machen   to close, shut
zur, zu der   to the
Zürich   city in Switzerland
zurück·kommen*, kam zurück, zurückgekommen   to come back
zurück·senden   to send back
zuviel   too much
zuwenig   too little
zwanzig   twenty
zwanzigst-   twentieth
zwei   two
zweimal   twice
zweit   second
zweiundzwanzig   twenty-two
die Zweizimmerwohnung, -en   two-room apartment
zwölf   twelve

English/German Vocabulary

This is a selective *English-German* Vocabulary which is based on this text and should aid you to complete the English-to-German activities and exercises. We offer it for your convenience, but it is no substitute for a complete English-German dictionary, which we recommend for any student of German. The definitions given are limited to the context of a particular exercise. Irregular and semi-irregular verbs are indicated with an *. Check their form on the list in the appendix.

A

a (an) ein
about über; etwa
accident der Unfall, ¨e
to be acquainted with kennen
to become acquainted with kennen·lernen
ad die Anzeige, -n
to be afraid sich fürchten vor, Angst haben vor + *dat.*
after nach; später
again wieder
airport der Flughafen, ¨
alarm clock der Wecker, -
all alle
almost fast, beinahe
alone allein
always immer
American der Amerikaner, *m.*; die Amerikanerin, -nen, *f.*; amerikanisch *adj.*
and und
to be annoyed sich ärgern über + *acc.*
answer die Antwort, -en
to answer antworten
apartment die Wohnung, -en
approximate ungefähr
area code die Vorwahl

to arrive an·kommen*
to ask fragen; bitten* um + *acc.*
at an; bei; zu
Austrian der Österreicher, *m.*; die Österreicherin, -nen, *f.*; österreichisch *adj.*
autumn der Herbst,

B

back zurück
bad schlecht, schlimm
bag die Tasche, -n; der Sack, ¨e
baggage das (Reise-) Gepäck
bath das Bad, ¨er
beautiful schön, hübsch
because weil
to become werden*
bed das Bett, -en
before vor; bevor
to begin an·fangen*; beginnen*
behind hinter
to believe glauben *dat.*
to belong gehören *dat.*
between zwischen
big groß; stark
book das Buch, ¨er
boring langweilig
born geboren
to bother stören

bottle die Flasche, -n
boy der Junge, -n
bread das Brot, -e
breakfast das Frühstück
to bring bringen*
brother der Bruder, ¨
to brush putzen
business das Geschäft, -e
but aber
to buy kaufen

C

cake der Kuchen, -
call der Anruf, -e
to call an·rufen*
can die Dose, -n
can, to be able to können*
car das Auto, -s; der Wagen, -
card die Karte, -n
careful vorsichtig
to celebrate feiern
to change ändern; wechseln; sich um·ziehen* (clothes)
cheap billig
chicken das Huhn, ¨er
to choose wählen, aus·suchen
church die Kirche, -n
city die Stadt, ¨e
classified ad die Anzeige, -n

clean   sauber, rein

clerk   die Angestellte, -n, *f.*; der Angestellte, -, *m.*

clock   die Uhr, -en

  at 8 o'clock   um acht Uhr

cold   kalt; die Erkältung (flu)

color   die Farbe, -n

to comb   (sich) kämmen

to come   kommen*

comfortable   bequem

to compare   vergleichen

to compute   aus·rechnen; be·rechnen

to complain   sich beklagen über *acc.*; sich beschweren

cool   kühl

to cook   kochen

corner   die Ecke, -n

correct   richtig

to cost   kosten

crazy   verrückt

cup   die Tasse, -n

D

to dance   tanzen

dangerous   gefährlich

daughter   die Tochter, ·

day   der Tag, -e

dear   lieb

to decide   entscheiden

degree   der Grad, -e

to demand   verlangen; fordern

to depart   ab·fahren*

departure   die Abfahrt, -en

to develop   entwickeln

dictionary   das Wörterbuch, ·er

different   verschieden, anders

difficult   schwierig, schwer

diligent   fleißig

dirty   schmutzig, dreckig

to disturb   stören

divorced   geschieden

to do   tun; machen

dog   der Hund, -e

door   die Tür, -en

dress   das Kleid, -er

to drink   trinken*

to drive   fahren*

driver   der Fahrer, -, *m.*; die Fahrerin, -nen, *f.*

dry   trocken

during   während

E

early   früh

to earn   verdienen

easy   leicht

to eat   essen*

education   die Erziehung; die Aus·bildung

electrician   der Elektriker, -, *m.*; die Elektrikerin, -nen, *f.*

embarrassing   peinlich, unan·genehm

to enjoy   genießen*; gern haben; gefallen* *dat.*

enough   genug

evening   der Abend, -e

every   jeder, jede, jedes

everything   alles

to examine   untersuchen; prüfen

to exchange   um·wechseln (Geld)

to excuse   sich entschuldigen

to exercise   üben; trainieren (Sport)

exit   der Ausgang, ·e

expense   die Ausgabe, -n; Kosten

expensive   teuer

to explain   erklären

express train   der Schnellzug, ·e

F

to fall   fallen*

false   falsch

family   die Familie, -n

famous   berühmt

far   weit

fast   schnell

father   der Vater, ·

to fear   fürchten

to feel   sich fühlen

to fill out   aus·füllen

to find   finden*

finished   fertig

firm   die Firma, die Firmen

flight   der Flug, ·e

foggy   nebelig

to follow   folgen *dat.*

for   für

to forget   vergessen*

fork   die Gabel, -n

free   frei

friend   der Freund, -e, *m.*

friend   die Freundin, -nen, *f.*

friendly   freundlich

full   voll, besetzt

fun   der Spaß

G

to gain weight   zu·nehmen*

game   das Spiel, -e

gasoline   das Benzin

genuine   echt

to get   bekommen*; erhalten*

girl   das Mädchen, -

to give   geben*

glass   das Glas, ·er

to go   gehen*; fahren*

good   gut

government   die Regierung, -en

group   die Gruppe, -n

guest   der Gast, ·e

guilty   schuldig

H

half   halb

to happen   geschehen*, passieren

happy   glücklich

to have   haben*

healthy   gesund

to hear   hören

to help   helfen* *dat.*

here   hier

high   hoch

to hike   wandern

home (adv.)   nach Hause

  at home   zu Hause

hope   hoffen

hot   heiß

hour   die Stunde, -n

how   wie

hunger   der Hunger

hungry   hungrig

to hurry   sich beeilen

to hurt   verletzen

  it hurts   es tut weh

I

ice cream   das Eis

idea   die Idee, -n

if   wenn

ill   krank

immediate(ly)   sofort; direkt

important   wichtig

independent   unabhängig

Independence Day   der Un·abhängigkeitstag

inexpensive   billig

to inform   informieren

inn   das Gasthaus, ·er

inside   innen, drinnen

interest   das Interesse, -n

  to be interested in   sich inter·essieren für + *acc.*

intersection   die Kreuzung, -en

to introduce   vor·stellen

invitation   die Einladung, -en

J

job   der Beruf, -e; der Job, -s

journey   die Reise, -n

judge   der Richter, -, *m.*; die Richterin, -nen, *f.*

just   gerade

K

to keep behalten*
key der Schlüssel, -
to kiss küssen
kitchen die Küche, -n
knapsack der Rucksack, ¨e
to know wissen*, kennen*

L

lake der See, -n
language die Sprache, -n
large groß
to last dauern
late spät
to laugh lachen
lawn der Rasen, -
lawyer der Rechtsanwalt, ¨e
lazy faul
to lead führen
to learn lernen
lease der Mietvertrag, ¨e
to lease mieten
to leave verlassen*; ab·fahren*
left links
to let lassen*
letter der Brief, -e
librarian der Bibliothekar, -e, *m.*;
    die Bibliothekarin, -nen, *f.*
to lie liegen*; lügen
light das Licht; leicht (adj.)
to like gern·haben
to listen zu·hören
to live leben; wohnen
long lang
lost (adj.) verloren
to look schauen, an·schauen
to lose verlieren*
loud laut
to love lieben
lovely hübsch; wunderschön
luggage das Gepäck
lunch das Mittagessen, -

M

mail die Post
to make machen
man der Mann, -¨er; der Mensch,
    -en
many viele
to marry heiraten
    married verheiratet
to mean bedeuten
meat das Fleisch
mechanic der Mechaniker, -, *m.*;
    die Mechanikerin, -nen, *f.*
medicine die Medizin; das Medika-
    ment, -e
to meet treffen*

menu die Speisekarte, -n
milk die Milch
minister der Pfarrer, -; der Pastor,
    -en, *m.*; die Pastorin, -nen, *f.*
to miss verpassen; versäumen;
    vermissen
Monday der Montag, -e
month der Monat, -e
more mehr
morning der Morgen, -
    in the morning morgens
mother die Mutter, ¨
mountain der Berg, -e
to move um·ziehen*
to move out aus·ziehen*
to mow mähen
much viel
too much zuviel
mushroom der Pilz, -e
must müssen*

N

naturally natürlich
to need brauchen
neighbor der Nachbar, -n
never nie
new neu
news die Nachricht, -en
newspaper die Zeitung, -en
next nächst
nice nett; fein
night die Nacht, ¨e
no nein
nobody niemand
nonsmoker der Nichtraucher, -
noon der Mittag, -e
nothing nichts
now jetzt, nun
number die Nummer, -n
nurse der Krankenpfleger, *m.*; die
    Krankenschwester, -n, *f.*

O

occupied besetzt
of von
offer das Angebot, -e
to offer an·bieten*
often oft
oil das Öl, -e
old alt
on auf
once einmal
to open öffnen; auf·machen
open offen
opinion die Meinung, -en
to order bestellen
other ander-
out aus; hinaus

over über
    over there dort drüben

P

page die Seite, -n
pain der Schmerz, -en
parents die Eltern
passport der Paß, ¨sse
to pay zahlen
peace der Frieden
peak der Gipfel, -
people die Leute
perhaps vielleicht
to phone telefonieren; an·rufen*
physician der Arzt, ¨e, *m.*; die
    Ärztin, -nen, *f.*
to pick up ab·holen
picture das Bild, -er
piece das Stück, -e
place der Ort, -e; die Stelle, -n;
    der Platz, ¨e
to play spielen
please bitte
to please gefallen* *dat.*
poor arm
police die Polizei
polite höflich
possible möglich
post office die Post; das Postamt,
    ¨er
postage stamp die Briefmarke,
    -n
to practice üben
to prefer vor·ziehen*; lieber
    haben
to press drücken
pretty hübsch; schön
price der Preis, -e
profession der Beruf, -e
prohibited verboten
to protect schützen, beschützen
to prove beweisen*
punctual pünktlich
pure rein
to push drücken
to put legen; stellen; setzen

Q

quality die Qualität, -en
quarter das Viertel, -
question die Frage, -n
quick schnell
quiet leise; ruhig
quite ganz; ziemlich

R

racket der Schläger, -
railroad der Zug, ¨e; die Bahn,
    -en

rain   der Regen, -
to rain   regnen
rather   zeimlich
to reach   erreichen
to read   lesen*
ready   bereit; fertig
reason   der Grund, ¨e
to recommend   empfehlen*
record   die Platte, -n; der Rekord, -e
to regret   bedauern
relative   der Verwandte, -n
to remain   bleiben*
to remember   sich erinnern an + acc.
rent   die Miete, -n
to rent   mieten, vermieten
to repair   reparieren
to report   berichten
to request   bitten*, ersuchen um + acc.
to require   verlangen, erfordern
to reserve   reservieren
retired   pensioniert
to return   zurück·kommen*
right   das Recht, -e
right (adj.)   richtig; rechts
river   der Fluß, ¨sse
road   die Straße, -n
room   das Zimmer, -
round trip   die Hin- und Rückfahrt, -en
rule   die Regel, -n

S

salesman   der Verkäufer, -
saleswoman   die Verkäuferin, -nen
satisfied   zufrieden
Saturday   der Samstag, -e
to save   sparen
to say   sagen
schedule   der Fahrplan, ¨e; die Liste, -n
school   die Schule, -n
to search   suchen; ausfindig machen
secretary   der Sekretär, -e, *m.*; die Sekretärin, -nen, *f.*
to see   sehen*
to seem   scheinen
seldom   selten
to select   aus·suchen; auswählen
to sell   verkaufen
to send   schicken, senden
to serve   bedienen; servieren
several   mehrere
to shave   (sich) rasieren
shoe   der Schuh, -e
short   kurz; klein

should   sollten
to show   zeigen
shower   die Dusche, -n
sick   krank
sign   das Schild, -er; das Zeichen, -
similar   ähnlich
to sing   singen*
single   ledig, unverheiratet
single room   das Einzelzimmer, -
to sit   sitzen*
sister   die Schwester, -n
to sleep   schlafen*
small   klein
to smoke   rauchen
snow   der Schnee
sold out   ausverkauft
some   einige; irgendein
something   irgend etwas
sometimes   manchmal
sorry!   es tut mir leid!
to speak   sprechen*
spoon   der Löffel, -
stamp   die Briefmarke, -n
to stand   stehen*
to stop   auf·hören; halten*
straight ahead   geradeaus
street   die Straße, -n
streetcar   die Straßenbahn, -en
strong   stark
to study   studieren; lernen
student   der Student, -en; der Schüler, *m.*; die Studentin, -nen; die Schülerin, -nen, *f.*
stuffed   gefüllt
stupid   dumm
to swim   schwimmen*
to succeed   gelingen*
successful   erfolgreich
to suggest   vor·schlagen*
suitcase   der Koffer, -
sun   die Sonne
sunglasses   die Sonnenbrille, -n

T

table   der Tisch, -e
to take   nehmen*
to take along   mit·nehmen*
to talk   sprechen*, reden
to taste   schmecken *dat.*
tax   die Steuer, -n
to teach   lehren
teacher, m.   der Lehrer, -
telephone call   der Telefonanruf, -e
television   das Fernsehen
television set   der Fernseher, -
to tell   sagen; erzählen
terrible   schrecklich
thanks   danke

that   daß (conjunction); das (demonstrative pronoun)
then   dann, damals
there   dort
   there is, there are   es gibt + acc.
thing   das Ding, -e; die Sache, -n
to think   denken*
thirsty   durstig
ticket   die Karte, -n
till   bis
time   die Zeit, -en
tip   das Trinkgeld, -er
today   heute
tomato   die Tomate, -n
tomorrow   morgen
tonight   heute abend
too   auch; zu
tough   zäh
town   die Stadt, ¨e
traffic   der Verkehr
train   der Zug, ¨e
to translate   übersetzen
to travel   reisen
to treat   behandeln
tree   der Baum, ¨e
to try   versuchen

U

umbrella   der Regenschirm, -e
uncle   der Onkel, -
under   unter
to understand   verstehen*
unfortunately   unglücklicherweise
unknown   unbekannt
unpleasant   unangenehm
until   bis
to use   verwenden*; gebrauchen

V

vacant   leer; frei; unbesetzt
vacation   die Ferien; der Urlaub, -e
vacation apartment   die Ferienwohnung, -en
valid   gültig
vegetable   das Gemüse, -
very   sehr
visit   der Besuch, -e
to visit   besuchen
vocabulary   das Vokabular, -e; der Wortschatz

W

to wait   warten
waiter   der Kellner, -

waitress   die Kellnerin, -nen
to wake up   auf·wachen
to walk   gehen*
to want   wünschen
to wash   waschen*
water   das Wasser
way   der Weg, -e
to wear   tragen*
weather   das Wetter
week   die Woche, -n
weight   das Gewicht
well   gut; wohl
well-done   gut durchgebraten

what   was
when   wann; als
where   wo
whether   ob
which   welch
who   wer
whom   wem
why   warum
to win   gewinnen*
window   das Fenster, -
to wish   wünschen
with   mit
without   ohne

woman   die Frau, -en
word   das Wort, ¨er
to work   arbeiten
would like   möchten
to write   schreiben*
wrong   falsch; unrichtig

Y

year   das Jahr, -e
yes   ja
yesterday   gestern
young   jung